Machine Learning for iOS Developers

Machine Learning for iOS Developers

Abhishek Mishra

WILEY

To my wife, Sonam, for her love and support through all the years we've been together.

To my daughter, Elana, for bringing joy and happiness into our lives.
—Abhishek

About the Author

Abhishek Mishra has been active in the IT industry for more than 19 years and has extensive experience with a wide range of programming languages, enterprise systems, service architectures, and platforms. He earned his master's degree in computer science from the University of London and currently provides consultancy services to Lloyds Banking Group in London as a security and fraud solution architect. He is the author of several books including *Machine Learning in the AWS Cloud* and *Amazon Web Services for Mobile Developers*.

About the Technical Editor

Paul Pires has been developing iOS apps professionally for the past five years, having worked within a range of industries such as finance, media, and fashion. He earned his bachelor's degree in computer science from City University in London and currently works as a freelance iOS consultant.

Acknowledgments

This book would not have been possible without the support of the team at Wiley, including Jim Minatel, Kenyon Brown, Kezia Endsley, Kim Wimpsett, and Pete Gaughan.

I would also like to thank Paul Pires for his keen eye for detail.

It has been my privilege working with all of you. Thank you.

Contents at a Glance

Contents

Introduction

Machine learning is one of the hottest trends in computing and deals with the problem of creating computer programs that can generalize and predict information reliably, quickly, and with accuracy, resembling what a human would do with similar information. With the recent hype in mainstream media around novel applications of machine learning, you may be inclined to think that machine learning is a relatively new discipline, but that is far from the truth. In fact, machine learning has been around for several decades, and it is because of recent advances in storage, processor, and GPU technology that it is possible to build and deploy machine learning systems at scale and get results in real time.

This book is targeted at intermediate/advanced iOS developers who are looking to come to grips with the fundamentals of machine learning, learn about some of the common tools used by data scientists, and learn how to build and deploy models into their iOS applications. This book at all times attempts to balance theory and practice, giving you enough visibility into the underlying concepts while providing you with the best practices and practical advice that you can apply to your workplace right away.

Machine learning is a rapidly evolving field. I have made every attempt to keep the content up-to-date and relevant. Even though this makes the book susceptible to being outdated on a few rare instances, I am confident the content will remain useful and relevant through the next releases of iOS.

What Does This Book Cover?

This book covers the fundamental concepts of machine learning as well as the use of these concepts to build real-world models and use them in your iOS apps.

Chapter 1: Introduction to Machine Learning This chapter introduces the different types of machine learning models commonly found in real-world applications as well as tools and libraries used by data scientists to build these models. The chapter also includes examples of real-world applications of machine learning and sources of training data.

Chapter 2: The Machine-Learning Approach This chapter examines a hypothetical scenario in which a rule-based system is used to process credit card applications. The limitations of the rule-based system are examined, and a machine learning system is devised to address some of those limitations. The chapter concludes with an overview of the steps involved in building a typical machine learning solution.

Chapter 3: Data Exploration and Preprocessing   This chapter focuses on the data exploration and feature engineering stage, specifically the use of popular Python libraries NumPy, Pandas, and Scikit-learn for tabular data. The chapter also explores feature selection techniques.

Chapter 4: Implementing Machine Learning on Mobile Apps   This chapter explores the options available to you as an iOS developer to integrate machine learning techniques on your apps. The chapter compares the pros and cons of an edge-based versus server-based deployment model and introduces both Apple offerings as well as other third-party offerings that can be used from within your apps.

Chapter 5: Object Detection Using Pre-trained Models   This chapter focuses on the use of pre-trained models for object detection in your iOS apps. The chapter also covers the basics of artificial neural networks (ANNs) and convolutional neural networks (CNNs).

Chapter 6: Creating an Image Classifier with the Create ML App   This chapter covers the use of Apple's Create ML app to train a machine learning model that can detect the dominant object in an image. The model is trained on a subset of the Kaggle Dogs vs. Cats dataset and exported to the Core ML format. The exported model is used within an iOS app.

Chapter 7: Creating a Tabular Classifier with Create ML   This chapter covers the use of Apple's Create ML app to train a classification model on tabular data. The model is trained on the popular UCI ML wine dataset and exported to the Core ML format using the Create ML app. The trained model is then used in an iOS app that allows users to input the chemical characteristics of wine and learn the quality of the beverage.

Chapter 8: Creating a Decision Tree Classifier   This chapter focuses on the use of Scikit-learn to create a decision tree classification model on the popular Iris flowers dataset. The trained model is then exported to the Core ML format using the Core ML Tools Python library and used in an iOS app.

Chapter 9: Create a Logistic Regression Model Using Scikit-learn and Core ML   This chapter focuses on the use of Scikit-learn to create a logistic regression model on the popular Pima Indians diabetes dataset. The trained model is then exported to the Core ML format using the Core ML Tools Python library and used in an iOS app.

Chapter 10: Building a Deep Convolutional Neural Network with Keras   This chapter covers the creation and training of a popular deep convolutional neural network architecture called Inception V4 using the Keras functional API. The Inception V4 network is trained on a small publicly available dataset and then used in an iOS app.

Appendix A: Anaconda and Jupyter Notebook Setup   This appendix helps you install Anaconda Navigator on your computer, set up a Python environment that includes several common machine learning libraries, and configure Jupyter Notebook.

Appendix B: Introduction to NumPy and Pandas   This appendix shows you how to use NumPy and Pandas. These libraries are commonly used during the data exploration and feature engineering phases of a project.

Additional Resources

In addition to this book, here are some other resources that can help you learn more about machine learning.

Apple Machine Learning Journal: `https://machinelearning.apple.com`

Scikit-learn User Guide: `https://scikit-learn.org/stable/user_guide.html`

Core ML Developer Documentation: `https://developer.apple.com/documentation/coreml`

Core ML Tools Documentation: `https://apple.github.io/coremltools/`

Keras Documentation: `https://keras.io`

Reader Support for This Book

We provide support for this book in a couple of ways.

Companion Download Files

As you work through the examples in this book, the project files you need are all available for download from `www.wiley.com/go/machinelearningforiosdevelopers`.

How to Contact the Publisher

If you believe you've found a mistake in this book, please bring it to our attention. At John Wiley & Sons, we understand how important it is to provide our customers with accurate content, but even with our best efforts an error may occur.

To submit your possible errata, please email it to our customer service team at `wileysupport@wiley.com` with the subject line "Possible Book Errata Submission."

Part 1

Fundamentals of Machine Learning

Chapter 1

Introduction to Machine Learning

WHAT'S IN THIS CHAPTER

- ◆ Introduction to the basics of machine learning

- ◆ Tools commonly used by data scientists

- ◆ Applications of machine learning

- ◆ Types of machine learning systems

Hello, and welcome to the exciting world of machine learning. If you have never heard of machine learning until now, you may be tempted to think that it is a recent innovation in computer science that will result in sentient computer programs, significantly more intelligent than humans that will one day make humans obsolete. Fortunately, there is very little truth in that idea of machine learning. For starters, it is not a recent development; computer scientists have been researching for decades ways to make computers more intelligent by attempting to find ways to teach computers to make generalizations and predictions much like humans do. However, intelligence is not just about recognizing things, and even the best machine learning systems today are not capable of reasoning like human beings. The machine learning systems that exist today are essentially pattern recognizers and can, for instance, examine a picture and detect a cup of tea close to the edge of a table. They cannot, however, reason that the cup could accidentally fall off the table, as it is too close to the edge.

Machine learning specifically deals with the problem of creating computer programs that can generalize and predict information reliably, quickly, and with accuracy resembling what a human would do with similar information. Machine learning algorithms require a lot of processing and storage space and until recently were only possible to deploy in large companies or in academic institutions. Recent advances in storage, processor, and GPU technology have provided the processing power required to build and deploy machine learning systems at scale and get results in real time.

In the past, lack of quality data was also a factor that prevented widespread adoption of machine learning. With the advent of social media and analytics applications, developers have access to lot more data about their customers than they did in the past.

Another factor that has contributed to the recent increase in machine learning applications is the availability of excellent tools and frameworks such as Core ML, Create ML, Pandas, Matplotlib, TensorFlow, Scikit-learn, PyTorch, and Jupyter Notebooks, which have made it possible for newcomers to start building real-world machine learning applications without having to delve into the complex underlying mathematical concepts. In this chapter, you will learn about what machine learning is, how machine learning systems are classified, and examples of real-world applications of machine learning.

What Is Machine Learning?

Machine learning is a discipline within artificial intelligence that deals with creating algorithms that learn from data. Machine learning traces its roots to a computer program created in 1959 by a computer scientist Arthur Samuel while working for IBM. Samuel's program could play a game of checkers and was based on assigning each position on the board a score that indicated the likelihood of leading toward winning the game. The positional scores were refined by having the program play against itself, and with each iteration, the performance of the program improved. The program was in effect learning from experience, and the field of machine learning was born.

A machine learning system can be described as a set of algorithms based on mathematical principles that can mine data to find patterns in the data and then make predictions on new data as it is encountered. Rule-based systems can also make predictions on new data; however, rule-based systems and machine learning systems are not the same. A rule-based system requires a human to find patterns in the data and define a set of rules that can be applied by the algorithm. The rules are typically a series of if-then-else statements that are executed in a specific sequence. A machine learning system, on the other hand, discovers its own patterns and can continue to learn with each new prediction on unseen data.

Tools Commonly Used by Data Scientists

As an iOS developer, Core ML is likely to be your framework of choice when it comes to deploying a machine learning model in your app. Training a machine learning model, on the other hand, involves several steps and, except for the simplest of cases, is performed offline and using a different set of tools. Apple provides a number of tools to train Core ML models and convert pre-trained models built using other frameworks such as Scikit-learn and Keras to the Core ML format. The reason you may want to use a non-Apple framework like Scikit-learn or Keras to train a model is because the library may provide an implementation of a model that is not possible to train using Apple's toolset or may simply be updated more frequently.

Depending on the type of model you are trying to build, there may be a lot of steps involved even before you get to the point when you can start training—such as data preprocessing, feature engineering, and data visualization. Data scientists frequently use a set of tools to assist them with these steps. In this section, you will learn about some of the tools commonly used by data scientists to build machine learning solutions.

Although R has historically been the language of choice for statisticians, most data scientists and machine learning engineers today work in Python. The popularity of Python in the machine learning space is due to the abundance of machine learning–specific libraries that assist with all steps of the machine learning process from preparing data, feature engineering, information visualization, to training models with the latest algorithms. Where Python code is presented, this book will use Python 3.6.5. The following are the most popular Python machine learning tools:

◆ **Jupyter Notebook:** This is a popular web-based interactive development environment for data science projects. A notebook combines code, execution results, and visualization results all in a single document. Jupyter Notebook is a successor to an older project called IPython Notebook. You can find out more about Jupyter Notebooks at http://jupyter .org. Appendix A contains instructions on installing Anaconda Navigator and setting up Jupyter Notebooks on your own computer.

◆ **Anaconda Navigator:** This is a commonly used package manager for data scientists. It allows users to conveniently install and manage Python libraries and quickly switch between different sets of libraries and Python versions. It also includes popular tools such as Jupyter Notebooks and Spyder Python IDE. You can find more information on Anaconda at `https://www.anaconda.com`.

◆ **Scikit-learn:** This is a Python library that provides implementations of several machine learning algorithms for classification, regression, and clustering applications. It also provides powerful data preprocessing and dimensionality reduction capabilities. You can find more information on Scikit-learn at `https://www.scikit-learn.org`.

◆ **NumPy:** This is a Python library that is commonly used for scientific computing applications. It contains several useful operations such as random number generation and Fourier transforms. The most popular NumPy features for data scientists are N-dimensional data arrays (known as *ndarrays*) and functions that manipulate these arrays. NumPy ndarrays allow you to perform vector and matrix operations on arrays, which is significantly faster than using loops to perform element-wise mathematical operations. You can find more information on NumPy at `https://www.numpy.org`.

◆ **Pandas:** This is a Python library that provides a number of tools for data analysis. Pandas builds upon the NumPy ndarray and provides two objects that are frequently used by data scientists—the *series* and the *dataframe*. You can find more information on Pandas at `https://pandas.pydata.org`.

◆ **Matplotlib:** This is a popular 2D plotting library. It is used by data scientists for data visualization tasks. You can find more information on Matplotlib at `https://matplotlib.org`.

◆ **Pillow:** This is a library that provides a variety of functions to load, save, and manipulate digital images. It is used when the machine learning system needs to work with images. You can find more information on Pillow at `https://python-pillow.org`.

◆ **Google TensorFlow:** This is a Python library for numerical computation. It was developed by Google and eventually released as an open source project in 2015. Google TensorFlow is commonly used to build deep learning systems. It uses a unique computation graph-based approach and requires users to build a computation graph where each node in the graph represents a mathematical operation and the connections between the nodes represent data (tensors). You can find out more information on TensorFlow at `https://www.tensorflow.org`.

◆ **Keras:** This is another popular Python library for training and using deep learning networks. It was designed to facilitate rapid experimentation with neural networks and acts like a higher-level abstraction to popular deep learning frameworks like Google TensorFlow. As of TensorFlow 2.0, Keras is included with TensorFlow.

Common Terminology

In this section, we examine some of the common machine learning–specific terminology that you are likely to encounter. While this list is not exhaustive, it should be useful to someone looking to get started.

◆ **Machine learning model:** This is the algorithm that is used to make predictions on data. It can also be thought of as a function that can be applied to the input data to arrive at the output predictions. The machine learning algorithm often has a set of parameters associated with it that influence its behavior; these parameters are determined by a process known as *training*.

◆ **Data acquisition:** This is the process of gathering the data needed to train a machine learning model. This could include activities ranging from downloading ready-to-use CSV files to scraping the Web for data.

◆ **Input variables:** These are the inputs that your machine learning model uses to generate its prediction. A collection of N input variables is generally denoted by lowercase x_i with $i = 1, 2, 3, \ldots N$. Input variables are also known as *features*.

◆ **Feature engineering:** This is the process of selecting the best set of input variables and often involves modifying the original input variables in creative ways to come up with new variables that are more meaningful in the context of the problem domain. Feature engineering is predominantly a manual task.

◆ **Target variable:** This is the value you are trying to predict and is generally denoted by a lowercase *y*. When you are training your model, you have a number of training samples for which you know the expected value of the target variable. The individual values of the target variable for N samples are often referred to as y_i with $i = 1, 2, \ldots N$.

◆ **Training data:** This is a set of data that contains all the input features as well as any engineered features and is used to train the model. For each item in the set, the value of the target variable is known.

◆ **Test data:** This is a set of data that contains all the input features (including engineering features) as well as the values of the target variable. This set is not used while training the model but instead is used to measure the accuracy of the model's predictions.

◆ **Regression:** This is a statistical technique that attempts to find a mathematical relationship between a dependent variable and a set of independent variables. The dependent variable is usually called the *target*, and the independent variables are called the *features*.

◆ **Classification:** This is the task of using an algorithm to assign observations to a label from a fixed set of predefined labels.

◆ **Linear regression:** This is a statistical technique that attempts to fit a straight line to a set of data points. Linear regression is commonly used to create machine learning models that can be used to predict continuous values (such as height, width, age, etc.).

◆ **Logistic regression:** This is a statistical technique that uses the output of linear regression and converts it to a probability between 0 and 1 using a sigmoid function. Logistic regression is commonly used to create machine learning models that can predict class-wise probabilities. An example is the probability that a person will develop an illness later in life or the probability that an applicant will default on a loan payment.

- **Decision tree:** This is a tree-like data structure that can be used for classification and prediction problems. Each node in the tree represents a condition, and each leaf represents a decision. Building a decision tree model involves examining the training data and determining the node structure that achieves the most accurate results.

- **Error function:** This is a mathematical function that takes as input the predicted and actual values and returns a numerical measure that captures the error in prediction. The goal of the training function is to minimize the error function.

- **Neural networks:** This is a machine learning model that mimics the structure of the human brain. A neural network consists of multiple interconnected nodes, organized into distinct layers—the input layer, the in-between layers (also known as the *hidden layers*), and the output layer. Nodes are commonly known as *neurons*. The number of neurons in the input layer correspond to the number of input features, and the number of neurons in the output layer correspond to the number of classes that are being predicted/classified.

- **Deep learning:** This branch of machine learning utilizes multilayer neural networks with a large number of neurons in each layer. It is also quite common for deep learning models to use multiple deep neural networks in parallel.

Real-World Applications of Machine Learning

Machine learning is transforming business across several industries at an unprecedented rate. In this section, you will learn about some of the applications of machine-learning-based solutions:

- **Fraud detection:** Machine learning is commonly used in banks and financial institutions to make a decision on the overall risk associated with a payment instruction. Payments in this context include money transfers and purchases (payments to providers) using cards. The risk decision is based on several factors including the transactional history. If the risk is low, the transaction is allowed to proceed. If the risk is too high, the transaction is declined. If the risk is deemed to lie in an acceptable threshold, the customer may be asked to perform some form of step-up authentication to allow the transaction to proceed.

- **Credit scoring:** Whenever a customer applies for a credit product such as a loan or credit card, a machine learning system computes a score to indicate the overall risk of the customer not being able to repay the loan.

- **Insurance premium calculation:** Machine learning systems are commonly used to compute the insurance premium that is quoted to a customer when they apply to purchase an insurance product.

- **Behavioral biometrics:** Machine learning systems can be trained to build a profile of a user based on the manner in which they use a website or a mobile application. Specifically, such systems create a profile of the user based on analyzing information on from where they access the platform, at what times of the day, where they click a page, how long they stay on a page, how quickly they move their mouse across a page, etc. Once the system has been trained, it can be used to provide real-time information on the likelihood that someone is impersonating a customer.

◆ **Product recommendation:** Machine learning systems are commonly used by online retailers (such as Amazon) to provide a list of recommendations to a customer based on their purchase history. These systems can even predict when a customer is likely to run out of groceries and send them reminders to order items.

◆ **Churn prediction:** Machine learning systems are commonly used to predict which customers are likely to cancel their subscription to a product or service in the next few days. This information gives businesses an opportunity to try to retain the customer by offering a promotion.

◆ **Music and video recommendations:** Online content providers such as Netflix and Spotify use machine learning systems to build complex recommendation engines that analyze the movies and songs you listen to and provide recommendations on other content that you may like.

◆ **Text prediction:** Smart keyboards like the one on your iPhone use machine learning models to predict the next word you are likely to type, and the top three predictions are surfaced as suggestions on top of the iPhone keyboard as you type.

◆ **Conversational interfaces:** Machine learning models are used with chatbots to map natural language inputs from users into an input that the chatbot can understand. For example, a chatbot that allows users to access banking functions will use machine learning to interpret slightly differing natural language instructions such as "I want to pay somebody," "I want to make a payment to my mother," "Make a payment," and "Transfer some money" to all map to the same internal banking process, perhaps called "Make payments."

◆ **Text analysis:** Machine learning models can be used to analyze text documents to extract information on entities referenced in the document and the overall sentiment of the document. The document in this context does not have to be a lengthy Microsoft Word document; it could be a short Twitter message. Such a system could be used to monitor a Twitter feed and inform you about trending topics or the overall sentiment of your followers' responses to a post you made.

◆ **Scene analysis and recognition:** Machine learning models (particularly deep learning models) are commonly used for scene analysis and object recognition in digital images and video feeds. Scene analysis involves feeding in an image (or a video) to the machine learning model and the model providing a description of the contents of the image—such as *man riding a green bicycle on a sunny day*. Object recognition involves feeding an image to the machine learning model and getting a list of objects detected in the image along with bounding boxes that represent the location of the objects in the image.

Types of Machine Learning Systems

There are several different ways in which you can go about classifying machine learning systems; one of the most common approaches is to base the classification on the manner in which the system is trained and the manner in which the system can make predictions. Based on this approach, machine learning systems can be classified as follows:

◆ Supervised learning

◆ Unsupervised learning

- Semisupervised learning
- Reinforcement learning
- Batch learning
- Incremental learning
- Instance-based learning
- Model-based learning

These labels are not mutually exclusive; it is quite common to come across a machine learning system that falls into multiple categories. For example, a system that uses behavioral usage data to detect potential fraudsters on a banking website could be classified as a supervised model–based machine learning system. Let's examine these classification labels in more detail.

Supervised Learning

Supervised learning refers to the training phase of the machine learning system. During the supervised training phase, the machine learning algorithm is presented with sets of training data. Each set consists of inputs that the algorithm should use to make predictions as well as the desired (correct) result (see Figure 1.1).

FIGURE 1.1
Supervised learning

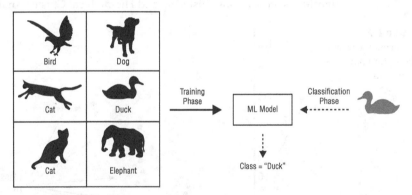

Labeled Training Set

Training consists of iterating over each set, presenting the inputs to the algorithm, and comparing the output of the algorithm with the desired result. The difference between the actual output and the desired output is used to adjust parameters of the algorithm to make the output of the algorithm closer to (or equal to) the desired output.

Human supervision is typically needed to define the desired output for each input in the training set. Once the algorithm has learned to make predictions on the training set, it can make predictions on data it has not previously encountered.

Most real-world machine learning applications are trained using supervised learning techniques. Some applications of supervised learning are the following:

- Finding objects in digital images
- Spam filtering

◆ Predicting the possibility of developing a medical condition based on lifestyle factors

◆ Predicting the likelihood of a financial transaction being fraudulent

◆ Predicting the price of property

◆ Recommending a product to a customer based on historical purchasing data

◆ A music streaming servicing suggesting a song to a customer based on what the customer has been listening to

Unsupervised Learning

Unsupervised learning also refers to the training phase of a machine learning system. However, unlike supervised learning, the algorithm is not given any information on the class/category associated with each item in the training set. Unsupervised learning algorithms are used when you want to discover new patterns in existing data. Unsupervised learning algorithms fall into two main categories:

◆ **Clustering:** These algorithms group the input data into a number of clusters based on patterns in the data. Visualizing these clusters can give you helpful insight into your data. Figure 1.2 shows the results of a clustering algorithm applied to the data on the heights and ages of children under six years of age. Some of the most popular clustering algorithms are k-means clustering and Hierarchical Cluster Analysis (HCA).

FIGURE 1.2
Clustering technique used to find patterns in the data

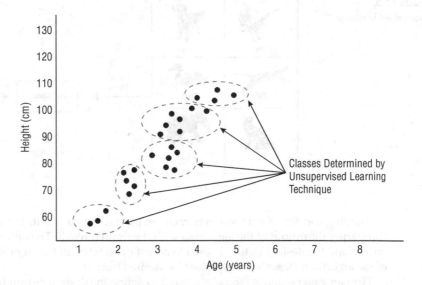

◆ **Dimensionality reduction:** These algorithms are used to combine a large number of input features into a smaller number of features without losing too much information, Typically the features that are combined have a high degree of correlation with each other. Dimensionality reduction reduces the number of input features and, therefore, the risk of overfitting; it also reduces the computational complexity of a machine learning model. Some examples of algorithms in this category are Principal Component Analysis (PCA), Linear Discriminant Analysis (LDA), and Autoencoding.

Semisupervised Learning

Semisupervised learning is a mix of both supervised and unsupervised learning. In many situations, it is practically impossible for a data scientist to label millions of samples for a supervised learning approach; however, the data scientist is already aware that there are known classifications in the data. In such a case, the data scientist labels a small portion of the data to indicate what the known classifications are, and the algorithm then processes the unlabeled data to better define the boundaries between these classes as well as potentially discover new classes altogether. Figure 1.3 depicts the results of applying semisupervised learning to the same data on the heights and ages of children under six years of age, with some of the samples labeled to indicate the level of education.

FIGURE 1.3
Semisupervised learning

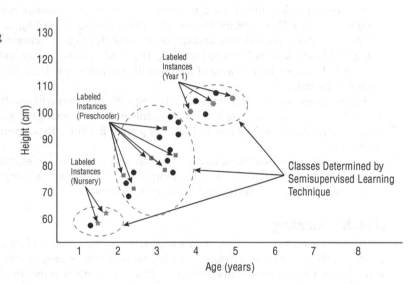

Real-world problems that involve extremely large datasets use this approach. Applications include speech recognition, natural language parsing, and gene sequencing.

A distinct advantage of semisupervised learning is that it is less prone to labeling bias than supervised learning. This is because a data scientist is labeling only a small portion of the data, and the effects of any personal labeling bias introduced by the scientist can be corrected by the unsupervised learning part of the algorithm based on the sheer number of unlabeled samples it will process.

Semisupervised learning algorithms make an assumption that the decision boundaries are geometrically simple; in other words, points that are close to each other are actually related in some way.

Reinforcement Learning

Reinforcement learning is a computational approach that attempts to learn using techniques similar to how humans learn—by interacting with their environment and associating positive and negative rewards with different actions. For instance, human beings have learned over time that touching a fire is a bad thing; however, using the same fire for cooking or providing warmth is a good thing. Therefore, when we come across a fire, we use it in positive ways.

A reinforcement learning–based system is typically called an *agent* and has a number of fixed actions that it can take at any given point in time. With each action is an associated reward or penalty. The goal of the system is to maximize cumulative reward over a series of actions. The knowledge gained by the agent is represented as a set of policies that dictate the actions that must be taken when the agent encounters a given situation. Reinforcement learning systems are used with two types of tasks.

◆ **Episodic tasks:** This is when the problem has a finite end point, such as winning a game.

◆ **Continuous tasks:** This is when the problem has no end point, such as maximizing the value of a stock portfolio.

Reinforcement learning algorithms often work in an environment where the results of choices are often delayed. Consider, for instance, an automated stock trading bot. It has several real-time inputs, manages several stocks, and can take one of three given actions at any point in time: buy a stock, sell a stock, or hold on to the stock. The result of several buy and sell decisions could be an eventual increase in the value of the portfolio (reward) or a decrease in the value of the portfolio (penalty).

The bot does not know beforehand if taking a given action will result in reward or penalty. The bot must also incorporate a delay mechanism and not attempt to gauge reward/penalty immediately after making a transaction. The goal of the bot is to maximize the number of rewards.

In time, the bot would have learned of trading strategies (policies) that it can apply in different situations. Reinforcement learning coupled with deep learning neural networks is a hotly researched topic among machine learning scientists.

Batch Learning

Batch learning, also known as *offline learning*, refers to the practice of training a machine learning model on the entire dataset before using the model to make predictions. A batch learning system is unable to learn incrementally from new data it encounters in the future. If you have new additional data for use in training a batch learning system, you need to create a new model on all the previous data plus the new data. You must then replace the older version of the model with this newly trained one.

Batch learning systems work in two distinct modes—learning and prediction. In learning mode, the system is in training and cannot be used to make predictions. In prediction mode, the system does not learn from observations.

The training process can be quite lengthy and require several weeks and several computing resources. You also need to retail all training data in the event that you need to train a new version of the model. This can be problematic if the training data is large and requires several gigabytes of storage.

Incremental Learning

Incremental learning, also known as *online learning*, refers to the practice of training a machine learning model continuously using small batches of data and incrementally improving the performance of the model. The size of a mini batch can range from a single item to several hundred items. Incremental learning is useful in scenarios where the training data is available in small chunks over a period of time or the training data is too large to fit in memory at once. The aim of incremental learning is to not have to retrain the model with all the previous training data; instead, the model's parameters (knowledge) are updated by a small increment with each new mini batch that it encounters. Incremental learning is often applied to real-time streaming data or very large datasets.

Instance-Based Learning

Instance-based learning, also known as *memory-based learning*, attempts to make predictions on new unseen data by picking the closest instance from instances in the training dataset. In effect, the machine learning system memorizes the training dataset, and prediction is simply a matter of finding the closest matching item. The training phase of instance-based learning systems involves organizing all the training data in an appropriate data structure so that finding the closest item during the prediction phase will be quicker. There is little (if any) model tuning involved, although some level of preprocessing may have been performed on the training data before presenting it to the machine learning system.

The advantage of an instance-based learning system is that both training and prediction are relatively quick, and adding more items to the training set will generally improve the accuracy of the system. It is important to note that the prediction from an instance-based system will be an instance that exists in the training set. For example, consider an instance-based machine learning system that predicts the shoe size of an individual given a height and weight value as input. Let's assume this system is trained using a training set of 100 items, where each item consists of a height weight and shoe size value.

If this instance-based machine learning system were to be used to predict the shoe size for a new individual given a height and weight of the new individual as input values, the predicted shoe size would be the value of the closest matching item in the training set. To put it another way, the machine learning system would never output a shoe size that was not in the training set to start with.

Model-Based Learning

Model-based learning systems attempt to build a mathematical, hierarchical, or graph-based model that models the relationships between the inputs and the output. Prediction involves solving the model to arrive at the result. Most machine learning algorithms fall into this category.

While model-based systems require more time to build, the size of the model itself is a fraction of the size of the training data, and the training data need not be retained (or presented to the model) in order to get a prediction. For example, a model built from a training dataset of over a million items could be stored in a small five-element vector.

Common Machine Learning Algorithms

Machine learning systems are also sometimes classified on the basis of the type of algorithm that is used to implement the model, and by now it should come as no surprise that there are several different types of machine learning algorithms, and this is an area of active research. You may have also encountered the term *classical machine learning models* to encompass all the algorithms that are not deep learning based. This may lead you to think that deep learning models are the only kind that matter and are the only kind that should be used to implement new solutions.

This is not true; non-deep-learning models have several use cases and are often the first choice for many tasks where the need to explain the result is just as important as its accuracy. In this section, you will learn about some of the different types of machine learning algorithms. This list is not exhaustive.

Linear Regression

Linear regression is a statistical technique that aims to find the equation of a line (or hyperplane) that is closest to all the points in the dataset. To understand how linear regression works, let's assume you have a training dataset of 100 rows, and each row consists of three features: X1, X2, and X3, and a known target value Y. Linear regression will assume that the relationship between target variable Y and input features X1, X2, and X3 is linear and can be expressed by the following equation:

$$Y_i = \alpha X1_i + \beta X2_i + \gamma X3_i + \varepsilon.$$

where:

◆ Y_i is the predicted value of the ith target variable.

◆ $X1_i$ is the ith value of feature X1.

◆ $X2_i$ is the ith value of feature X2.

◆ $X3_i$ is the ith value of feature X3.

◆ α, β, γ are the coefficients (or the slopes) of the features X1, X2, X3.

◆ ε is a constant term, also known as the bias term or intercept.

The training process will iterate over the entire training set multiple times and calculate the best values of α, β, γ, and ε. A set of values is considered better if they minimize an error function. An error function is a mathematical function that captures the difference between the predicted and actual values of X_i. Root mean square error (RMSE) is a commonly used error function and is expressed mathematically as follows:

$$RMSE = \sqrt{\frac{\sum_{i=1}^{N}(Y_i' - Y_i)^2}{N}}$$

where Y' is the predicted value and Y is the reference or actual value.

In effect, linear regression attempts to find the best line (or hyperplane in higher dimensions) that fits all the data points. The output of linear regression is a continuous, unbounded value. It can be a positive number or a negative number, and it can have any value depending on the inputs with which the model was trained. Therefore, linear regression models are commonly used to predict a continuous numeric value.

Linear regression with a large number of variables can be difficult to visualize. Figure 1.4 is a scatter plot of two variables: the feature variable X and the target variable Y.

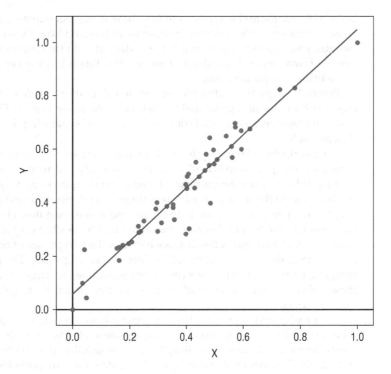

FIGURE 1.4
A simple linear
regression model

The values of both variables have been normalized to ensure they lie between 0.0 and 1.0. The regression line is also depicted in the plot, and as you can see, although it does not fit every single point perfectly, it appears to be the best-fitting overall line. The equation of this line can be represented as follows:

$$Y_i = \alpha X1_i + \varepsilon$$

The coefficient α and the intercept term ε of the regression line are values that are determined by the training process, and once you know those values, you can fit them into the equation to calculate the predicted Y value for any X value.

Support Vector Machines

A *support vector machine* (SVM) is a versatile model that can be used for a variety of tasks including classification, regression, and outlier detection. The original algorithm was invented in 1963 by Vladmir Vapnik and Alexey Chervonenkis as a binary classification algorithm. During the training process, support vector machine models aim to create a decision boundary that can partition the data points into classes. If the dataset has just two features, then this decision boundary is two-dimensional and can be conveniently represented in a scatter plot. If the decision boundary is linear, it will take the form of a straight line in two dimensions, a plane in three dimensions, and a hyperplane in n-dimensions. As humans, we cannot visualize more than three dimensions, which is why in order to understand how SVMs work, we'll consider a two-dimensional example with a fictional dataset with two features, with each point belonging to one of two classes. Let's also assume that the data is linearly separable—that is, one can draw a line that can separate them.

Figure 1.5 depicts a scatter plot of feature values of points from this fictional dataset, with one class of observations represented as circles and the other as stars. Figure 1.5 also presents three possible linear decision boundaries, each capable of separating the observations into two different sets.

The red decision boundary is too close to the first set of observations, and there is a risk that a model with that decision boundary could misclassify real-world observations if they are only slightly different from the training set. The green decision boundary has a similar problem in that it is too close to the second set of observations. The decision boundary in blue is optimal because it is as far away as possible from both classes and at the same time clearly separates both classes. SVM models aim to find this blue line or, to put it in another way, aim to find the decision boundary that maximizes the distance between the two classes of observations on either side. The half-width of the margin is denoted by Greek letter ε (epsilon). The points on the edges of the margin are called *support vectors* (the vector is assumed to originate at the origin and terminate at these points). In effect, one could say these vectors are supporting the margins—hence the name *support vectors*.

Most real-world data is not linearly separable as the dataset depicted in Figure 1.5 and, therefore, linear decision boundaries are unable to clearly separate the classes. Furthermore, even when the data is linearly separable, there is a possibility that the margin of separation is not as wide as the fictional example in Figure 1.5. Data points are often too close together to allow for wide, clear margins between the decision boundary and the support vectors on either side, and to handle this, SVM implementations include the concept of a tolerance parameter that controls the number of support vectors that can be inside the margins, which in turn has an impact on the width of the margin. Setting a large tolerance results in a wider margin with more samples in the margin, whereas setting a small tolerance value will result in a narrow margin. Having a wide margin is not necessarily a bad thing, as long as most of the points in the margin are on the correct side of the decision boundary.

The real power of SVM-based classifiers is their ability to create nonlinear decision boundaries. Support vector models use a mathematical function called a *kernel* that is used to transform each input point into a higher-dimensional space where a linear decision boundary can be found. This will be easier to understand with an example. Figure 1.6 shows a scatter plot of another fictional dataset with two features per data point, with each data point belonging to one of two classes. In this case, it is quite clear that there is no linear decision boundary (straight line) that can classify all data points correctly—no matter which way you draw a straight line, you will always end up with some samples on the wrong side of the line.

If, however, you were to add an extra dimension (z-axis) to the data, and compute z values for each point using the equation $z = x^2 + y^2$, then the data becomes linearly separable along the z-axis using a plane at $z = 0.3$. This is depicted in Figure 1.7.

FIGURE 1.5
Three potential decision boundaries

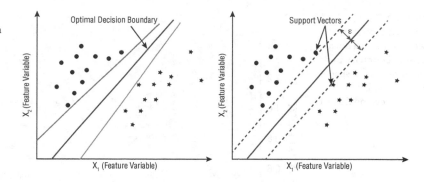

FIGURE 1.6
Data that cannot be classified using a linear decision boundary in two-dimensional space

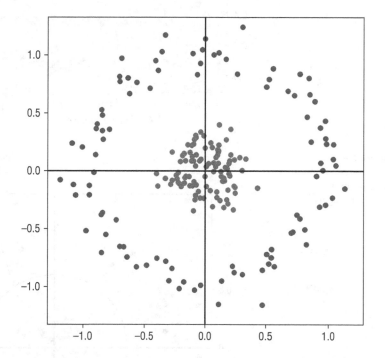

Since z was computed as $x^2 + y^2$, the decision plane at $z = 0.3$ implies $x^2 + y^2 = 0.3$, which is nothing but the equation of a circle in two dimensions. Therefore, the linear decision boundary in three-dimensional space has become a nonlinear decision boundary in two-dimensional space. This is illustrated in Figure 1.8.

This is an over-simplification of how kernels work, and if you are interested in learning more about SVM kernels, you should read *An Introduction to Support Vector Machines and Other Kernel-based Learning Methods* by Nello Cristianini and John Shawe-Taylor at `https://www.cambridge.org/core/books/an-introduction-to-support-vector-machines-and-other-kernelbased-learning-methods/A6A6F4084056A4B23F88648DDBFDD6FC`.

FIGURE 1.7
Data that cannot be classified using a linear decision boundary in two-dimensional space can be classified in three-dimensional space.

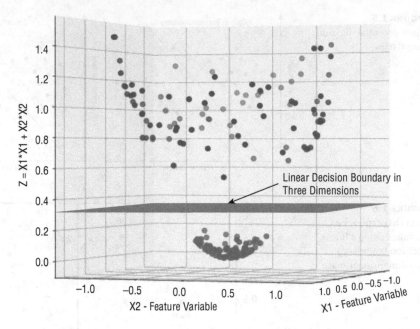

Linear Decision Boundary in Three Dimensions

$Z = X1*X1 + X2*X2$

X2 - Feature Variable

X1 - Feature Variable

FIGURE 1.8
Nonlinear decision boundary in two-dimensional space

Nonlinear Decision Boundary
$Z = X^2 + Y^2 = 0.3$

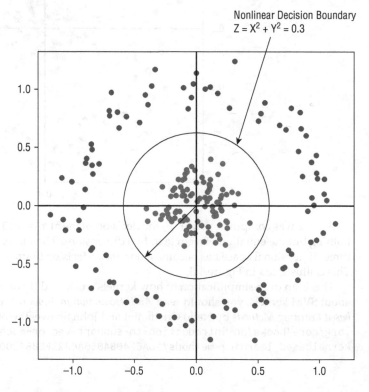

Logistic Regression

Logistic regression, despite having the word *regression* in its name, is a technique that can be used to build binary and multiclass classifiers. Logistic regression (also known as *logit regression*) builds upon the output of linear regression and returns a probability that the data point is of one class or another. Recall that the output of linear regression is a continuous unbounded value, whereas probabilities are continuous bounded values—bounded between 0.0 and 1.0.

To use a continuous value for binary classification, logistic regression converts it into a probability value between 0.0 and 1.0 by feeding the output of linear regression into a logistic function. In statistics, a logistic function is a type of function that converts values from [-infinity, + infinity] to [0, 1].

In the case of logistic regression, the logistic function is the sigmoid function, which is defined as follows:

$$\text{Sigmoid}(x) = \frac{1}{1 + e^{-x}}$$

The graph of the sigmoid function is presented in Figure 1.9. The output of the sigmoid function will never go below 0.0 or above 1.0, regardless of the value of the input.

FIGURE 1.9

The sigmoid function

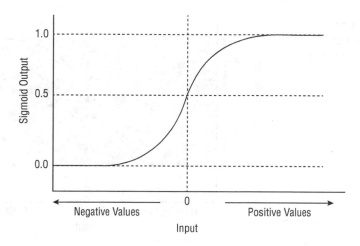

The output of the sigmoid function can be used for binary classification by setting a threshold value and treating all values below that as class A and everything above the threshold as class B (see Figure 1.10).

Logistic regression is inherently a binary classifier, but it can be used as a multiclass classifier for datasets where the target variable can belong to more than two classes. There are two fundamental approaches that can be used with a binary classifier for multiclass problems.

◆ **One-versus-rest approach:** This is also known as the OVR approach, and it involves creating a number of binary classification models with each model predicting the probability that the output is one of the subclasses. This approach will create N models for N classes, and the final class output by the multiclass classifier corresponds to the model that predicted the highest probability. Consider the popular Iris flowers dataset, where the target variable can have one of three values [0, 1, 2], corresponding to the type of Iris flower. In this case, the OVR approach would involve training three logistic regression models. The first model would predict the probability that the output class is 0 or not 0. Likewise, the second model would only predict the probability that the output class is 1 or not 1, and so on. The one-versus-rest approach is sometimes also referred to as the one-versus-all (OVA) approach.

♦ **One-versus-one approach:** This is known as the OVO approach, and it also involves creating a number of binary classification models and picking the class that corresponds to the model that output the largest probability value. The difference between the OVO approach and the OVR approach is in the number of models created. The OVO approach creates one model for each pairwise combination of output classes. In the case of the Iris flowers dataset, the OVO approach would also create three models.

   ♦ Logistic regression model that predicts output class as 0 or 1

   ♦ Logistic regression model that predicts output class as 0 or 2

   ♦ Logistic regression model that predicts output class as 1 or 2

FIGURE 1.10
Using the sigmoid function for binary classification

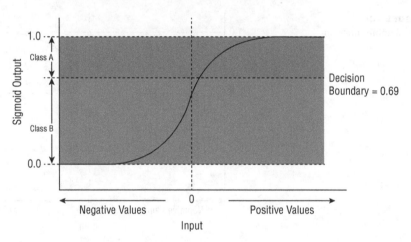

As you can see, the number of models generated increases with the number of features.
   While training an ensemble of binary models is one way to build models capable of multiclass classification, some algorithms like logistic regression can be modified to inherently support multiclass classification. In the case of logistic regression, the modification involves training multiple linear regression models internally and replacing the sigmoid function with another function—*the softmax function*. The softmax function is capable of receiving inputs from multiple linear-regression models and outputting class-wise probabilities. The softmax function is also known as the normalized exponential function, and its equation is illustrated in Figure 1.11.

FIGURE 1.11
Softmax logistic
regression

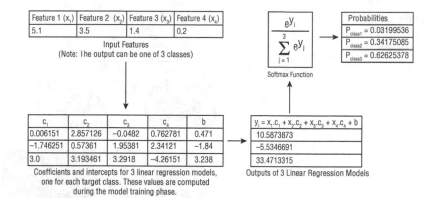

To understand how this function works, consider a dataset where each row contains four continuous numeric attributes and a multiclass target with three possible output classes: 0, 1, 2. When a softmax logistic regression model is trained on this dataset, it will contain three linear regression models within it, one for each target class. When the model is used for making predictions, each linear regression model will output a continuous numeric value that will be fed into the softmax function, which will in turn output three class-wise probabilities.

Decision Trees

Decision trees are, as their name suggests, tree-like structures where each parent node represents a decision boundary and child nodes represent outcomes of the decision. The topmost node of the tree is known as the root node. Building a decision tree model involves picking a suitable attribute for the decision at the root node and then recursively partitioning the tree into nodes until some optimal criteria is met.

Decision trees are versatile and can be used for both classification and regression tasks. When used for classification tasks, they are inherently capable of handling multiclass problems and are not affected by the scale of individual features. Predictions made by decision trees also have the advantage of being easy to explain; all you need to do is traverse the nodes of the decision tree, and you will be able to explain the prediction. This is not the case for models such as neural networks where it is not possible to explain why the model predicts something. Models such as decision trees, which allow you to easily understand the reasoning behind a prediction, are called *white-box models*, whereas models such as neural networks that do not provide the ability to explain a prediction are called *black-box models*.

Figure 1.12 depicts a decision tree trained on the popular Iris flowers dataset. The dataset consists of 150 rows, and each row contains four feature variables and one target variable. The four feature variables are the sepal length, sepal width, petal length, and petal width in cm. The target variable is a string that can take three possible values—setosa, virginica, and versicolor—and indicate the species of the Iris flower. You will learn more about decision trees in Chapter 8.

FIGURE 1.12
Decision tree
visualization

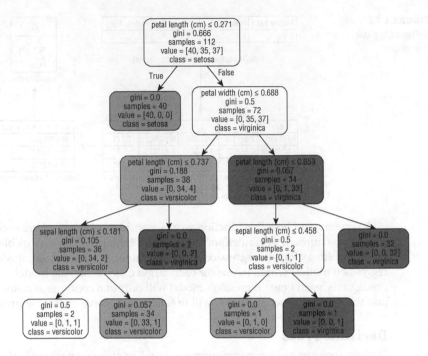

Table 1.1 contains a sample of five rows from the Iris flowers dataset that was used to train the decision tree.

TABLE 1.1:   Type and Range of Data Across 100 Sample Application

SEPAL LENGTH (CM)	SEPAL WIDTH (CM)	PETAL LENGTH (CM)	PETAL WIDTH (CM)
5.1	3.5	1.4	0.2
4.9	3.0	1.4	0.2
4.7	3.2	1.3	0.2
4.6	3.1	1.5	0.2
5.0	3.6	1.4	0.2

To make predictions with this decision tree, you start with the condition on the root node: `petal length <= 0.271`. There are two branches from this node; the branch on the left should be traversed if the condition is met, and the branch on the right is traversed if the condition is not met. You then repeat this process until you reach a leaf node, and the class associated with the leaf node will be the prediction. A decision tree can also be used for regression problems, with the key difference being that each node predicts a numeric value instead of a class.

Artificial Neural Networks

Artificial neural networks (ANNs) are computing tools that were developed by Warren McCulloch and Walter Pitts in 1943, and their design is inspired by biological neural networks. Figure 1.13 depicts the structure of a simple artificial neural network.

FIGURE 1.13

Structure of an ANN

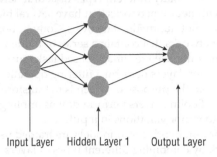

Input Layer   Hidden Layer 1   Output Layer

ANNs consist of units called *neurons* and are organized into a series of layers. There are three types of layers.

◆ **Input layer:** Directly receives inputs for the computation. There is only one input layer in an artificial neural network.

◆ **Output layer:** Provides the output of the computation. There can be one or more neurons in this layer depending on the type of problem the network is used to solve.

◆ **Hidden layer:** Sits between the input and the output layer. Neurons in the input layer are connected to neurons in the hidden layer, and neurons in the hidden layer are connected to the neurons in the output layer. When all of the neurons in one layer are connected to every neuron in the previous layer, the network is called a *fully connected network*. A simple neural network may not necessarily have a hidden layer, and complex neural networks such as deep learning networks have several hidden layers each with a large number of neurons in them.

Each of the connections between neurons has a weight value associated with it; the weight multiplies the value of the neuron the connection originated from. Each neuron works by computing the sum of its inputs and passing the sum through a nonlinear activation function. The output value of the neuron is the result of the activation function. Figure 1.14 depicts a simple neural network with two neurons in the input layer and one neuron in the output layer.

FIGURE 1.14

A simple neural network

If x_1, x_2 are the values loaded into the neurons in the input layer, if w_1, w_2 are the connection weights between the input layer and the output layer, and if f() is the activation function of the neuron in the output layer, then the output value of the neural network in Figure 1.14 is $f(w_1.x_1 + w_2.x_2)$.

There are many different types of activation functions with their own advantages and disadvantages. The reason to have an activation function is to ensure that the network is not just one big linear model. When a neural network is instantiated, the weights are set to random values. The process of training the neural network involves finding out the values of the weights.

There are many different types of neural network architectures; the field of deep learning deals with neural networks that have several hidden layers, and each layer can have several dozens, if not hundreds of neurons. Convolutional neural networks (CNNs) are a class of deep neural networks that contain a series of hidden layers called *convolution* and *pooling* layers. CNNs are commonly used for image-based tasks such as object detection and scene analysis. Convolution layers perform a filtering operation known in the image processing community as a *convolution*, the purpose of which is to transform the input data in such a way to find useful features. Pooling layers perform downsampling, and the purpose is to make the resulting model robust to minor variations in input.

Neural-network-based models are trained using libraries that allow you to quickly create a network by combining different types of layers. These libraries often provide efficient means to train the network. You can either create a CNN architecture from scratch or, more typically, use a well-known CNN architecture such as LeNet, AlexNet, VGGNet, and ResNet50. Since training a neural network is a time-consuming task and requires a lot of data, Apple provides several pre-trained models at `https://developer.apple.com/machine-learning/models/` based on popular CNN architectures.

The advantage of neural network-based models is their ability to handle complex problem spaces such as speech recognition, image understanding, etc. The disadvantage of neural network models is that they require a large amount of data to train, and it is not possible to determine why a neural-network-based model produces a certain output.

Sources of Machine Learning Datasets

Training a machine learning model requires high-quality data. In fact, lack of quality training data can result in the poor performance of models built using the best-known machine learning algorithms. *Quality* in this case refers to the ability of the training data to accurately capture the nuances of the underlying problem domain and to be reasonably free of errors and omissions. Some of the common sources for publicly available machine learning data are explored next.

Scikit-learn Datasets

The datasets package within Scikit-learn includes downsampled versions of popular machine learning datasets such as the Iris, Boston, and Digits datasets. These datasets are often referred to as *toy* datasets, and they are helpful when you are learning to use existing machine learning algorithms or are building a new algorithm and need a small well-known dataset to work with.

Scikit-learn provides functions to load a toy dataset into a dictionary-like object with the following attributes:

◆ **DESCR:** Returns a human-readable description of the dataset.

◆ **data:** Returns a NumPy array that contains the data for all the features.

◆ **feature_names:** Returns a NumPy array that contains the names of the features. Not all toy datasets support this attribute.

◆ **target:** Returns a NumPy array that contains the data for the target variable.

◆ **target_names:** Returns a NumPy array that contains the values of categorical target variables. The digits, Boston house prices, and diabetes datasets do not support this attribute.

The process of data exploration and feature engineering is typically performed using Jupyter Notebooks and Python. The following Python 3.6 snippet loads the toy version of the popular Iris dataset and explores the attributes of the dataset. The corresponding notebook file `Iris_dataset_exploration.ipynb` is included with the resources that accompany this chapter.

```
#load Scikit-learn's downsampled iris dataset
from sklearn import datasets
iris_dataset = datasets.load_iris()

# explore the dataset
print (iris_dataset.DESCR)
Iris Plants Database
====================

Notes
-----
Data Set Characteristics:
    :Number of Instances: 150 (50 in each of three classes)
    :Number of Attributes: 4 numeric, predictive attributes and the class
    :Attribute Information:
        - sepal length in cm
        - sepal width in cm
        - petal length in cm
        - petal width in cm
        - class:
                - Iris-Setosa
                - Iris-Versicolour
                - Iris-Virginica
    :Summary Statistics:

    ============== ==== ==== ======= ===== ====================
                    Min  Max  Mean    SD   Class Correlation
    ============== ==== ==== ======= ===== ====================
    sepal length:   4.3  7.9  5.84   0.83    0.7826
    sepal width:    2.0  4.4  3.05   0.43   -0.4194
    petal length:   1.0  6.9  3.76   1.76    0.9490  (high!)
    petal width:    0.1  2.5  1.20   0.76    0.9565  (high!)
    ============== ==== ==== ======= ===== ====================

    :Missing Attribute Values: None
    :Class Distribution: 33.3% for each of 3 classes.
    :Creator: R.A. Fisher
    :Donor: Michael Marshall (MARSHALL%PLU@io.arc.nasa.gov)
    :Date: July, 1988
```

```
This is a copy of UCI ML iris datasets.
http://archive.ics.uci.edu/ml/datasets/Iris

.....

print (iris_dataset.data.shape)
(150, 4)

print (iris_dataset.feature_names)
['sepal length (cm)', 'sepal width (cm)', 'petal length (cm)', 'petal
width (cm)']

print (iris_dataset.target.shape)
(150,)

print (iris_dataset.target_names)
['setosa' 'versicolor' 'virginica']
```

The following are the toy datasets included with Scikit-learn:

- **Boston house prices dataset:** This is a popular dataset used for building regression models. The toy version of this dataset can be loaded using the `load_boston()` function. The full version of this dataset can be found at `https://archive.ics.uci.edu/ml/machine-learning-databases/housing/`.

- **Iris plants dataset:** This is a popular dataset used for building classification models. The toy version of this dataset can be loaded using the `load_iris()` function. The full version of this dataset can be found at `https://archive.ics.uci.edu/ml/datasets/iris`.

- **Onset of diabetes dataset:** This is a popular dataset used for building regression models. The toy version of this dataset can be loaded using the `load_diabetes()` function. The full version of this dataset can be found at `http://www4.stat.ncsu.edu/~boos/var.select/diabetes.html`.

- **Handwritten digits dataset:** This is a dataset of images of handwritten digits 0 to 9 and is used in classification tasks. The toy version of this dataset can be loaded using the `load_digits()` function. The full version of this dataset can be found at `http://archive.ics.uci.edu/ml/datasets/Optical+Recognition+of+Handwritten+Digits`.

- **Linnerud dataset:** This is a dataset of exercise variables measured in middle-aged men and is used for multivariate regression. The toy version of this dataset can be loaded using the `load_linnerud()` function. The full version of this dataset can be found at `https://rdrr.io/cran/mixOmics/man/linnerud.html`.

- **Wine recognition dataset:** This dataset is a result of chemical analysis performed on wines grown in Italy. It is used for classification tasks. The toy version of this dataset can be loaded using the `load_wine()` function. The full version of this dataset can be found at `https://archive.ics.uci.edu/ml/machine-learning-databases/wine/`.

- **Breast cancer dataset:** This dataset describes the characteristics of cell nuclei of breast cancer tumors. It is used for classification tasks. The toy version of this dataset can be loaded using the `load_breast_cancer()` function. The full version of this dataset can be found at `https://goo.gl/U2Uwz2`.

AWS Public Datasets

Amazon hosts a repository of public machine learning datasets that can be easily integrated into applications that are deployed onto AWS. The datasets are available as S3 buckets or EBS volumes. Datasets that are available in S3 buckets can be accessed using the AWS CLI, AWS SDKs, or the S3 HTTP query API. Datasets that are available in EBS volumes will need to be attached to an EC2 instance. Public datasets are available in the following categories:

◆ **Biology:** Includes popular datasets such as the Human Genome Project.

◆ **Chemistry:** Includes multiple versions of PubChem and other content. PubChem is a database of chemical molecules that can be accessed at `https://pubchem.ncbi .nlm.nih.gov`.

◆ **Economics:** Includes census data and other content.

◆ **Encyclopedic:** Includes Wikipedia content and other content.

You can browse the list of AWS public datasets at `https://registry.opendata.aws`.

Kaggle.com Datasets

Kaggle.com is a popular website that hosts machine learning competitions. Kaggle.com also contains a large number of datasets for general use that can be accessed at `https://www .kaggle.com/datasets`. In addition to the general use datasets listed on the page, competitions on Kaggle.com also have their own datasets that can be accessed by taking part in the competition. The dataset files can be downloaded onto your local computer and can then be loaded into Pandas dataframes. You can get a list of current and past competitions at `https://www.kaggle .com/competitions`.

UCI Machine Learning Repository

The UCI machine learning repository is a public collection of more than 450 datasets that is maintained by the Center for Machine Learning and Intelligent Systems at UC Irvine. It is one of the oldest sources of machine learning datasets and is often the go-to destination for beginners and experienced professionals alike. The datasets are contributed by the general public and vary in the level of preprocessing you will need to perform in order to use them for model building. The datasets can be downloaded onto your local computer and then processed using tools like Pandas and Scikit-learn. You can browse the complete list of datasets at `https://archive.ics. uci.edu/ml/datasets.php`.

A small selection of the most popular UCI machine learning repository datasets is also hosted at Kaggle.com and can be accessed at `https://www.kaggle.com/uciml`.

NOTE To follow along with the examples in this chapter, ensure you have installed Anaconda Navigator and Jupyter Notebooks, as described in Appendix A.

You can download the code files for this chapter from Wrox.com or from GitHub using the following URL:

`https://github.com/asmtechnology/iosmlbook-chapter1.git`

Summary

- Machine learning is a discipline within artificial intelligence that deals with creating algorithms that learn from data.

- Machine learning deals with the problem of creating computer programs that can generalize and predict information reliably and quickly.

- Machine learning is commonly used to implement fraud detection systems, credit scoring systems, authentication decision engines, behavioral biometric systems, churn prediction, and product recommendation engines.

- The type of training data that is required to train a machine learning system can be used to classify the machine learning system into supervised, unsupervised, or semisupervised learning.

- Batch learning refers to the practice of training a machine learning model on the entire dataset before using the model to make predictions.

- Incremental learning, also known as online learning, refers to the practice of training a machine learning model continuously using small batches of data and incrementally improving the performance of the model.

- Instance-based learning systems make a prediction on new unseen data by picking the closest instance from instances in the training dataset.

- Model-based learning systems attempt to build a mathematical, hierarchical, or graph-based model that models the relationships between the inputs and the output.

Chapter 2

The Machine-Learning Approach

WHAT'S IN THIS CHAPTER

♦ Comparing traditional and machine-learning systems

♦ Techniques to evaluate binary classification models

♦ A summary of the key steps involved in building machine-learning applications

In the previous chapter, you learned about the basics of machine learning, terminology associated with machine-learning systems, and different types of models. In this chapter, you will examine a hypothetical scenario in which a rule-based system is devised to process credit card applications. The limitations of the rule-based system will then be examined, and a machine-learning system will be devised to address some of those limitations. The chapter will conclude with an overview of the steps involved in building a typical machine-learning solution.

By the time you finish this chapter, you should have a better understanding of how machine-learning systems are built and their strengths over traditional approaches.

The Traditional Rule-Based Approach

As humans, we are familiar with the concept of learning. Learning takes two major forms—memorization and understanding. There is a clear difference between memorizing your password and learning to drive a car. The latter involves understanding how the vehicle works and how to react in different situations on the road. You do not memorize the exact sequence of activities you need to perform to drive between your home and your place of work; instead, you apply the understanding you have gained while assessing the situation on the road.

The capabilities of machine-learning algorithms are not as sophisticated as human learning. Machines do not have the capability to understand and reason; however, they can predict and generalize, and they are capable of processing data much faster than humans. In this section, you will examine a hypothetical situation and understand how a machine-learning system can be applied to solve the problem at hand.

Imagine you have been hired by the credit cards team at a bank and tasked with creating a solution to offer a new credit card product to customers. Eligible customers can, under this new product, get cards with credit limits up to $25,000 at low interest rates. The bank would like to keep its losses to a minimum and requires that the credit card be offered only to customers who are likely to pay the money back to the bank.

To start with, you decide to create a new application form that customers will need to complete in order to apply for this credit card. On the application form, you ask for the following information:

◆ Name

◆ Age

◆ Gender

◆ Number of years lived at current address

◆ Number of addresses in the last five years

◆ Number of credit cards held with other banks

◆ Total amount of loan (excluding mortgage)

◆ Total income after tax

◆ Estimated regular monthly outgoings

◆ Total monthly repayments

◆ Homeowner status

◆ Marital status

◆ Number of dependents in the household

In a real-world scenario, you would ask for a lot more information and would also use a credit scoring company to provide the applicant's credit rating, but for the purposes of this example, this list will do. Let's also assume that the mechanism to allow customers to apply for the credit card is available on the bank's website, and the data from all application forms is available in a table in a SQL database within the bank.

When the product is launched, your bank expects the product to be popular with customers, so you need to have a plan in place to process a large number of applications each week. It is also crucial for your bank to remain competitive in the credit cards space, and therefore, you cannot keep applicants waiting for weeks to find out the outcome of a credit card application. You need to ensure that the bank's standard terms of service apply to your new product, and therefore, at least 51 percent of all credit applications need to be decided within a few minutes of the application being received by the bank.

Clearly, it is not cost effective to hire a few hundred analysts to scrutinize loan applications as they come in and make the necessary checks to arrive at a decision. You have two choices before you:

◆ You can build a rule-based decision system.

◆ You can build a machine-learning system.

In this section, you will examine how a rule-based system can be built and applied to the problem of scrutinizing loan applications. In the next section, you will examine how a similar system could be built using machine-learning algorithms.

To implement a rule-based system, you decide to store the business rules in a database and encapsulate the logic to apply the rules to a new loan application into a server-side application. You plan to have a cluster of these servers that can be scaled up as necessary to deal with increased volumes. Figure 2.1 depicts the architecture of the proposed system.

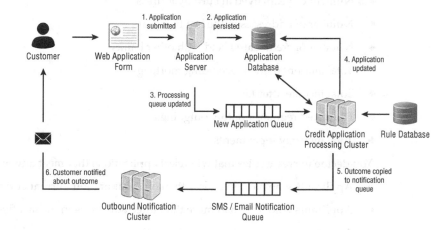

FIGURE 2.1
Architecture of a rule-based decision system

When an applicant submits a credit card application on the bank's website, a unique card application identifier is generated, and a row is added to a database by the web application. The web application also publishes a message onto a message queue. The contents of that message contain the unique application identifier. A cluster of loan processing servers subscribes to the message queue, and the first available servers will pick up the message and begin processing the credit card application. When the server reaches a decision, it will update the loan application in the database and publish a message on another message queue. The contents of this new message will contain all the information needed to send an SMS or email notification to the customer, informing the customer of the outcome.

How do you define the rules that will be used to make the decision? To start with, you need to create the rules based on your experience of the problem domain and qualities of the loan application forms that you feel are favorable. If your business has another rule-based system that your solution is trying to replace, then you may also be able to port some of the rules from the existing system.

Let's assume you do not have access to the existing system and need to define the business rules yourself. Looking at the fields in your loan application form, you decide that the following fields can be discarded from the decision-making process, as you feel they are not likely to have any impact on the ability of the individual to keep up their monthly repayments:

◆ Name

◆ Gender

◆ Marital status

◆ Number of dependents in the household

◆ Homeowner status

You are now left with the following information that you can use to build your rules:

◆ Number of years lived at current address

◆ Number of addresses in the last five years

◆ Number of credit cards held with other banks

◆ Total amount of loan (excluding mortgage)

◆ Total income after tax

◆ Estimated regular monthly outgoings

◆ Total monthly repayments

You decide to create rules that will reject applications that meet any of the following criteria:

◆ Applicants who have lived less than one year at their current address

◆ Applicants who have had more than three addresses in the last five years

◆ Applicants who have two or more credit cards with other banks

◆ Applicants whose disposable monthly income is less than 15 percent of their total income after tax

These rules can be coded in any programming language using if-then-else statements. Figure 2.2 contains a flowchart that depicts the decision-making process using the rules you have defined.

There is a possibility that the rules you have created and the initial assumptions you have made were not optimal, but you can always tailor the rules if you observe the losses due to missed payments exceeding the bank's risk threshold. In time, as the volumes of credit applications increase, you will need to tailor your business rules to deal with the increased volumes. You are likely to encounter a few problems:

◆ Your rules become complicated and interdependent; it becomes increasingly complex to replace old rules with new ones.

◆ Your rules have not been based on any numerical analysis; they have been created ad hoc to address increasing demand.

◆ Your rules do not account for changing patterns in the economy. For example, in the midst of a recession, a larger number of people may end up missing their payments even though your rules predict that they should not. You will need to constantly update your rules, which can be a costly and time-consuming process.

Let's now see how a machine-learning system could be used to address these problems.

FIGURE 2.2
A flowchart depicting the decision-making process for a rule-based system

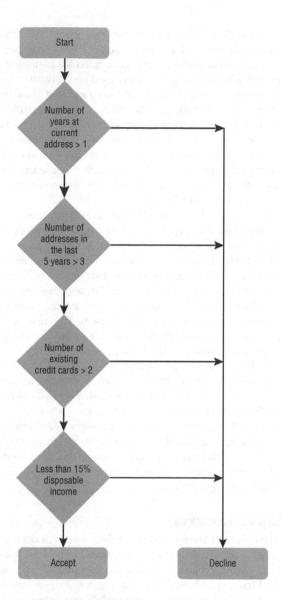

A Machine-Learning System

Unlike a rule-based solution, you cannot create a machine-learning solution without historical data from previous applicants. It is important to have data that is accurate and relevant to the problem you are trying to solve. You may be tempted to build your machine-learning model using data from a different loan product, such as a personal loan. This is not recommended, as there could be trends in that data that are applicable only to personal loan applications.

You may be wondering why there was no need for historical data while building the rule-based system and why defining the rules based on an intuitive understanding of the questions alone was sufficient. The reason is that in the rule-based approach, you were defining the rules based on your personal knowledge and experience of the problem domain. A machine-learning system, on the other hand, does not start with any prior knowledge of the problem domain and does not have the intuitive capability of a human being. Instead, a machine-learning system attempts to make its own inferences purely from the data it encounters. Not only do you need data, but you need it to be relevant. If the data that is used to train the machine-learning system is significantly different from what the system will encounter when asked to make predictions, the predictions are likely to be incorrect.

Just how much data will you need? There is no simple answer to that question. In general, machine-learning algorithms require a lot of data to be trained effectively, but it is not just the quantity that matters, it is also the quality of the data. If your data has too many samples that follow a particular trend, then your machine-learning system will be biased toward that trend.

For the purpose of this example, let's assume you have decided to pick the data for 5,000 applicants randomly from your database and export these rows to a CSV file. These are all applicants who have applied for your credit card product and have either kept up with their regular payments or missed at least one payment. The input variables in this case would be answers to the questions asked on the form; the target variable will be a Boolean that indicates whether the applicant missed at least one payment.

This type of data, where you already know the value of the target variable, is known as *labeled data* and is commonly used for training machine-learning models. Not all data is labeled; in fact, the vast majority of data in the world is unlabeled. Using unlabeled (or partially labeled) data to train machine-learning algorithms is an active area of research.

What if you want to build a machine-learning solution but have absolutely no data of your own and can't wait for months (or years) to collect high-quality labeled data? Your best option in that case would be to find existing datasets from free/paid sources on the Internet that are as close as possible to the problem domain you are working in. Chapter 1 provided links to several public machine-learning datasets.

Picking Input Features

Once you have collected the labeled input data, you will need to perform basic statistical analysis on the data to pick input variables that are most likely to be relevant and prepare the input data for the machine-learning model. Having the data in a CSV file makes it easy to load into data analysis tools. Most cloud-based data analysis tools allow you to upload CSV files, and some also support importing data from cloud-based relational databases.

Data visualization techniques are commonly used to get an indication of the spread and correlation of individual features. You will most likely build and train a model using an initial set of features and calculate the value of a performance metric while making predictions with the model. You will then retrain the model with additional input features and repeat as necessary as long as you observe a significant improvement in the value of the performance metric.

The number of features you choose will also impact the size of the training dataset you are likely to need. A model with three features could be built using a dataset of 500 items, whereas a model with 10 features will likely need a training dataset that consists of several thousands of items.

It may surprise you to learn that the bulk of a data scientist's job is looking at data and working out ways to use it. This work is often referred to as *data munging*, and it involves several steps including but not limited to the following:

◆ Finding out whether there are any missing values in the data

◆ Working out the best way to handle missing values

◆ Examining the statistical distribution of the data

◆ Examining the correlation between input variables

◆ Creating new input variables by splitting or combining existing input variables

NOTE   *Munge* is a technical term coined by MIT students and means to transform data using a series of reversible steps to arrive at a different representation. Data munging is also known as *data wrangling* and *feature engineering*.

Python, Jupyter Notebook, NumPy, Pandas, and Matplotlib are commonly used for statistical analysis and feature engineering. Appendix B provides an introduction to NumPy and Pandas; basic feature engineering techniques are covered in Chapter 3.

Let's now examine the questions on the application form and perform some simple feature engineering, based on personal experience, to arrive at the inputs to our first machine-learning model. Table 2.1 lists all the questions on the loan application form with their data types, range of expected values, and range of actual values as observed in 5,000 samples.

TABLE 2.1:   Type and Range of Data Across 5,000 Sample Applications

QUESTION	TYPE OF DATA	ACTUAL RANGE	MAXIMUM RANGE
Name	Free text	Characters A–Z; some special characters	Characters A–Z; some special characters
Age	Continuous numeric	22–45	18–150
Sex	Categorical	Male, Female, Undisclosed	Male, Female, Undisclosed
Number of years lived at current address	Continuous numeric	0–7	0–150
Number of addresses in the last five years	Continuous numeric	1–6	1–10
Number of credit cards held with other banks	Discrete numeric	1,2,3	1,2,3,4,5,6,7,8,9,10

TABLE 2.1:   Type and Range of Data Across 5,000 Sample Applications *(CONTINUED)*

QUESTION	TYPE OF DATA	ACTUAL RANGE	MAXIMUM RANGE
Total amount of loan (excluding mortgage)	Continuous numeric	0–17500	0–10 million
Total income after tax	Continuous numeric	50000–200000	0–10 million
Estimated regular monthly outgoings	Continuous numeric	3000–15000	0–10 million
Total monthly repayments	Continuous numeric	0–1500	0–10 million
Homeowner status	Categorical	Yes or No	Yes or No
Marital Status	Categorical	Single, Married, Undisclosed	Single, Married, Undisclosed
Number of dependents in the household	Discrete numeric	1,2,3	1,2,3,4,5,6,7,8,9,10

It is quite clear that some of the answers are categorical, while others are numeric. The numeric features themselves are either discrete or continuous and have different ranges of values.

Most machine-learning models are designed to perform better on one type of feature over the other. Some statistical-based learning models are also sensitive to large numeric values. After examining the type of questions on the application form, the range of input values, and sample data for 5,000 applicants, you decide that you want to use all of the answers on the application form as input features, except for the following:

- Name of the applicant
- Number of dependents
- Number of cards held with other banks

You also decide to engineer a new feature called Total Disposable Income and convert the three categorical features into numeric features, as listed in Table 2.2.

TABLE 2.2:   Transforming Categorical Features Into Numeric Features

ORIGINAL CATEGORICAL FEATURE	NEW NUMERIC FEATURE	ALLOWED VALUES/RANGE
Sex	SexIsMale	0 or 1
	SexIsFemale	0 or 1
	SexIsUndisclosed	0 or 1

TABLE 2.2:   Transforming Categorical Features Into Numeric Features   *(CONTINUED)*

ORIGINAL CATEGORICAL FEATURE	NEW NUMERIC FEATURE	ALLOWED VALUES/RANGE
Homeowner status	IsHomeOwner	0 or 1
	IsNotHomeOwner	0 or 1
Marital status	MaritalStatusIsSingle	0 or 1
	MaritalStatusIsMarried	0 or 1
	MaritalStatusIsUndisclosed	0 or 1

The newly engineered feature called Total Disposable Income is defined as follows:

Total Disposable Income = Total Income After Tax – Regular
Monthly outgoings – Monthly Loan Repayments

Feature engineering techniques are covered in Chapter 3, but it's worth noting that questions that have been answered as undisclosed are being treated as first-class values, and the fact that an answer was not provided is captured by creating the feature variables SexIsUndisclosed and MaritalStatusIsUndisclosed. Were the absence of an answer not to be treated as meaningful data, you would either need to reject the application form or attempt to substitute the missing answer with the mean or median value.

Table 2.3 lists the new set of input and engineered features, the expected range of values for each feature, and the actual range of values, as observed in 5,000 sample application forms.

TABLE 2.3:   Modified Input Features

FEATURE NAME	FEATURE DESCRIPTION	TYPE OF DATA	OBSERVED RANGE	MAXIMUM RANGE
F1	Age	Continuous Numeric	22–45	18–150
F2	SexIsMale	Discrete Numeric	0, 1	0 or 1
F3	SexIsFemale	Discrete Numeric	0, 1	0 or 1
F4	SexIsUndisclosed	Discrete Numeric	0, 1	0 or 1
F5	Number of years lived at current address	Continuous Numeric	0–7	0–150
F6	Number of addresses in the last 5 years	Continuous Numeric	1–6	0–10
F7	Total disposable income	Continuous Numeric	0–5000	0–10 million

TABLE 2.3:   Modified Input Features   *(CONTINUED)*

FEATURE NAME	FEATURE DESCRIPTION	TYPE OF DATA	OBSERVED RANGE	MAXIMUM RANGE
F8	Total amount of loan (excluding mortgage)	Continuous Numeric	0–17500	0–10 million
F9	Total income after tax	Continuous Numeric	50000–200000	0–10 million
F10	Estimated regular monthly outgoings	Continuous Numeric	3000–15000	0–10 million
F11	Total monthly repayments	Continuous Numeric	0–1500	0–10 million
F12	IsHomeOwner	Discrete Numeric	0, 1	0 or 1
F13	IsNotHomeOwner	Discrete Numeric	0, 1	0 or 1
F14	MaritalStatusIsSingle	Discrete Numeric	0, 1	0 or 1
F15	MaritalStatusIsMarried	Discrete Numeric	0, 1	0 or 1
F16	MaritalStatusIsUndisclosed	Discrete Numeric	0, 1	0 or 1

It is quite clear that the range of allowed values for the features are not all the same. For example, the F1 values lie in the range [18,100], whereas other feature values lie in the ranges [0,1], [0, 150], [1,10], and [0, 10000000]. Before you can use this data, you will need to normalize the values of all the features to lie in the same range [0, 1]. Normalization is covered in Chapter 3 and involves transforming the value of each feature so that it lies in the interval [0, 1]. You will need to normalize both the training data as well as data on which your solution will make predictions.

You could also have chosen to transform the numeric features into categorical features by defining ranges of allowed values. For example, a given response to the *total income after tax* question—which is a continuous value between 0 and 10 million—could be converted into one of the following categorical values:

- `Between0and100000`

- `Between100001And500000`

- `Above500001`

There is no right or wrong way to engineer features. Sometimes the choice of machine-learning algorithm dictates the type of features (numerical or categorical). Some algorithms, such as linear regression, work better with numeric features. Others that are based on decision trees work better with categorical features. Sometimes you start with a set of features only to realize that the predictive accuracy of the model trained on those features is not good enough and you need to start from scratch with new features, perhaps a different algorithm or training technique.

Preparing the Training and Test Set

Before you can build a machine-learning model, you need to create separate training and testing datasets. The training set is used to build the model, whereas the test set is used to evaluate the performance of the model. The reason to have a separate training and test sets is that a well-trained model will always perform well on the training set, as it has learned all the items in the training set.

To truly measure the performance of the model, you need to present data that it has not encountered during training. Often the training dataset is split into further training and validation datasets, therefore resulting in a three-way split of the original data—the training dataset, the validation dataset, and the test dataset. The purpose of the validation dataset is to help tune the model, and sometimes the validation set is the same as the test set, although this is not recommended.

Typically, you will hold out 30 percent of the data you have collected for testing and use the remaining 70 percent for model building. The training and validation subsets can be created by splitting the 70 percent of the data reserved for model building into two smaller subsets, using, once again, a 70/30 split. When preparing training, validation, and test datasets, it is important to ensure that the members of the dataset are well distributed and do not exhibit bias toward any particular trend. For instance, if the training dataset consisted of a large proportion of applicants that were female and had annual incomes exceeding $100,000, the model is likely to incorporate this trend as part of its learning and perform poorly on other types of applicants. When a model performs well on the training set and poorly on the test set, the model is said to *overfit* the training data.

Cross-validation can help minimize the possibility of the model picking up on unexpected bias in the training set. The idea behind cross-validation is to shuffle the entire model building dataset randomly and divide it into a number of smaller sets (known as *folds*). If, for instance, the data was divided into 10 equal folds, then 10 different models would be trained and evaluated. For each model, the same hyperparameters will be used. The only difference between the models will be the data that is used during the training and evaluation cycle. One of the folds will be held out as the test set, and the remaining nine will make the training set. This is illustrated in Figure 2.3.

FIGURE 2.3
Cross-validation using four folds

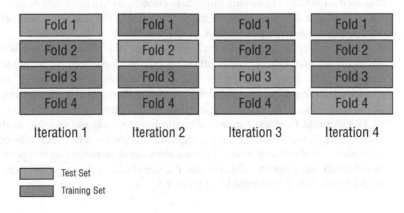

Fold 1	Fold 1	Fold 1	Fold 1
Fold 2	Fold 2	Fold 2	Fold 2
Fold 3	Fold 3	Fold 3	Fold 3
Fold 4	Fold 4	Fold 4	Fold 4
Iteration 1	Iteration 2	Iteration 3	Iteration 4

Test Set
Training Set

The performance of each model on the respective test set is recorded, and the average value of the performance metric is used to assess the quality of the model.

Sometimes the bias is introduced during the data collection phase (also known as *sampling bias*) and no amount of cross-validation can help remove it. For instance, you may be working with a dataset that captures consumer shopping trends and was collected from people in shopping centers during the Christmas holiday season. This data will be biased toward trends that are specific to holiday shopping, and a model built using this data will perform poorly if it's used to predict what consumers may buy over the course of the entire year. In such cases, the best option is to collect more data to remove the sampling bias.

Picking a Machine-Learning Algorithm

There are a number of machine-learning algorithms that can be used for classification tasks. In the current example, the objective is to decide, at the point of application, whether an applicant should be issued a credit card. The machine-learning system that makes this decision will be trained on data that is labeled to indicate if the customer has historically missed any payments (negative outcome) or if the customer did not miss a single payment (positive outcome).

The decision to issue the credit card is directly related to whether the machine-learning system indicates the customer will default or not. This is a typical classification problem and a number of algorithms could be used:

- Logistic regression

- Decision trees

- Random forests

- XGBoost

- Neural networks

- Clustering-based techniques

The choice of algorithm is often influenced by factors such as desired accuracy, number of classes desired (binary versus multiclass classification), availability of sufficient training data, time taken to train the model, memory footprint of the trained model, and resources required to deploy the model into production.

In this example, we will use an algorithm called *logistic regression*, which is an algorithm that performs well for binary classification problems. These are problems that involve classifying something into one of two classes and were introduced in Chapter 1. Logistic regression models work by training a linear regression model and then passing the continuous real-valued output of the linear model to a mapping function such as the sigmoid function.

The sigmoid function converts a continuous real-valued number in the range $[-\infty, +\infty,]$ to the range $[0, 1]$. Since the output of the sigmoid function is a number between 0 and 1, you can select a suitable threshold and treat all values above that threshold as the positive outcome (issue the credit card) and treat all values below the threshold as the negative outcome (do not issue the credit card). This is illustrated in Figure 2.4.

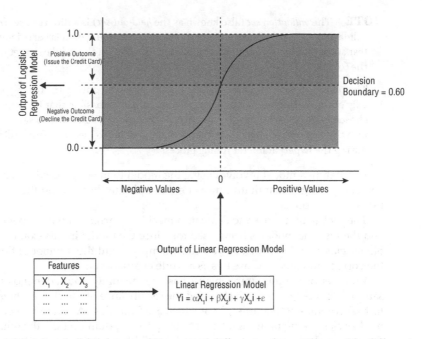

The choice of the threshold value is arbitrary, and different values will provide different results. The threshold value in a logistic regression model is a hyperparameter and can be tuned to get better results. Logistic regression is simple to understand; however, it may fail to provide good results if the relationship between the target variable and the input features is complex. In such cases, you can consider using a tree-based model such as decision trees or an instance-learning based clustering model such as k-means.

Evaluating Model Performance

Once you have built a model that can be used to determine whether an applicant should be issued a credit card, you need to be able to quantitatively measure its performance and ideally make tweaks to the model to improve performance. The purpose of evaluating a model is to determine how well it works on data that it has not encountered during training. The first model you build is usually called a *baseline model*, and its performance is evaluated on a labeled test set, which was not used during the training process. Once you have a baseline model, you will typically try different combinations of hyperparameters to find a model that performs better than the baseline version.

However, the final performance of a model is evaluated using a separate labeled validation set that was set aside during the dataset preparation phase.

NOTE   The *validation set* (also known as the *held-out set*) is a different set from the test set. The validation set is usually set aside even before the training data is partitioned into the training and test subsets. When cross-validation is used, the data in the validation set does not appear in any of the folds.

The reason to have a separate validation set is because during the tuning phase, the model is repeatedly encountering the values of the test set, and it is possible that the hyperparameters that are chosen begin to create models that overfit the test set. You can also say that values in the test set leak into the hyperparameters. It is, therefore, important to have one final validation set that's not used during the hyperparameter tuning process.

Evaluating a model involves using the model to make predictions on the test/validation test and computing a quantitative measure that indicates how far off the predictions are from the expected outcomes.

The metric that is used to evaluate a machine-learning model depends on the type of model and the task the model is being used for. Since the model in this example attempts to solve a binary classification problem, you could simply count the number of times the model predicted the correct outcome and use this as a crude evaluation metric.

Whether or not this simple metric has any meaning would depend on the proportion of samples that belong to each class and the significance of the classes themselves. For instance, if a test set contains 100 samples, 50 of which are from class A and the other 50 belong to class B, with neither class being more significant to the problem domain than the other, a model that predicts the correct class 80 percent of the time is straightforward to understand.

If, however, 95 items in the test set were from class A and only five were from class B, then a model that predicts the correct class 80 percent of the time is not so good after all. The problem can be significantly worse if the model was meant to predict whether an individual had a deadly illness, and the five samples from class B were the only ones that indicated a presence of the illness. This is not as an impossible situation as you might think. There is a high possibility that a random sample of the general population will have a few number of individuals with a specific illness.

To get a better idea of the model's performance, what you need is a set of metrics that capture the class-wise performance of the model. The most commonly used primary metrics for binary classification are listed next. These metrics assume one of the two target classes represents a positive outcome, whereas the other represents a negative outcome. In the case of the credit card application processing system, issuing the credit card to an applicant could be defined as the positive outcome.

- **True positive count:** The number of times the model predicted a positive outcome and the prediction was correct

- **False positive count:** The number of times the model predicted a positive outcome and the prediction was incorrect

- **True negative count:** The number of times the model predicted a negative outcome and the prediction was correct

- **False negative count:** The number of times the model predicted a negative outcome and the prediction was incorrect

This class-wise prediction accuracy is also sometimes referred to as the class-wise *confusion*, and when these four primary metrics are placed in a 2×2 matrix, the resulting matrix is called the *confusion matrix*. Figure 2.5 depicts a confusion matrix and explains what the individual numbers mean.

FIGURE 2.5

A class-wise confusion matrix

Features			Actual Target	Predicted Target
X_1	X_2	X_3	Y	Y
...	...	...	Y	Y
...	...	...	N	Y
...	...	...	Y	Y
...	...	...	Y	Y
...	...	...	Y	Y
...	...	...	N	N
...	...	...	N	N
...	...	...	N	N
...	...	...	N	Y
...	...	...	Y	N
...	...	...	Y	N
...	...	...	Y	N

	Predicted Class: Positive	Predicted Class: Negative	
Actual Class: Positive	4/12 True Positives	3/12 False Negatives	Total Number of Actual Positives = 4 + 3 = 7
Actual Class: Negative	2/12 False Positives	3/12 True Negatives	Total Number of Actual Negatives = 3 + 2 = 5

Total Number of Positive Predictions = 4 + 2 = 6   Total Number of Negative Predictions = 3 + 3 = 6

In addition to these primary statistical metrics, data scientists use the following secondary metrics for binary classification models. The values of these metrics are computed from the primary metrics.

◆ **Accuracy:** This is defined as (TP + TN) / (total number of predictions). This is basically the same as counting the number of times the model predicted the correct value.

◆ **Precision:** This is defined as TP / (TP + FP). If you look at Figure 2.5, you will notice that the denominator is the total number of positive predictions made by the model. Therefore, precision can also be written as TP / (total number of positive predictions), and it measures how precise your model is. Precision is a good measure to use when there is a high cost associated with a false positive. The closer the value is to 1.0, the more precise are the positive predictions.

◆ **Recall:** This is defined as TP / (TP + FN). Looking at Figure 2.5, you will notice that the denominator of this expression is the actual number of positive samples in the dataset. Therefore, the expression to compute recall can be rewritten as TP / (total number of positive samples in the test set). Recall is a good measure to use when there is a high cost associated with false negatives.

Data scientists often use a visualization tool called the receiver operating characteristics (ROC) curve and a metric called the area under ROC curve (AUC) to evaluate the quality of a classification model. The ROC curve is computed by plotting the true positive rate on the x-axis, against the false-positive rate on the y-axis for a number of different confusion matrices, computed for threshold values between 0.0 and 1.0. Figure 2.6 depicts ROC curves obtained from two different types of binary classification models trained on the same data.

When comparing the performance of different binary classification models, the model with the larger AUC metric generally performs better.

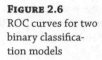

FIGURE 2.6
ROC curves for two
binary classifica-
tion models

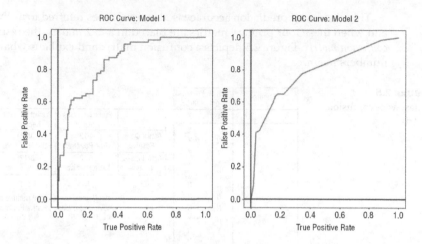

The Machine-Learning Process

In the previous section, you learned about the differences between the traditional and machine-learning approaches. In this section, you will obtain a summary of the steps involved in building a machine-learning system.

Data Collection and Preprocessing

This is the first stage of the process, and it is usually where the data scientist spends most of his time. Few data scientists have readily available, high-quality data at their disposal. Often, companies that want to train and deploy a machine-learning solution have to wait for sufficient training data to be captured through various means such as real-time sensors, analytics feeds, customer surveys, application logs, and so on. Even when sufficient quantities of data become available, the data is unlikely to be usable in its initial form. For instance, analytic data captured by a typical mobile application will be a JSON or XML object that captures information such as time stamps, the name of the screen the user is viewing and the name of the user interface element that the user clicked, the IP address, and so on. If the data is a log message, then it is probably even more cryptic and decipherable by only a handful of people who understand the conventions used while creating the log message.

As you can imagine, a significant amount of time and effort is invested in cleaning up, enriching, and combining data from multiple sources so that meaningful features can be engineered. If the algorithm the data scientist wants to use requires supervised training, then the data scientist has to also label all the data in some way.

Preparation of Training, Test, and Validation Datasets

Once you have sufficient training data, the next step involves shuffling and splitting the master dataset into separate training, test, and validation datasets. The purpose of each dataset is described here:

- **Training dataset:** The training dataset consists of labeled items and is used to train the model. In other words, your machine-learning model will process and learn patterns from this data.

- **Test dataset:** The test dataset consists of labeled items and is different from the training dataset. The purpose of the test dataset is to calculate the performance of the model on data that it has not encountered during the training phase. If the performance of the model is not found to be good enough, the data scientist adjusts one or more hyperparameters of the model, re-trains the model on the training set, and evaluates the result of the tuning process on the test set. While the model does not directly learn patterns from the test dataset, the fact that the performance of the test dataset influences the specific combination of hyperparameters tuned by the data scientist implies that the validation dataset has an indirect effect on the model.

- **Validation dataset:** The validation dataset consists of labeled items that do not belong to either the training or test sets. It is used as the gold standard to evaluate the performance of the model and ensures the model is not overfitting the training or test data. The performance of the model on the validation dataset is not used to influence any hyperparameter tuning or feature selection decisions that the data scientist makes. Sometimes the same dataset is used for testing and validation, but this approach is not recommended.

Model Building

After the training, test, and validation datasets are prepared, you can build the machine-learning model. The process of building a model is also known as *training* the model, and it involves submitting observations from the training dataset to some code that implements a machine-learning algorithm. The observations can be submitted one at a time, or in mini batches. Depending on the type of model you are training, it may be possible to harness the power of parallel processing to speed up the training process. The result of model building is a trained machine-learning model.

Model Evaluation

The evaluation stage of the machine-learning process involves using the model with the test dataset to make predictions on observations within the dataset and computing a metric that represents how far off the predictions are from the expected values. The metric you use will depend on a number of factors such as the type of model you are using and the nature of the problem you are trying to solve. For example, if you are working on a classification problem, the problem domain will influence decisions such as whether accuracy, precision, or recall is the preferred metric you will optimize for.

Model Tuning

Rarely does a machine-learning model perform well on the test dataset the first time you evaluate the model. After feature engineering, model tuning is the next area where a data scientist will spend his time. Depending on the type of model you are using, you may have a number of hyperparameters that you could adjust to get different results. Sometimes, no matter how many hyperparameters you adjust, the performance of the model is just not good enough. In such a case, you may need to revisit your initial choice of features from the training data and perhaps change the number of features or engineer new features entirely and repeat the entire training and evaluation process again.

Model Deployment

To use your trained and tuned machine-learning model in your applications, you will need to export (serialize) the model into a file and deploy the model in a suitable execution (runtime) environment. As an iOS developer, the obvious choice for you is Apple's Core ML, which both defines a file format and provides an execution environment. However, Apple's Core ML format isn't the only serialization format; a popular format is the RecordIO protobuf format, which is commonly used to serialize models trained with Google TensorFlow and deploy them into a variety of server-side hosting environments, including Google's TFServe, AWS SageMaker, and others.

The manner in which you interact with your machine-learning model from your application is dictated by the execution environment. Models executed within Apple's Core ML environment can be interfaced with using Swift code. Models deployed in server-side execution environments use HTTPS RESTful APIs to allow applications to interact with the model. In addition to TFServe, which is a server-side deployment option, Google also provides TensorFlow Lite, which is a framework that can execute Google TensorFlow models on iOS devices without using Core ML.

Summary

- Rule-based systems require a domain expert to define the business rules based on the expert's experience of the problem domain. Rule-based systems can therefore be created without any training data.

- The rules in a rule-based system can, over time, become interdependent and complex, thereby making it difficult to replace old rules with new ones.

- Rule-based systems need to be continually updated and maintained to ensure the rules are relevant and account for changing social and economic patterns.

- Machine-learning systems require you to have sufficient quantities of training data and will infer the rules from the data.

- The bulk of a data scientist's time is spent cleaning up input data and feature engineering.

- Building a machine-learning model is an iterative process and involves several steps, including feature engineering, model building, evaluation, and tuning.

- During the creation of the baseline model and subsequent hyperparameter optimization, models are evaluated using the labeled test set that was set aside during the dataset preparation phase. Evaluating a model involves using the model to make predictions on the test set and computing a quantitative measure that indicates how far off the predictions are from the expected outcomes.

- Once the final optimized model is created, it is evaluated on a separate validation set to ensure that the hyperparameter optimization has not resulted in a model that is overfitting the test set. The validation set is not used during the hyperparameter optimization stage.

Chapter 3

Data Exploration and Preprocessing

◆ Techniques to explore data

◆ Techniques to impute missing values

◆ Feature engineering techniques

◆ Feature selection techniques

In the previous chapter, you examined a hypothetical scenario and learned about the differences between traditional and machine-learning based approaches as well as the high-level steps involved in building a machine-learning solution. In this chapter, you will learn to use NumPy, Pandas, and Scikit-learn to explore data, perform common feature engineering tasks, and select the features that you will use to train your models.

NOTE To follow along with this chapter, ensure that you have installed Anaconda Navigator and Jupyter Notebook, as described in Appendix A.

You can download the code files for this chapter from wrox.com or from GitHub at the following URL:

https://github.com/asmtechnology/iosmlbook-chapter3.git

Data Preprocessing Techniques

In Chapter 1, you learned about the different types of machine-learning systems and the general process for building a machine-learning solution. It should come as no surprise that the performance of a machine-learning system is heavily dependent on the quality of training data. In this section, you will learn some of the common ways in which data is prepared for machine-learning models. The examples in this section will use datasets commonly found on the Internet, and they are included with the downloads that accompany this lesson.

Obtaining an Overview of the Data

When building a machine-learning model, one of the first things you will want to do is explore the data to get an overview of the variables and the target. This section uses the Titanic dataset in a Jupyter Notebook with NumPy and Pandas. The Titanic dataset is a popular dataset that contains information on the demographic and ticket information of 1309 passengers on board the Titanic, with the goal of predicting which of the passengers were more likely to survive.

The full dataset is available from the Department of BioStatistics at the Vanderbilt University (http://biostat.mc.vanderbilt.edu/wiki/Main/DataSets). Versions of the titanic3 dataset are also available from several other sources, including a popular Kaggle.com competition titled "Titanic: Machine Learning From Disaster," at https://www.kaggle.com/c/titanic.

The Kaggle version of the dataset is included with the resources that accompany this chapter, and it has the benefit of being shuffled and pre-split into a training and validation set. The training set is contained in a file called train.csv, and the validation set is called test.csv.

The attributes of the Kaggle version of the Titanic dataset are as follows:

- PassengerId: A text variable that acts as a row identifier.

- Survived: A Boolean variable that indicates whether the person survived the disaster. 0 = No, 1 = Yes.

- Pclass: A categorical variable that indicates the ticket class. 1 = first class, 2 = second class, and 3 = third class.

- Name: The name of the passenger.

- Sex: A categorical variable that indicates the gender of the passenger.

- Age: A numeric variable that indicates the age of the passenger.

- SibSp: A numeric variable that indicates the number of siblings/spouses traveling together.

- Parch: A numeric variable that indicates the number of parents and children traveling together.

- Ticket: A text variable containing the ticket number.

- Fare: A numeric variable that indicates the fare paid in pre-1970 British pounds.

- Cabin: A textual variable that indicates the cabin number.

- Embarked: A categorical variable that indicates the port of embarkation. C = Cherbourg, Q = Queenstown, and S = Southampton.

To load the Titanic training set from a CSV file located on your computer into a Pandas dataframe, use the following snippet:

```
import numpy as np
import pandas as pd


# load the contents of a file into a pandas Dataframe
input_file = './datasets/titanic_dataset/original/train.csv'
df_titanic = pd.read_csv(input_file)
```

The first thing to do is get information on the number of rows and columns of the dataset. The shape attribute of the dataframe can be used to provide this information:

```
df_titanic.shape

(891, 12)
```

You can see that the dataframe has 891 rows and 12 columns (or attributes). The following snippet can be used to get the names of the columns:

```
# titles of the 12 columns
print (df_titanic.columns.values)

['PassengerId' 'Survived' 'Pclass' 'Name' 'Sex' 'Age' 'SibSp' 'Parch'
 'Ticket' 'Fare' 'Cabin' 'Embarked']
```

One of the most common problems that data scientists have to deal with is that of missing values. Raw datasets often have missing values in one or more columns. There can be a number of reasons why the values are missing, ranging from human error to data simply being unavailable for that observation. When you load a CSV file into a Pandas dataframe, Pandas uses NaN as a marker to signify missing values. There are various ways to find out whether a column in a dataframe contains missing values. One way is to use the info() function, as illustrated in the following snippet:

```
# how many missing values?
df_titanic.info()

<class 'pandas.core.frame.DataFrame'>
Int64Index: 891 entries, 1 to 891
Data columns (total 11 columns):
Survived    891 non-null int64
Pclass      891 non-null int64
Name        891 non-null object
Sex         891 non-null object
Age         714 non-null float64
SibSp       891 non-null int64
Parch       891 non-null int64
Ticket      891 non-null object
Fare        891 non-null float64
Cabin       204 non-null object
Embarked    889 non-null object
dtypes: float64(2), int64(4), object(5)
memory usage: 83.5+ KB
```

Looking at the results of the info() function, it is clear that most columns have 891 values, whereas three columns—Age, Cabin, and Embarked—have fewer than 891 values. Using the info() function to detect missing values works only if the value is truly missing in the CSV file, which means Pandas has been able to detect the missing value and substitute it with a NaN marker in the dataframe. If, however, the process by which the data was generated used a blank space or a special character sequence such as ## to represent a missing value, then Pandas will not automatically interpret these characters to represent missing data.

Another way to get information on missing values is to chain the output of the Pandas isnull() function with the sum() function. The isnull() function, when applied on a dataframe, returns a dataframe of Boolean values with the same dimensions as the original dataframe. Each position in the new dataframe has a value of True if the corresponding position in the original dataframe has a value of None or NaN. The sum() function, when applied to the new dataframe of Boolean values, will return a list with the number of values in each column that are True.

The following snippet shows the result of chaining the isnull() and sum() functions to obtain the number of missing values in each column of the dataframe:

```
# another way to determine the number of missing
# values in a dataframe.
df_titanic.isnull().sum()
```

```
PassengerId      0
Survived         0
Pclass           0
Name             0
Sex              0
Age            177
SibSp            0
Parch            0
Ticket           0
Fare             0
Cabin          687
Embarked         2
dtype: int64
```

It is quite clear from these results that a significant number of Age and Cabin values are missing. We will look at ways to deal with missing values later in this chapter.

Sometimes the best way to get a feel for the data is to visually inspect the contents of the dataframe. You can use the head() function of the dataframe object to view the contents of the first few rows of the dataframe (see Figure 3.1).

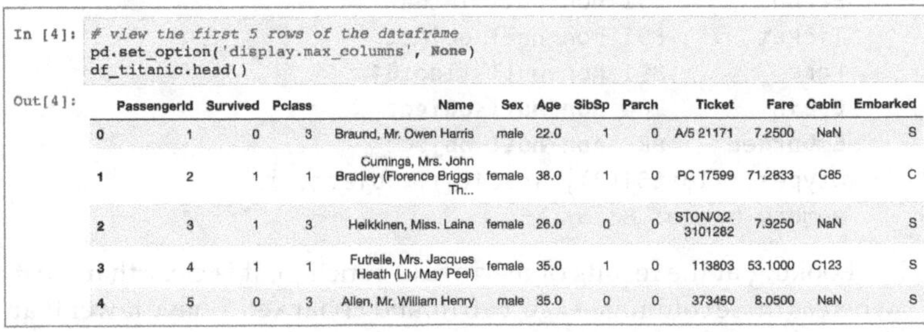

FIGURE 3.1
The head() function displays rows from the beginning of a Pandas dataframe.

```
In [4]:  # view the first 5 rows of the dataframe
         pd.set_option('display.max_columns', None)
         df_titanic.head()
```

Out[4]:	PassengerId	Survived	Pclass	Name	Sex	Age	SibSp	Parch	Ticket	Fare	Cabin	Embarked
0	1	0	3	Braund, Mr. Owen Harris	male	22.0	1	0	A/5 21171	7.2500	NaN	S
1	2	1	1	Cumings, Mrs. John Bradley (Florence Briggs Th...	female	38.0	1	0	PC 17599	71.2833	C85	C
2	3	1	3	Heikkinen, Miss. Laina	female	26.0	0	0	STON/O2. 3101282	7.9250	NaN	S
3	4	1	1	Futrelle, Mrs. Jacques Heath (Lily May Peel)	female	35.0	1	0	113803	53.1000	C123	S
4	5	0	3	Allen, Mr. William Henry	male	35.0	0	0	373450	8.0500	NaN	S

If the number of columns is too many for Pandas to fit horizontally into a single line, then by default Pandas displays a subset of the columns of the dataframe. The subset consists of a few columns from the left of the dataframe, and a few from the right. Figure 3.2 illustrates the effect of using the head() function on a dataframe with 30 columns.

FIGURE 3.2
The head() function
displays truncated data
for large dataframes.

```
In [10]:  # load the contents of a file with many columns into a pandas Dataframe
          input_file2 = './datasets/random_30column.csv'
          df_random30 = pd.read_csv(input_file2)
          df_random30.head()
```

Out[10]:

	attribute_1	attribute_2	attribute_3	attribute_4	attribute_5	...	attribute_26	attribute_27	attribute_28	attribute_29	target
0	457	430	295	778	420	...	211	836	651	8	1
1	679	597	940	859	590	...	774	630	138	253	1
2	278	326	998	885	974	...	439	865	557	706	0
3	909	604	10	876	845	...	138	522	457	263	1
4	622	26	272	67	520	...	595	880	77	675	1

5 rows × 30 columns

You can change the maximum number of columns that will be displayed by Pandas by setting the display.max_columns Pandas property. For example, the following snippet will ensure Pandas displays no more than four columns:

```
pd.set_option('display.max_columns', 4)
df_random30.head()
```

```
     attribute_1.   attribute_2    ...    attribute_29   target
0      457            430          ...         8            1
1      679            597          ...         253          1
2      278            326          ...         706          0
3      909            604          ...         263          1
4      622            26           ...         675          1
```

```
5 rows × 30 columns
```

If you would like all columns to be displayed, set the value of display.max_columns to None.

```
pd.set_option('display.max_columns', None)
```

Astute readers may have noticed that the PassengerId attribute of the Titanic dataset is a numeric row identifier and does not provide any useful input as far as model building is concerned. Every Pandas dataframe can have an index that contains a unique value for each row of the dataframe. By default, Pandas does not create an index for a dataframe. You can find out if a dataframe has an index by using the following snippet:

```
# Does this dataframe have a named index? If so, what is it?
print (df_titanic.index.name)
```

```
None
```

To make the PassengerId attribute the index of the df_titanic dataframe, use the following snippet:

```
df_titanic.set_index("PassengerId", inplace=True)
```

Figure 3.3 shows the results of applying the head() function to the df_titanic dataframe before and after the index has been set up.

FIGURE 3.3
Impact of the set_
index function on
a dataframe

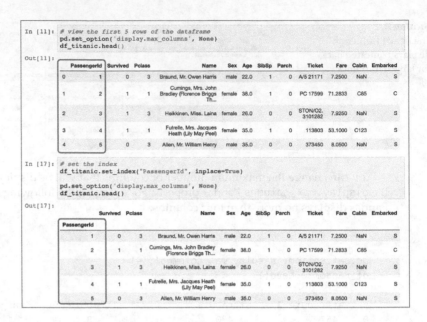

FIGURE 3.3
Impact of the set_
index function on
a dataframe

If you use the shape attribute of the dataframe to get the number of rows and columns, you will notice that the number of columns is now reported as 11 instead of 12. This is illustrated in the following snippet:

```
# how many rows and columns in the dataframe
# after the index has been set?
df_titanic.shape
```

```
(891, 11)
```

You may have noticed that the Survived attribute is one of the 11 remaining attributes in the df_titanic dataframe after PassengerId has been used as the index. During the training process, you need to ensure you do not include the target attribute as one of the input features. There are various means by which you could ensure this, but perhaps the simplest option is to separate the feature variables and the target variables into separate dataframes.

The following snippet will extract the Survived attribute from the df_titanic dataframe into a separate dataframe called df_titanic_target, and it will separate the 10 feature variables from the df_titanic dataframe into a separate dataframe called df_titanic_features.

```
# extract the target attribute into its own dataframe
df_titanic_target = df_titanic.loc[:,['Survived']]

# create a dataframe that contains the 10 feature variables
df_titanic_features = df_titanic.drop(['Survived'], axis=1)
```

The Survived attribute is a binary attribute in which a value of 1 implies that the individual survived. When the target that your machine-learning model is trying to predict is categorical (binary, or multiclass), it is useful to know the distribution of values in the training dataset per category. You can get the distribution of target values in this example by using the following snippet:

```
# what is the split between the two classes of the target variable?
df_titanic_target['Survived'].value_counts()


0    549
1    342
Name: Survived, dtype: int64
```

The default behavior of the value_counts() function is that it will not pick out NaN values. To have the value_counts() function include counts of NaN markers, include the dropna=false parameter, as demonstrated in the following snippet:

```
# unique values and counts of categorical attribute 'Embarked'
# includes NaN markers
df_titanic_features['Embarked'].value_counts(dropna=False)


S      644
C      168
Q       77
NaN      2
Name: Embarked, dtype: int64
```

If you prefer a visual representation of the distribution of target values, you can use the following snippet to create a histogram. The histogram is depicted in Figure 3.4.

```
# histogram of target variable
%matplotlib inline
import matplotlib.pyplot as plt
df_titanic_target.hist(figsize=(5,5))
```

FIGURE 3.4
Distribution of values for the survived attribute

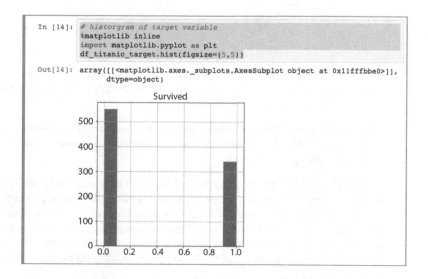

In addition to a histogram of the target variables, it is also useful to use histograms to get an overview of the distribution of feature values. The `hist()` function provided by the Pandas dataframe object will only generate histograms for numeric values. The only numerical features in the Titanic dataset are `Age`, `Fare`, `Pclass`, `Parch`, and `SibSp`. The following snippet can be used to generate histograms of numeric features. The resulting feature histograms are depicted in Figure 3.5.

```
#histogram of features
df_titanic_features.hist(figsize=(10,10))
```

FIGURE 3.5

Histogram of numeric features

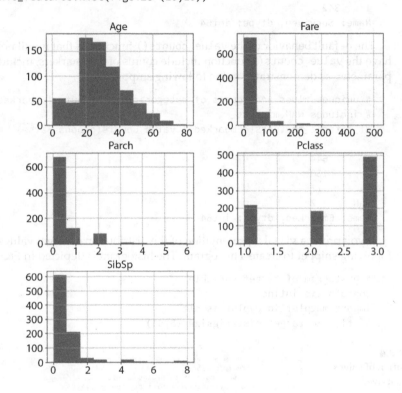

NOTE   Pandas provides a function called `hist()` that can be used to create histograms from the contents of a dataframe. Behind the scenes, this function uses a popular Python plotting library called Matplotlib to create the histogram.

The plotting capabilities of Pandas are a small subset of what is possible with Matplotlib. A detailed discussion of Matplotlib is outside the scope of this book; however, you can find more information at `https://matplotlib.org`.

If you have a background in statistics, you will be aware that a *histogram* is an estimate of the probability distribution of a continuous variable, and the first step in creating a histogram is to convert the continuous range of values taken by the variable into a discrete number of values. This conversion is performed by splitting the continuous range into a set of nonoverlapping intervals (or bins). The bars of the histogram then correspond to the number of items in the corresponding interval, and the appearance of the histogram is influenced by the width of the intervals.

For example, assume for a moment that you have a dataset of the heights of 50 individuals measured in centimeters and want to create a histogram. If you chose to plot the 50 points on a graph, what you would get would not be a histogram; it would be a scatter plot. To get a histogram, you need to decide how many bars you want. If you decide that you want five bars in your histogram, you need to define five intervals (such as 0 cm to 60 cm, 60 cm to 120 cm, 120 cm to 180 cm, 180 cm to 240 cm, 240 cm to 300 cm) and place all the 50 values into one of these five intervals.

The choice of the number of intervals is entirely up to you, and had you chosen a different number, the histogram would look different. Data scientists often generate multiple histograms of the same variable with different interval widths to get a better understanding of the distribution of the data.

The following snippet can be used to create a histogram of a single numeric attribute and to specify the number of equal intervals along the x-axis. Figure 3.6 depicts the histograms obtained by choosing a number of different interval widths for the same numerical feature.

```
#histogram of single feature - Age
# it is a good idea to try different bin widths to get a better idea of
# the distribution of values.
df_titanic_features.hist(column='Age', figsize=(5,5), bins=2)
```

FIGURE 3.6
Histogram of numeric feature Age using different widths (2, 3, 5, 80)

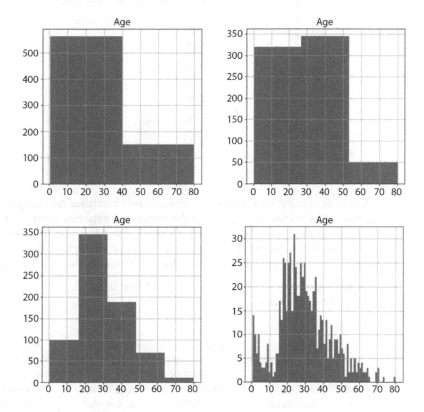

Pandas' plotting capabilities relies on a library called Matplotlib, which refers to these intervals as *bins*. In the preceding snippet, the bins = 2 moniker should be read as two equal-width, nonoverlapping intervals.

The value_counts() function works on both discrete numeric and categorical features. Therefore, you could generate a histogram of a categorical feature by using the output of the value_counts() function. The following snippet demonstrates this approach on the Embarked categorical feature. The resulting histogram is depicted in Figure 3.7.

```
# histogram of categorical attribute 'Embarked'
# computed from the output of the value_counts() function
vc = df_titanic_features['Embarked'].value_counts(dropna=False)
vc.plot(kind='bar')
```

FIGURE 3.7

Histogram of categorical feature, Embarked

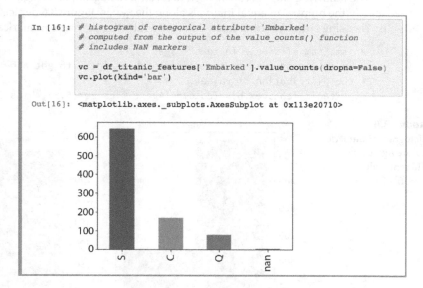

In addition to information on the distribution of features and target variables, the statistical characteristics of these variables and the correlation between them can provide useful insights into the training data. Pandas provides a describe() function that can be used on dataframes to obtain statistical information on the numerical attributes within the dataframe. The following snippet shows the results of the describe() function on the df_titanic_features dataset:

```
# get statistical characteristics of the data
df_titanic_features.describe()
```

	Pclass	Age	SibSp	Parch	Fare
count	891.000000	714.000000	891.000000	891.000000	891.000000
mean	2.308642	29.699118	0.523008	0.381594	32.204208
std	0.836071	14.526497	1.102743	0.806057	49.693429
min	1.000000	0.420000	0.000000	0.000000	0.000000
25%	2.000000	20.125000	0.000000	0.000000	7.910400

50%	3.000000	28.000000	0.000000	0.000000	14.454200
75%	3.000000	38.000000	1.000000	0.000000	31.000000
max	3.000000	80.000000	8.000000	6.000000	512.329200

Information provided by the describe() function includes the minimum value, maximum value, mean value, standard deviation, and quartiles of each numerical feature. A quartile is a value below which a certain percentage of observations can be found. For example, the first quartile is the value below which 25 percent of the observations can be found. The first quartile of the Age feature is 20.12, which means that 25 percent of the people captured by the dataset were younger than 20 years old.

Information on quartiles and statistical characteristics of a feature is often represented using a box plot. You can use the boxplot() function of the dataframe to create a box plot of all numeric features. The following snippet demonstrates the use of the boxplot() function. The resulting box plot is depicted in Figure 3.8.

```
# create a box plot of numeric features.
df_titanic_features.boxplot(figsize=(10,6))
```

FIGURE 3.8
Box plot of
numeric features

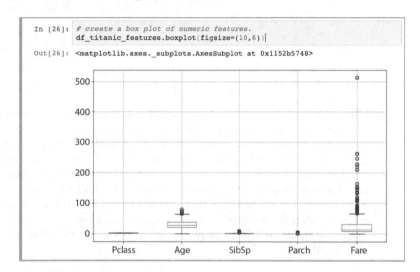

Handling Missing Values

In the previous section, you learned about techniques that can be used to explore the data. While exploring the Titanic dataset, you learned that the Age, Cabin, and Embarked class have missing values. Age is a numeric feature, and you can use a box plot to get a quick overview of the statistical characteristics of the values that make up this feature using the following snippet. Figure 3.9 depicts a box plot of the Age feature variable.

```
# boxplot of 'Age'
%matplotlib inline
import matplotlib.pyplot as plt
df_titanic_features.boxplot(column='Age', figsize=(7,7))
```

FIGURE 3.9
Box plot of the Age
feature variable

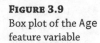

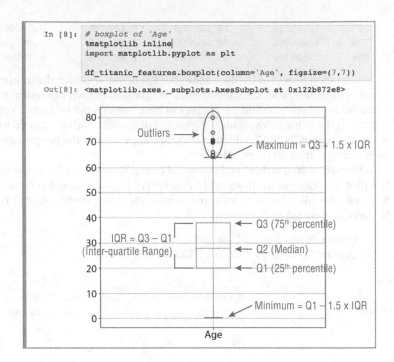

FIGURE 3.9
Box plot of the Age
feature variable

NOTE   A box plot is a diagram that shows information on five key statistical attributes of a variable. The attributes are—the minimum, first quartile (Q1), second quartile (median), third quartile (Q3), and maximum. The distance between the first and third quartiles forms the "box" portion of the graph and is also known as the inter-quartile range (IQR). The minimum and maximum values that are plotted on a box plot are not the lowest and highest values of the dataset; instead, they are computed using the following equations: minimum = Q1 – 1.5 × IQR, and maximum = Q3 + 1.5 × IQR. Any values lesser than or greater than the minimum and maximum values of the plot are marked as outliers. This is illustrated in Figure 3.9. Using the information in a box plot, you can obtain information of the spread, and the symmetry of your data. You can also obtain information on the outliers in your distribution.

A box plot also provides a convenient mechanism to compare different variables (features) against each other. This is illustrated in Figure 3.8.

The median value of the age, according to the box plot, is just under 30. Pandas provides the `fillna()` function, which can be used to replace missing values with a new value. The following snippet uses the `fillna()` function to replace the missing values of the Age attribute with the median value:

```
# fill missing values with the median
median_age = df_titanic_features['Age'].median()
print (median_age)
28.0

df_titanic_features["Age"].fillna(median_age, inplace=True)
```

NOTE Although it is not demonstrated in this section, you must ensure that any feature engineering, or imputation, that is carried out on the training data must also be carried out on the test and validation data. Ideally this process should be performed before you split out the master data into training, test, and validation sets.

The Embarked attribute is categorical, and since the number of missing values is small (just two), a reasonable approach is to substitute the missing values with the most frequent occurring value in the Embarked column. The following snippet uses the fillna() function to achieve this:

```
# fill missing values of the Embarked attribute
# with the most common value in the column
embarked_value_counts = df_titanic_features['Embarked'].value_counts(dropna=True)
most_common_value = embarked_value_counts.index[0]

print (most_common_value)
S


df_titanic_features["Embarked"].fillna(most_common_value, inplace=True)
```

The Cabin attribute is also categorical but has a large number of missing values (687 missing values). Using the same strategy that was used to impute missing values for the Embarked attribute will not work in this case, as you will create a significant bias in the data. The best approach in this situation is to create a new Boolean feature called CabinIsKnown, which will have a value of True if the Cabin attribute is known, and False otherwise. You may be tempted to use the integer 1 to signify known cabin values and 0 to signify missing cabin values, but if you were to do this, then you will create an unintentional order in the data (1 being greater than 0), and this could influence the output of some models.

The following snippet creates a new column called CabinIsKnown and drops the original Cabin column from the dataframe:

```
# create a Boolean feature 'CabinIsKnown'
# which will have True if the Cabin column
# does not have missing data
df_titanic_features['CabinIsKnown'] = ~df_titanic_features.Cabin.isnull()

# drop the Cabin column from the dataframe
df_titanic_features.drop(['Cabin'], axis=1, inplace=True)
```

With the changes described in this section, you have imputed missing values where possible and created a new column in the dataframe. There should be no missing values in the dataframe, a new column called CabinIsKnown should be visible in the dataframe, and the Cabin column should have been deleted from the dataframe. All of these changes can be validated by executing the following snippet:

```
# display the columns of the dataframe.
print (df_titanic_features.columns.values)

# display number of missing values in the columns
df_titanic_features.isnull().sum()
```

```
['Pclass' 'Name' 'Sex' 'Age' 'SibSp' 'Parch' 'Ticket' 'Fare' 'Embarked'
 'CabinIsKnown']
Out[10]:
Pclass           0
Name             0
Sex              0
Age              0
SibSp            0
Parch            0
Ticket           0
Fare             0
Embarked         0
CabinIsKnown     0
dtype: int64
```

Creating New Features

If you observe the descriptions of the columns of the Titanic dataset, you will come across the SibSp and Parch columns. From the description of the dataset:

◆ SibSp: A numeric variable that indicates the number of siblings/spouses traveling together

◆ Parch: A numeric variable that indicates the number of parents and children traveling together

It may make sense to combine these values into a single numeric value that represents the size of the family traveling together. It is not possible to tell at this stage if the model will perform better with this additional synthesized feature, but having this new feature in the data will give you more options when it comes to building and evaluating models. The following snippet creates a new attribute in the dataframe called FamilySize, which is computed as the arithmetic sum of the SibSp and Parch attributes.

```
# create a numeric feature called FamilySize that is
# the sum of the SibSp and Parch features.
df_titanic_features['FamilySize'] = df_titanic_features.SibSp + df_titanic_
features.Parch
```

NOTE   Although it is not demonstrated in this section, you must ensure that any feature engineering that is carried out on the training data is also carried out on the test and validation data.

The Age and Fare features are numeric and take on a range of values. It may be useful to bin the value of these features and create categorical features. During model building you may discover that the categorical (binned) values of Age and Fare provide better results. To create a new categorical feature called AgeCategory, you can use the Pandas cut() function, as demonstrated in the following snippet:

```
# generate new categorical feature AgeCategory
bins_age = [0,20,30,40,50,150]
labels_age = ['<20','20-30','30-40','40-50','>50']
```

```
df_titanic_features['AgeCategory'] = pd.cut(df_titanic_features.Age,
                                            bins=bins_age,
                                            labels=labels_age,
                                            include_lowest=True)
```

Figure 3.10 depicts the output of the head() function on the df_titanic_features dataframe after the AgeCategory feature has been created.

FIGURE 3.10 Dataframe with engineered feature AgeCategory

```
In [11]: # examine the first 10 rows of the dataset
         df_titanic_features.head(10)
Out[11]:
```

PassengerId	Pclass	Name	Sex	Age	SibSp	Parch	Ticket	Fare	Embarked	CabinIsKnown	FamilySize	AgeCategory
1	3	Braund, Mr. Owen Harris	male	22.0	1	0	A/5 21171	7.2500	S	False	1	20-30
2	1	Cumings, Mrs. John Bradley (Florence Briggs Th...	female	38.0	1	0	PC 17599	71.2833	C	True	1	30-40
3	3	Heikkinen, Miss. Laina	female	26.0	0	0	STON/O2. 3101282	7.9250	S	False	0	20-30
4	1	Futrelle, Mrs. Jacques Heath (Lily May Peel)	female	35.0	1	0	113803	53.1000	S	True	1	30-40
5	3	Allen, Mr. William Henry	male	35.0	0	0	373450	8.0500	S	False	0	30-40
6	3	Moran, Mr. James	male	28.0	0	0	330877	8.4583	Q	False	0	20-30
7	1	McCarthy, Mr. Timothy J	male	54.0	0	0	17463	51.8625	S	True	0	>50
8	3	Palsson, Master. Gosta Leonard	male	2.0	3	1	349909	21.0750	S	False	4	<20
9	3	Johnson, Mrs. Oscar W (Elisabeth Vilhelmina Berg)	female	27.0	0	2	347742	11.1333	S	False	2	20-30
10	2	Nasser, Mrs. Nicholas (Adele Achem)	female	14.0	1	0	237736	30.0708	C	False	1	<20

The cut() function has several parameters. In this example, the bins parameter contains a sequence of numbers that define the edges of the bins. The lowest and highest values are deliberately chosen to be outside the range of values observed in the Age feature. The labels parameter contains a list of strings that serve as the labels of the bins (and the values of the categorical feature that will be generated as a result of executing the cut() function). The include_lowest parameter is set to True to indicate that the first interval is left-inclusive. You can find information about the full list of parameters for the cut() function at https://pandas.pydata.org/pandas-docs/version/0.23.4/generated/pandas.cut.html.

There is no set formula to determine the correct number of bins and the widths of the bins. During the model building process, you may find yourself experimenting with different binning strategies and picking the strategy that results in the best performing model.

If you want to split a continuous numeric variable into a categorical variable by using the quantiles as bin boundaries, you can use the Pandas qcut() function. The following snippet uses the qcut() function to create a new categorical feature called FareCategory using the quartiles as bin boundaries:

```
# generate new categorical feature FareCategory
df_titanic_features['FareCategory'] = pd.qcut(df_titanic_features.Fare,
                                              q=4,
                                              labels=['Q1', 'Q2', 'Q3', 'Q4'])
```

The second parameter, q=4, indicates that you want to use the quartiles as bin boundaries. Information about the qcut() function is available at https://pandas.pydata.org/pandas-docs/stable/reference/api/pandas.qcut.html.

Figure 3.11 depicts the output of the head() function on the df_titanic_features dataframe after the FareCategory feature has been created.

FIGURE 3.11
Dataframe with
engineered feature
FareCategory

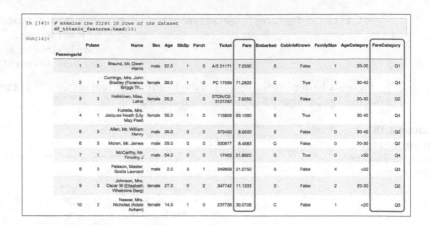

Transforming Numeric Features

After having created the categorical features AgeCategory and FareCategory in the previous section, you may want to drop the original Age and Fare attributes from the dataset. The decision to drop the original numerical values will largely depend on the type of model you are going to build.

When building a model with continuous numeric variables, you may need to transform numeric attributes. Several machine-learning models converge faster and work better when the values of numeric attributes are small and have a distribution that is close to a standard normal distribution with mean 0 and variance 1. For example, if you were training a linear regression model with two features, the first of which had values in the range [0, 100] and the second in the range [10,000 to 1 million], then the larger numeric values of the second feature will introduce a bias in the model.

NOTE In statistics, standard deviation (SD) is a quantity that measures the dispersion of a set of values around the mean (average) value. A low standard deviation value of a set of numbers means that the numbers are located quite closely around the mean of the numbers. Variance is another statistical quantity that is defined as the square of the standard deviation value. While both variance and standard deviation convey information on the spread of a set of values around the mean, the calculation of the variance uses squares, and therefore penalizes outliers more heavily than standard deviation. The use of squares in the computation of the variance also implies that the variance is not expressed in the same units as the numbers themselves. For example, if your data consisted of 100 heights measured in centimeters, the units of standard deviation would be cm, but the units for variance would be cm^2.

Normalization and standardization are the two most common types of transformations performed on numerical attributes. The result of normalizing a feature is that the values of the feature will be scaled to fall within 0 and 1. The result of standardizing a feature is that the distribution of the new values will have a mean of 0 and a standard deviation of 1, but the range of the standardized values is not guaranteed to be between 0 and 1. Standardization is used when the model you want to build assumes the feature variables have a Gaussian distribution. Normalization is often used with neural network models, which require inputs to lie within the range [0, 1].

Scikit-learn provides a number of classes to assist in scaling numeric attributes. The MinMaxScaler class is commonly used for normalizing features, and the StandardScaler class is for standardization. The following snippet creates two new columns, called NormalizedAge and StandardizedAge, in the df_titanic_features dataframe. Figure 3.12 compares the histogram of the Age, NormalizedAge, and StandardizedAge features.

```
# generate new feature NormalizedAge using MinMaxScaler
from sklearn import preprocessing

minmax_scaler = preprocessing.MinMaxScaler()
ndNormalizedAge = minmax_scaler.fit_transform(df_titanic_features[['Age']].values)
df_titanic_features['NormalizedAge']  = pd.DataFrame(ndNormalizedAge)

# generate new feature StandardizedAge using StandardScaler
standard_scaler = preprocessing.StandardScaler()
ndStandardizedAge = standard_scaler.fit_transform(df_titanic_features
[['Age']].values)
df_titanic_features['StandardizedAge']  = pd.DataFrame(ndStandardizedAge)

# histogram of Age, NormalizedAge, StandardizedAge
df_titanic_features[['Age', 'NormalizedAge', 'StandardizedAge']].hist(figsize
=(10,10), bins=5)
```

FIGURE 3.12
Histogram of Age, NormalizedAge, and StandardizedAge

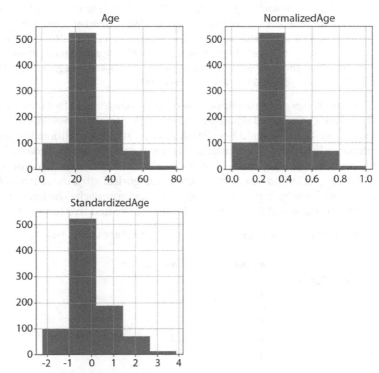

One-Hot Encoding Categorical Features

Let's now look at techniques to convert categorical features into numeric features using one-hot encoding. You may be wondering why you would want to convert categorical features to numeric, especially since a previous section in this chapter discussed techniques to do the opposite—convert numeric features into categorical.

Not all machine-learning algorithms can deal with categorical data. For example, linear regression and logistic regression are only capable of using numeric features. Algorithms like XGBoost and Random Forests are capable of using categorical features without any problems.

One-hot encoding is a technique that converts a categorical feature into a number of binary numeric features, one per category. Pandas provides the get_dummies() function to help with one-hot encoding. The following snippet will convert the categorical features Sex, Embarked, CabinIsKnown, AgeCategory, and FareCategory into binary numeric features and list the columns of the dataframe:

```
# use one-hot encoding to convert categorical attributes
# into binary numeric attributes
df_titanic_features = pd.get_dummies(df_titanic_features,
columns=['Sex','Embarked','CabinIsKnown','AgeCategory','FareCategory'])

# display the columns of the dataframe.
print (df_titanic_features.columns.values)

['Pclass' 'Name' 'Age' 'SibSp' 'Parch' 'Ticket' 'Fare' 'FamilySize'
 'NormalizedAge' 'StandardizedAge' 'Sex_female' 'Sex_male' 'Embarked_C'
 'Embarked_Q' 'Embarked_S' 'CabinIsKnown_False' 'CabinIsKnown_True'
 'AgeCategory_<20' 'AgeCategory_20-30' 'AgeCategory_30-40'
 'AgeCategory_40-50' 'AgeCategory_>50' 'FareCategory_Q1' 'FareCategory_Q2'
 'FareCategory_Q3' 'FareCategory_Q4']
```

As can be seen in this snippet, the original categorical attributes are no longer present in the df_titanic_features dataframe; however, a number of new columns have been added to the dataframe. To understand how Pandas has created the additional columns, consider the Sex categorical attribute. This attribute has two values, male and female. To convert this categorical attribute into a binary numeric attribute, Pandas has created two new columns in the dataframe, called Sex_male and Sex_female. Other categorical attributes such as Embarked, CabinIsKnown, and so on, have been processed using a similar approach. The following snippet lists the values of the Sex_male and Sex_female columns for the first five rows of the dataframe:

```
df_titanic_features[['Sex_male', 'Sex_female']].head()

              Sex_male      Sex_female
PassengerId
1             1             0
2             0             1
3             0             1
4             0             1
5             1             0
```

Astute readers may notice that since the values taken by the Sex attribute in the original df_titanic_features dataset are either male or female, you don't need both the Sex_male and Sex_female attributes, because you can infer one from the other. The situation is similar to the CabinIsKnown_False and CabinIsKnown_True features. The following snippet drops the Sex_female and CabinIsKnown_False attributes along with non-numeric attributes Name and Ticket to arrive at a dataframe that contains only numeric attributes:

```
# drop the Name, Ticket, Sex_female, CabinIsKnown_False features
# to get a dataframe that can be used for linear or logistic regression
df_titanic_features_numeric = df_titanic_features.drop(['Name', 'Ticket',
'Sex_female', 'CabinIsKnown_False'], axis=1)
```

Selecting Training Features

In the previous section, you learned about techniques to explore data, impute missing values, and engineer features. In this section, you will look at techniques that can be used to select the best set of training features, as well as reduce the number of features in large datasets.

Correlation

Information on the correlation between input features and the target can be helpful in picking out the best features from the data to use for model building and predictions. Information on the correlation between the features themselves can be helpful in reducing the number of features and the general risk of overfitting. Pandas provides a corr() function that can be used to compute Pearson's correlation coefficient between the columns of a dataframe. The results of applying the corr() function on the df_titanic dataframe are depicted in Figure 3.13.

FIGURE 3.13
Linear correlation between numeric columns

```
In [39]:  # correlation between the target variable and the features
          df_titanic.corr()

Out[39]:
```

	Survived	Pclass	Age	SibSp	Parch	Fare
Survived	1.000000	-0.338481	-0.077221	-0.035322	0.081629	0.257307
Pclass	-0.338481	1.000000	-0.369226	0.083081	0.018443	-0.549500
Age	-0.077221	-0.369226	1.000000	-0.308247	-0.189119	0.096067
SibSp	-0.035322	0.083081	-0.308247	1.000000	0.414838	0.159651
Parch	0.081629	0.018443	-0.189119	0.414838	1.000000	0.216225
Fare	0.257307	-0.549500	0.096067	0.159651	0.216225	1.000000

It is important to note that Pearson's correlation coefficient will only detect linear correlations between variables. The corr() function allows you to choose from standard correlation coefficients such as Pearson, Kendall, and Spearman. You can find more information at https://pandas.pydata.org/pandas-docs/stable/reference/api/pandas.DataFrame.corr.html.

The following snippet lists the correlation between the numeric features and the target variable Survived, sorted by descending value:

```
# what features show the strongest correlation with the target variable?
corr_matrix = df_titanic.corr()
corr_matrix['Survived'].sort_values(ascending=False)

Survived    1.000000
Fare        0.257307
Parch       0.081629
SibSp      -0.035322
Age        -0.077221
Pclass     -0.338481
Name: Survived, dtype: float64
```

Computing the values of correlation coefficients between pairs of attributes is not the only way to get information on the correlation between features. You can also create scatter plots between pairs of features to visualize their relationship. The following snippet uses the Pandas scatter_matrix() function to create scatter plots of all numeric features with each other. The resulting scatter plot is depicted in Figure 3.14.

```
# visualize relationship between features using a
# matrix of scatter plots.
from pandas.plotting import scatter_matrix
scatter_matrix(df_titanic, figsize=(12,12))
```

FIGURE 3.14
Matrix of scatter plots between pairs of numeric attributes

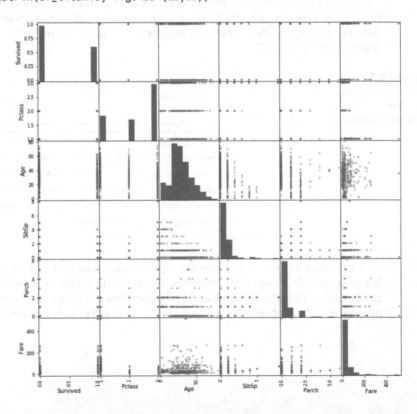

If you were to compute the correlation between the target attribute Survived and the numeric features engineered at the end of the previous section, you will see a significantly better correlation than achieved prior to feature engineering. The following snippet demonstrates this:

```
# to facilitate computation of Pearson's correlation
# coefficient, create a dataframe that contains all the attributes
# from df_titanic_features_numeric, and the survived attribute
df_temporary = pd.concat([df_titanic_features_numeric, df_titanic['Survived']],
axis=1)
df_temporary.head()

# what features show the strongest correlation with the target variable after
feature engineering?
corr_matrix = df_temporary.corr()
corr_matrix['Survived'].sort_values(ascending=False)
```

```
Survived               1.000000
CabinIsKnown_True      0.316912
Fare                   0.257307
FareCategory_Q4        0.233638
Embarked_C             0.168240
FareCategory_Q3        0.084239
Parch                  0.081629
AgeCategory_<20        0.076565
AgeCategory_30-40      0.057867
FamilySize             0.016639
Embarked_Q             0.003650
AgeCategory_40-50     -0.000079
NormalizedAge         -0.001654
StandardizedAge       -0.001654
AgeCategory_>50       -0.022932
SibSp                 -0.035322
Age                   -0.064910
AgeCategory_20-30     -0.093689
FareCategory_Q2       -0.095648
Embarked_S            -0.149683
FareCategory_Q1       -0.221610
Pclass                -0.338481
Sex_male              -0.543351
Name: Survived, dtype: float64
```

Note the particularly strong negative correlation between the chances of survival and the Sex_male engineered feature. This tells us that the chance of survival for men in general was poorer than that of women. Additionally, the strong positive correlation between the chances of survival and the engineered FareCategory_Q4 attribute implies that people who paid more for their tickets (first class passengers) were more likely to survive. All of this aligns well with historical records.

You may also have noticed the extremely weak correlation between the chances of survival and some of the attributes such as `NormalizedAge`, `StandardizedAge`, `AgeCategory_<20`, `AgeCategory_30-40`, `AgeCategory_40-50`, and `AgeCategory_>50`. Because of the weak correlation between these attributes and the target variable, you may want to exclude them from the model.

Principal Component Analysis

Many real-world datasets have several dozen (sometimes hundreds) attributes per data point. Having a large number of input features can make the model training process extremely slow, and it can be difficult to use visualization techniques to pick out the best attributes. As you have seen in the previous section, not all features exhibit a strong degree of correlation with the target variable. Excluding features that exhibit poor correlation is feasible only if you do not end up discarding too many features from the dataset. In large datasets, it is entirely possible that none of the features exhibits strong correlations with the target variable. Principal component analysis (PCA) is a statistical technique that can be used to reduce the number of features in the dataset yet maintain a large percentage of the variance of the original data.

A detailed discussion of PCA is outside the scope of this book. However, to understand how it works, consider a simple two-dimensional dataset, the scatter plot for which is depicted in Figure 3.15. The variance (spread) of data along each axis is also depicted in the figure.

FIGURE 3.15
Variance of data along
the x- and y-axes

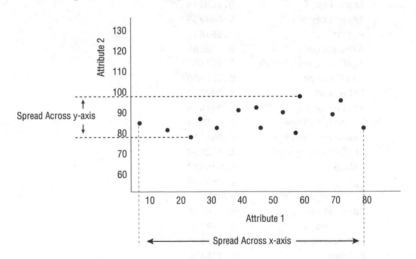

As you can clearly see, the data is not spread out uniformly across both axes. The variance along the x-axis is significantly more than that along the y-axis. You could say that the data points of this scatter plot do not use the full range of values available along the y-axis. This general behavior is also true for most real-world datasets with a large number of features. If you consider each feature to represent an axis in a higher-dimensional space and each axis normalized to [0, 1], then often most of the variance is confined to a small number of axes (dimensions), with the data not using the full range of values of the higher-dimensional axes. One solution may be to try to collect more data so as to try to improve the spread across all the axes; however, this is not always practical.

PCA attempts to find a new set of axes in a lower-dimensional space and project the data points from the original higher-dimensional space onto this new set of axes. The new set of axes is selected in such a manner as to preserve a large portion of the original variance. This idea is illustrated in Figure 3.16.

FIGURE 3.16

Projecting two-dimensional data onto a one-dimensional line

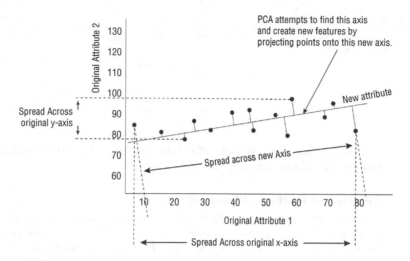

As you can see, the new axis depicted in Figure 3.16 captures almost 90 percent of the variance of the dataset, and by projecting the points from the original two-dimensional space on to this line, PCA has reduced the number of features per data point from 2 to 1. This same concept applies in higher dimensions.

Scikit-learn implements principal component analysis using the singular value decomposition (SVD) algorithm in the class called PCA, which is part of the sklearn.decomposition package. The following snippet uses the PCA class to reduce the number of features from the df_titanic_features_numeric dataframe so as to preserve 99.9 percent of the variance.

```
# use PCA to reduce the number of features in
# df_titanic_features_numeric so as to preserve
# 99.90% of the variance.

from sklearn.decomposition import PCA
pca_decomposer = PCA(0.9990)
PCAResult = pca_decomposer.fit_transform(df_titanic_features_numeric)

print (pca_decomposer.n_components_)
4
```

The n_components_ attribute of the PCA object contains the number of reduces axes (features), and the fit_transform() method can be used to project the features from the original higher-dimensional space into the lower-dimensional space.

The following snippet creates a dataframe with the projected feature values:

```
dfPCAResult = pd.DataFrame(data = PCAResult, columns = ['C1', 'C2', 'C3', 'C4'])
dfPCAResult.head()
```

The new features have been named C1, C2, C3, and C4. It is important to note that these features are not the same as the features in the df_titanic_features_numeric dataframe and that by using PCA, you are discarding some of the original data. Figure 3.17 contains the first few rows of the dataframe with the new features.

FIGURE 3.17
Features after principal component analysis

```
In [9]:  dfPCAResult = pd.DataFrame(data = PCAResult, columns = ['C1', 'C2', 'C3', 'C4'])
         dfPCAResult.head()

Out[9]:
              C1         C2         C3         C4
    0   -25.153063  -6.699775   0.071657   0.884335
    1    39.321840   7.596666   0.172549  -0.858967
    2   -24.378188  -2.672111  -1.012035   0.384358
    3    21.062323   5.092991   0.274836  -1.086400
    4   -24.008620   6.324614  -0.613897   0.397106
```

You can learn more about the PCA class at https://scikit-learn.org/stable/modules/generated/sklearn.decomposition.PCA.html.

Recursive Feature Elimination

The final topic in this chapter deals with a brute-force technique called *recursive feature elimination* (RFE), which can be used to assess the importance of features in the performance of a machine-learning model. The idea behind recursive feature elimination is to train a model using all the features in the dataset and then recursively train models by dropping one feature at a time. At the end of the process, the relative importance of each feature can be assessed. Recursive feature elimination, although computationally expensive, shows how much each feature contributes to the performance of the model.

Scikit-learn implements recursive feature elimination in the RFE class defined in the sklearn.feature_selection module. The following snippet uses recursive feature elimination to rank the importance of features in the df_titanic_features_numeric dataframe with a logistic regression model.

```
# use recursive feature elimination to work out
# the relative importance of the features in the
# df_titanic_features_numeric dataset
from sklearn.feature_selection import RFE
from sklearn.linear_model import LogisticRegression

#use logistic regression as the model
logisticRegressionClassifier = LogisticRegression(penalty='l2',
solver='liblinear', max_iter=500)
rfe = RFE(logisticRegressionClassifier, n_features_to_select=1)
rfe.fit(df_titanic_features_numeric, np.ravel(df_titanic_target))

print (rfe.ranking_)
[ 3 17  9 19 20 14  1 11 12 15  2  4  6  5 16 10 18 13  7  8]
```

The rank of each feature can be accessed by inspecting the ranking_ attribute of the RFE object. The result is an array of numbers, with each index containing the rank of the corresponding feature. You can learn more about the RFE class at https://scikit-learn.org/stable/

`modules/generated/sklearn.feature_selection.RFE.html`. Training a logistic regression model and using the model in an iOS app are covered in Chapter 5.

Feature engineering is the most laborious and time-consuming aspect of data science, and there is no set formula that can be applied to a given situation. In this chapter, you learned about some of the techniques that can be used to explore data, impute missing values, and engineer features.

Summary

- You can use the Pandas' `isnull()` and `sum()` functions together to obtain the number of missing values in each column of a dataframe.

- The `hist()` function exposed by the Pandas dataframe object will only generate histograms for numeric values.

- Pandas provides a `describe()` function that can be used on dataframes to obtain statistical information on the numerical attributes within the dataframe.

- Pandas provides a `corr()` function that can be used to compute Pearson's correlation coefficient between the columns of a dataframe.

- You can also create scatter plots between pairs of features to visualize their relationship.

- Pandas provides the `fillna()` function that can be used to replace missing values with a new value.

- Principal component analysis is a statistical technique that can be used to reduce the number of features in the dataset yet maintain a large percentage of the variance of the original data.

- Recursive feature elimination, although computationally expensive, helps us understand how much each feature contributes to the performance of the model.

Chapter 4

Implementing Machine Learning on Mobile Apps

WHAT'S IN THIS CHAPTER

- ◆ Differences between deploying models on an iOS device and on a server-side environment
- ◆ Introduction to Apple's machine-learning ecosystem
- ◆ Introduction to third-party machine-learning tools that can be leveraged by iOS developers
- ◆ Tools that can be used to convert models from popular formats to the Core ML format

The previous chapters of the book introduced several concepts of machine learning, including feature engineering and selection techniques. In this chapter, you will learn about the options available to you as an iOS developer to integrate machine learning in your apps. While choosing Apple's offerings will usually be your go-to choice, you will also learn about other third-party offerings that can be used from within your apps.

Device-Based vs. Server-Based Approaches

When you have finished training your machine-learning model, you will probably want to use the model in an application. To use the model, you will first need to export the model into a suitable file format on your computer's hard disk. Unfortunately, the combination of a large number of model-building libraries and the lack of standardization has led to a proliferation in the number of custom file formats for machine-learning models. Most model-building libraries have their own custom file format, and sometimes these formats are not interoperable. A variety of tools exist to convert models from one proprietary format to another. At the time of writing, the following were the most popular formats that seem to have industry-wide acceptance:

- ◆ **Pickle:** Pickle is a Python module that can be used to convert any Python object into a byte stream and save it to disk. You can use this library to serialize (and deserialize) machine-learning models built in Python, provided you intend to use them within a Python environment.

- ◆ **ONNX:** The Open Neural Network Exchange format is the most popular format for machine-learning models in the industry. Although it was initially designed for neural network models, Scikit-learn models can also be exported to this format.

♦ **Core ML:** Apple's Core ML is not just a runtime environment but also a file format. This is the format in which you need to save your models if you want to use them in an iOS app. Core ML Tools is a Python library that can be used to convert a number of models from popular formats into the Core ML format.

With the model saved to a file, you will need to deploy the model into a suitable runtime environment so that it can be used by your applications. The purpose of the runtime is to load the model and provide a programmatic interface that allows you to use the model to make predictions. The runtime environment can be a server-side environment such as Google TF Serve or an on-device environment such as Core ML. In the former case, your mobile app code will interact with the model via an HTTPS REST API, and in the latter case using Swift code.

With these two fundamentally different deployment options, which one should you choose? Some of the reasons that you may want to prefer *on-device inferencing* (also known as *edge-based* inferencing) over server-side inferencing are as follows:

♦ There are no server-side round-trips involved, so you do not need to worry about transport security, authentication, authorization, and credential management.

♦ The data on which inferences are sought will remain on the iOS device. You could choose to send the data to a server-side application for some other purpose, but this would have nothing to do with Core ML.

♦ The machine-learning aspects of your mobile app can work in the absence of Internet connectivity.

There are also situations where server-side inferencing may be the preferred approach. These are some of the reasons to favor server-side inferencing:

♦ Your model may need access to data from different real-time sources in addition to what you are able to submit from the mobile device. For example, a model that is used to decide whether an applicant should be issued a credit card could require the answers to the questions on the application form as well as data from previously generated analytics feeds to determine the length of time spent by the applicant on the page, the number of times the applicant moved away from the page, and so on.

♦ Your model may need access to data about the transactional history and other products associated with the user. For example, a model that is used to decide whether an applicant should be issued a credit card could require information on other accounts opened by the customer, the dates these were opened, and their balances.

♦ Your model may be based on a cutting-edge algorithm or framework that is not supported by Core ML. Machine learning is a fast-moving space, and with Apple only updating Core ML once a year, there is a real possibility that a new ground-breaking algorithm is not available in Core ML for a number of Core ML releases.

Even though you have a choice on where to deploy your trained model, training the model is almost always achieved using server-side resources. There are a few types of models that can be trained efficiently on resource-constrained environments, such as mobile devices, and this type of training usually involves making minor changes to a pretrained model (a process known as *transfer learning*). Table 4.1 summarizes the pros and cons of deploying models on server-side environments and on-device environments.

TABLE 4.1:   Pros and Cons of Server-Side and Edge-Based Deployment

ON-DEVICE MODEL DEPLOYMENT	SERVER-SIDE MODEL DEPLOYMENT
Pros: ♦ No server-side round-trips involved. ♦ The data on which inferences are sought will remain on the iOS device. ♦ Model can be used in the absence of Internet connectivity. Cons: ♦ You are restricted in the types of models you can deploy (only those supported by Core ML runtime). ♦ Updating the model requires a new app-release. ♦ You do not have access to other data that may be held on your servers for the user.	Pros: ♦ You can deploy a new model whenever you like; there is no need to update the app. ♦ You are not restricted to the Core ML format. You can use any number of cutting-edge algorithms that may not be supported by Core ML. ♦ Your model can access historical user data that you hold in your server-side databases. Cons: ♦ You will need to manage and pay for the infrastructure required to host the model. ♦ You will need to manage authentication and authorization. ♦ User data will be sent to your servers, which may require additional user consent, and in some cases may dictate the location of your servers.

Apple's Machine Learning Frameworks and Tools

Apple provides a number of frameworks to help integrate machine learning into your applications. These frameworks operate at different levels of abstraction but can broadly be classified into two main categories—task-level frameworks and model-level frameworks.

Task-Level Frameworks

Task-level frameworks provide methods that allow you to perform high-level tasks without having to explicitly deal with training and deploying a machine-learning model. The framework includes a number of pre-trained models and will pick one based on the task you want to perform. At the time of writing, the key task-level frameworks provided by Apple were as follows:

♦ **Vision:** This framework provides high-level APIs to perform tasks, such as face detection, landmark detection, barcode scanning, and object tracking. The framework also provides helpful methods that can be used to prepare images for use with other frameworks, such as Core ML. In fact, if you want to use custom Core ML format models to process images and videos in your apps, it is highly recommended to use Vision. You can learn more about the Vision framework at `https://developer.apple.com/documentation/vision`.

♦ **Natural Language:** This framework provides high-level APIs to analyze text and deduce language-specific elements such as nouns, verbs, adjectives, and named entities such as people, places, and organizations. It can also be used to detect the dominant language of a text document. You can learn more about the Natural Language framework at `https://developer.apple.com/documentation/naturallanguage`.

◆ **Speech:** This framework can be used to recognize spoken words in audio streams. The framework supports multiple languages and uses machine-learning models hosted on Apple's servers for much of its functionality. If you use this framework in your apps, your app will need an Internet connection. It is worth noting that Apple sets limits on the daily number of requests that can be made from an app. You can find out more about the Speech framework at `https://developer.apple.com/documentation/speech`.

Model-Level Frameworks

Model-level frameworks provide a mechanism to use a machine-learning model in your app. Core ML is Apple's model-level framework, and although there are other third-party frameworks that you can use instead of Core ML, it is usually the first choice for an iOS developer. The difference between task-level frameworks and Core ML is in the amount of work you will need to perform to do something. Task-level frameworks provide convenient high-level APIs that handle a lot of tasks such as pre-processing inputs, threading, using an appropriate model, and post-processing model outputs.

However, to implement the equivalent functionality using Core ML, you will need to perform the various pre- and post-processing operations. You may be tempted to ask why should I even bother using Core ML directly, given the extra overheads? There are two good reasons.

◆ Apple's task-level frameworks may not exist for the high-level task you need to perform. For instance, there is no task-level framework to predict stock price movements.

◆ Even when a task-level framework exists, the model internally used by the framework may not be good enough for your needs.

Apple provides a number of pre-trained models in the Core ML format, which can be down-loaded from `https://developer.apple.com/machine-learning/models/`. These models are open source, and Apple also provides links to the Python source code that was used to create the model.

In addition to models provided by Apple, you can also get models in the Core ML format from third-party Internet repositories. These model repositories are commonly referred to as *model zoos*. A quick Internet search for *Core ML model zoo* should return several options. It is worth mentioning that you are using these third-party models at your own risk.

Format Converters

Core ML Tools is a Python module provided by Apple that can be used to convert models created using popular open source tools—such as Scikit-learn, LightGBM, and XGBoost—into the Core ML format. You can find out more about Core ML Tools at `https://pypi.org/project/coremltools/`.

Some frameworks, like Google TensorFlow and Apache MXNet, are not supported by Core ML Tools. Google provides the TensorFlow to Core ML convertor Python module called `tf-coreml`, which can be used to convert TensorFlow models into the Core ML format. You can find out more about `tf-coreml` at `https://github.com/tf-coreml/tf-coreml`.

The Apache software foundation provides a Python-based convertor for Apache MXNet models called `mxnet-to-coreml`. You can find out more about the Apache MxNet to Core ML converter at `https://github.com/apache/incubator-mxnet/tree/master/tools/coreml`.

If you are using a framework that is not supported by Core ML Tools and does not come with a convertor that can convert models directly to the Core ML format, you can try to convert the model into the popular ONNX format and then use the ONNX to Core ML convertor Python module to convert from the ONNX format to the Core ML format. You can find out more about converting ONNX models to Core ML at `https://github.com/onnx/onnx-coreml`.

Transfer Learning Tools

Apple also provides tools that allow you to use a technique known as *transfer learning* to modify existing pre-trained models with your own data. Transfer learning is generally used with deep-learning models, and the key idea behind the approach is to save training time by reusing much of the knowledge in an existing model to work with different but related data.

For instance, training a good deep-learning model that is capable of detecting 10 different types of objects in an image is a time-consuming task and requires access to a large corpus of labeled training images. Once trained, this model is only capable of working with the 10 object classes it has been trained for. If you wanted a model to identify different types of objects, then in normal circumstances, you would need to retrain a new model from scratch.

However, certain types of deep-learning model architectures (such as convolutional neural networks—CNNs) have distinct feature-extraction and classification parts. The feature-extraction part of the network learns to extract a number of useful features from the input image, and the classification part of the network deals with mapping these features into the desired object classes. Transfer learning uses this architectural design and allows you to re-train just the classification part of an already trained model. The classification part of the model is usually just a couple of layers, and hence re-training is very quick.

This approach works only if the object classes for which you want to retrain the model are somewhat similar to the original object classes used while building the model. This is because the feature-extraction part of the model will be unmodified during transfer learning, and that part of the model has learned how to extract the best class of features from the images it was trained on. Therefore, transfer learning can be used if you have a model that can recognize different models of cars and you want to re-train it to recognize different models of trucks. However, if you tried to use transfer learning on a model trained to recognize cars, in an attempt to create a model capable of recognizing different breeds of dogs, then the results will not be satisfactory.

The two key offerings from Apple for transfer learning are Create ML and Turi Create, both of which operate at a task level. You specify what you want to do, and these tools pick the best pre-trained model and apply transfer learning to it.

TURI CREATE

Turi Create is an open source Python library that was released by Apple in 2017, and was essentially Apple's first transfer learning offering. The origins of the product can be traced to a startup called Turi, which Apple acquired in 2016. To use Turi Create, you will need to create a Python script file and execute the script in your Jupyter Notebook or on the command line. The Python script file will perform the transfer learning operation on a pre-trained model and output a Core

ML–compatible model file, which you can then use with Xcode. Turi Create allows you to use transfer learning to create models that can accomplish the following tasks:

◆ Create personalized recommendations

◆ Classify sounds

◆ Recognize objects in images

◆ Detect an activity from sensor data

◆ Analyze the sentiment of text messages

◆ Predict values using tree-based regression models

You can learn more about Turi Create at `https://github.com/apple/turicreate`.

CREATE ML

Create ML is a Swift library that was announced by Apple in 2018, and provided a subset of the capabilities of Turi Create to Swift developers. The initial version of Create ML could be used to perform transfer learning for object detection and sentiment analysis. In 2019, Apple announced Create ML app, which is a macOS application that allows you to use transfer learning to create Core ML models using drag-and-drop operations. At the time of writing, the Create ML app was in Beta and supported all the capabilities of Turi Create.

Third-Party Machine-Learning Frameworks and Tools

In addition to the tools provided by Apple, as an iOS developer, you can also choose to leverage a number of non-Apple-provided machine-learning frameworks and tools. This section summarizes some of the more popular options.

◆ **Google TensorFlow-lite:** TensorFlow is a popular machine-learning framework created by Google, and it is primarily used to create deep-learning models. Google provides a lightweight mobile optimized runtime called TensorFlow-lite that can be used to deploy TensorFlow models on both iOS and Android devices. You can find out more about TensorFlow-lite at `https://www.tensorflow.org/lite`.

◆ **Google ML Kit:** This is a machine learning SDK provided by Google that provides a number of task-specific capabilities for iOS and Android developers. Google is actively enhancing the capabilities of ML Kit, and at the time this book was written, ML Kit provided APIs for natural language processing (NLP), text translation, face detection, object detection, barcode scanning, and landmark detection. One of the key differences between Google's ML Kit and Apple's frameworks is that ML Kit is capable of working with models deployed both on-device and on the cloud. You can find out more about Google ML Kit at `https://developers.google.com/ml-kit/`.

◆ **Scikit-learn:** Scikit-learn is a popular Python machine learning framework used for a variety of tasks, such as feature engineering, cross-validation, and model-building. You can use Core ML Tools to convert Scikit-learn models into the Core ML format and execute them on-device with the Core ML framework. You can also use tools such as Amazon

SageMaker to deploy Scikit-learn models on the AWS cloud and use these models from your iOS apps. You can find out more about Scikit-learn at `https://scikit-learn.org/stable/`.

◆ **Amazon Web Services (AWS):** Amazon provides a number of cloud-based machine-learning services. Some of these services are task focused and use pre-trained models to allow you to perform tasks such as text to speech conversion, and others are general purpose and allow you to train your own models and deploy the models into AWS-hosted virtual machines. Amazon provides an SDK for iOS and Android that can be used to consume these server-based machine learning services. The following are some of the more popular AWS services for machine learning:

  ◆ **Amazon Comprehend:** This is a task-focused service that uses pre-trained models and allows you to build applications that need to understand the structure and content of text. Amazon Comprehend uses natural language processing to extract insights into the content of documents. The insights can be entities (people, places), key phrases, sentiment (positive, neutral, mixed, or negative), and syntax.

  ◆ **Amazon Lex:** This is a task-focused service that uses pre-trained models and allows you to build conversational interfaces (chatbots) that support both text and voice. Amazon Lex uses deep learning to implement natural language understanding (NLU) and automatic speech recognition (ASR) and is the same engine that is used in Amazon Alexa.

  ◆ **Amazon Rekognition:** This is a task-focused service that provides APIs for deep-learning based object detection and recognition in images and videos. You can think of this as Amazon's answer to Apple's Vision framework.

  ◆ **Amazon Translate:** This is a document translation service that uses pre-trained models to allow you to translate text among a variety of languages.

  ◆ **Amazon SageMaker:** This is Amazon's key offering for users who want to train their own machine-learning models and deploy them into the AWS cloud. Amazon SageMaker includes an integrated Jupyter Notebook, ready-to-use implementations of popular machine learning algorithms, and support for training (and hosting) models created with Scikit-learn, Keras, and Google TensorFlow.

You can find out more about Amazon's machine learning specific offerings at `https://aws.amazon.com/machine-learning/`. You can find out more about the AWS iOS SDKs at `https://aws.amazon.com/developers/getting-started/ios/`.

Summary

◆ Apple's Core ML is not just a runtime environment but also a file format. This is the format in which you need to save your models if you want to use them in an iOS app.

◆ The Open Neural Network Exchange format is the most popular format for machine-learning models in the industry. Although it was initially designed for neural network models, Scikit-learn models can also be exported to this format.

◆ Machine-learning models can be deployed in runtime environments that are on the user's iOS devices or in server-side environments.

◆ Core ML models are deployed on-device.

◆ Apple provides a number of task-level frameworks that allow you to perform high-level tasks without having to explicitly deal with training and deploying a machine-learning model.

◆ Apple provides a number of pre-trained models in the Core ML format, which can be downloaded from the Internet. You can also get Core ML models from third-party sites, called model zoos.

◆ Core ML Tools is a Python module provided by Apple that can be used to convert models created using popular open source tools—such as Scikit-learn, LightGBM, and XGBoost—into the Core ML format.

◆ Some frameworks, like Google TensorFlow and Apache MXNet, are not supported by Core ML Tools. In such cases, the frameworks themselves provide either a mechanism to directly export to the Core ML format, or a popular format like ONNX.

◆ ONNX models can be converted to the Core ML format by using the ONNX to Core ML converter Python module.

◆ Transfer learning is generally used with deep-learning models, and the key idea behind the approach is to save training time by reusing much of the knowledge in an existing model in order to work with different but related data.

◆ The two key offerings from Apple for transfer learning are Create ML and Turi Create; both of these operate at a task level.

◆ Besides the tools provided by Apple, as an iOS developer, you can also choose to leverage a number of non-Apple-provided machine-learning frameworks and tools.

Part 2

Machine Learning with CoreML, CreateML, and TuriCreate

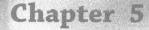

Chapter 5

Object Detection Using Pre-trained Models

WHAT'S IN THIS CHAPTER

- ◆ Introduction to object detection
- ◆ Introduction to artificial neural networks
- ◆ Introduction to convolutional neural networks
- ◆ Using a pre-trained model to implement object detection in an iOS app

In this chapter, you will learn about the basics of artificial neural networks (ANNs) and convolutional neural networks (CNNs) and use a pre-trained convolutional neural network model with Core ML to create an app that allows users to take a picture to detect the dominant object in the image.

NOTE   You can download the code files for this chapter from wrox.com or from GitHub using the following URL:

https://github.com/asmtechnology/iosmlbook-chapter5.git

What Is Object Detection?

Before we jump into the code to implement object detection in an app, it will be useful to understand what object detection is and how it works. Object detection is an application of computer vision techniques to detect one or more objects in an image. Computer vision is a discipline within artificial intelligence that deals with the development of algorithms that can be applied to the domain of digital images and video.

Early applications of object detection algorithms were primarily used for quality control in manufacturing facilities. Typically, a still or video camera would be used to take an image of a part (such as a circuit board), and this image would be processed by a computer to detect any anomalies in the image. If anomalies were detected, the part would be discarded. The same kind of inspection techniques could also be applied to other scenarios—such as inspecting freshly picked apples on a conveyor belt and discarding ones that do not exhibit some desirable characteristic (such as size/shape). Figure 5.1 illustrates the general principle behind this type of setup.

FIGURE 5.1
Object detection
techniques applied in
industrial inspection

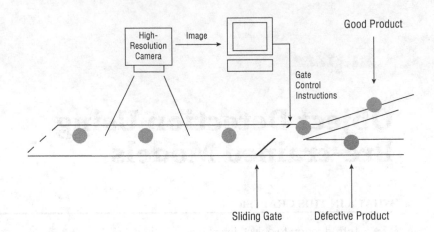

These early implementations of object detection involved three general stages (see Figure 5.2).

♦ **Preprocessing stage:** This stage involved running a series of predetermined image processing operations on the image, such as balancing the brightness levels in an image, converting it to grayscale, and applying popular edge detection algorithms to arrive at a black and white image where the dominant edges in the image were in white and the rest of the image was black.

♦ **Feature extraction stage:** This stage involved analyzing the output of the preprocessing stage (the image with information on dominant edges of the image) and trying to find geometric structures such as lines, rectangles, and, ellipses. The statistical characteristics of these shapes (size, orientation, etc.) were also computed during this stage.

♦ **Object detection stage:** The final stage involved creating domain-specific algorithms to combine the information from the feature extraction stage into a meaningful output. For instance, if two circles were detected in an image, separated by no more than 20 pixels, then the object was probably a pair of spectacles.

As you can probably infer, implementing object detection in this way required individuals with specialist knowledge, and solutions were not transferrable across different domains. A system to detect images of oranges on a conveyor belt could not be used to detect images of grapes.

The next generation of object detection algorithms were based on a new class of features called *wavelet features*, specifically *Haar features*. A popular approach called the Viola-Jones approach used Haar wavelet features to detect human faces in digital images with a good success rate. You can learn more about the Viola-Jones approach from their 2001 paper titled "Rapid Object Detection Using a Boosted Cascade of Simple Features," at https://www.cs.cmu .edu/~efros/courses/LBMV07/Papers/viola-cvpr-01.pdf.

Despite the high success rate of the Viola-Jones face detector, it still suffered from problems with scale and orientation. It required faces to be in a specific orientation. The individual must be facing the camera directly, could not be smiling, could not be blinking, etc. A number of approaches were taken to overcome some of these shortcomings, the most notable of which was the creation of the patented Scale Invariant Feature Transformation (SIFT) algorithm for object detection. For quite some time, SIFT was the dominant approach in problems such as object detection, match moving, and object tracking.

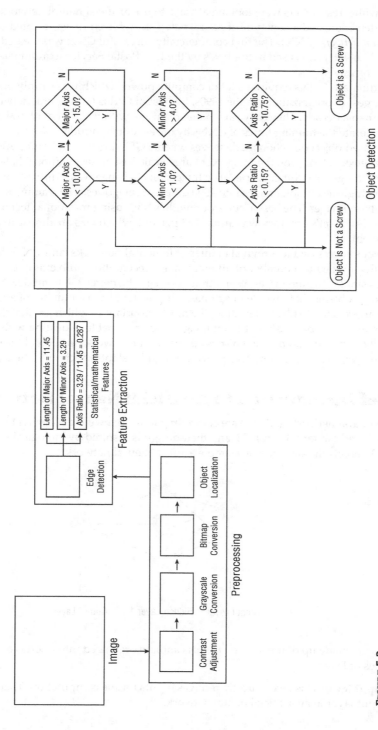

FIGURE 5.2
Object detection stages

Meanwhile, researchers were looking at ways to use artificial neural networks for the problem of object detection, and a new type of neural network architecture was created called the *convolutional neural network* (CNN). The first commercially successful CNN was created by Yann LeCun and called LeNet; it was used in the 1990s by the U.S. Postal Service to automate the reading of ZIP codes on envelopes.

Unfortunately, CNNs required a lot of compute power, which was simply not available to all but the largest of organizations in the 1990s. Interest in CNNs (and neural networks) died down for more than a decade. They only saw mainstream use with the advent of powerful GPUs that could accelerate the training times of CNNs by orders of magnitude.

CNN-based object detection made waves when a GPU-based CNN called AlexNet (created by Alex Krizhevsky et al.) won the ImageNet Large Scale Visual Recognition Challenge in 2012, by a significant margin over other entries. The ImageNet challenge was a difficult one and involved classifying high-resolution images into 1000 different categories. The training set alone was more than a million images. The best accuracy of models built using traditional techniques was around 74 percent. AlexNet's accuracy was around 83 percent, which was an almost 10 percent improvement.

AlexNet's success led to a revival in interest in neural networks, and CNNs have since been successfully applied to a number of different image recognition problems and are able to achieve accuracies similar to humans, and sometimes even a little better. CNN models today are the go-to models for problems that involve image-based inputs and have a number of advantages over previous approaches to object detection, the most important of which are that they require significantly less preprocessing of input images and are capable of dealing with different object scales and orientations. A detailed discussion of neural networks is beyond the scope of this book; however, the next section does provide a high-level introduction to the topic.

A Brief Introduction to Artificial Neural Networks

Artificial neural networks (ANNs) are computing tools that were developed by Warren McCulloch and Walter Pitts in 1943, and their design is inspired by biological neural networks. Figure 5.3 depicts the structure of a simple artificial neural network.

FIGURE 5.3
Structure of an artificial
neural network

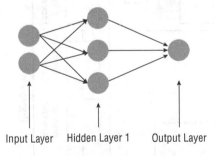

Input Layer   Hidden Layer 1   Output Layer

ANNs are made up of units called *neurons* and are organized into a series of layers. There are three types of layers.

◆ **Input layer:** This layer directly receives inputs for the computation. There is only one input layer in an artificial neural network.

◆ **Output layer:** This layer provides the output of the computation. There can be one or more neurons in this layer, depending on the type of problem the network is used to solve.

◆ **Hidden layer:** This layer sits between the input and output layers. Neurons in the input layer are connected to neurons in the hidden layer, and neurons in the hidden layer are connected to the neurons in the output layer. When all of the neurons in one layer are connected to every neuron in the previous layer, the network is called a *fully connected* (or dense) network. A simple neural network may not necessarily have a hidden layer, and complex neural networks such as deep-learning networks have several hidden layers, each with a large number of neurons in them.

Each of the connections between neurons has a weight value associated with it. The weight multiplies the value of the neuron the connection originated from. Each neuron works by computing the sum of its inputs and passing the sum through a nonlinear activation function. The output value of the neuron is the result of the activation function. Figure 5.4 depicts a simple neural network with two neurons in the input layer and one neuron in the output layer.

FIGURE 5.4

A simple neural network

If x_1, x_2 are the values loaded into the neurons in the input layer, w_1, w_2 are the connection weights between the input layer and the output layer, and f() is the activation function of the neuron in the output layer, then the output value of the neural network in Figure 5.4 is $f(w_1.x_1 + w_2.x_2)$.

There are many different types of activation functions with their own advantages and disadvantages. The reason to have an activation function is to ensure that the network is not just a one big linear model. When a neural network is instantiated, the weights are set to random values. The process of training the neural network involves finding out the values of the weights. During the training process, some training samples (for which you know the outcome) are fed into the network one at a time, and the predictions made by the network are compared with expected results. A mathematical error function (such as mean squared error) is used to capture the overall error in prediction, and the weights of the neural network are adjusted to reduce the value of this error function. Assuming you have several training samples, the computation of the error function and subsequent weight optimization can happen at one of three points in time during the training process.

◆ After each training sample has been processed by the network

◆ After a batch of training samples has been processed by the network (the *batch size* is assumed to be smaller than the total number of training samples)

◆ After all the training samples have been processed by the network

When the neural network has encountered all the training samples, one *training epoch* is said to have elapsed. Networks are typically trained for several epochs until the error in predictions has stopped reducing.

For a given value of the error function, the adjustment of the weights of the neurons happen layer by layer, starting from the last layer of the network and working back to the first layer of the network. The algorithm used to split the error across individual neurons is known as *back propagation* and uses the chain rule of differentiation to work out the individual contributions of each neuron to the overall network error. A detailed discussion of back propagation is beyond the scope of this book; however, it is important to keep in mind that back propagation requires the activation functions of the neurons to be differentiable. This means you cannot arbitrarily choose any activation function, only ones for which the derivative is defined.

A convolutional neural network architecture consists of two parts—a convolutional base and a regular dense neural network on top of the base. The purpose of the convolutional base is to extract useful features from the input image, and the purpose of the dense network is to use the outputs of the convolutional base to solve a typical binary or multiclass classification problem. In the case of a binary classification problem, the final output is a number that indicates the probability that the input image contains an object of a specific class. If the problem is a multi-class one, the final output of the network is an array of class-wise probabilities. Figure 5.5 depicts the structure of a simple CNN that could be used to solve a two-class classification problem.

As you can see from Figure 5.5, the convolutional base portion of the network consists of a number of layers stacked on top of each other. These layers can be of three types.

- **Convolutional layer:** This layer performs a convolution operation on its input. The convolution operation is a popular operation in image and signal processing. It involves using a small matrix of floating-point numbers called a *kernel* (usually 3×3) to modify the input image, by centering the kernel over each pixel position in the input image and computing the value of the corresponding pixel of the output image as a weighted sum of the neighboring pixels. The values of the kernel matrix serve as the weights. Figure 5.6 illustrates the convolution operation.

- If you are not familiar with the convolution operation in the image processing domain, this idea may seem quite abstract to you. The key point to understand about the operation is that a kernel with specially selected weights can transform the input image to accentu-ate certain features.

- Applying a sequence of convolution operations to an image (with different kernels) will result in an image that may not necessarily look anything like the original. A typical convolution layer can contain a number of kernels, and the output of these kernels can be used as inputs to another convolutional layer. Each successive convolutional layer adds a level of abstraction to the features detected by the previous layer. Figure 5.7 illustrates this concept with an image of a mobile phone.

- **Pooling layer:** This type of layer is used to reduce the size of the input image by a factor of 50 percent. The reduction can be achieved in a number of ways, but the most common way is to examine each 2×2 pixel neighborhood in the input image and use the highest input pixel value in the region as the value of the pixel in the output image. This operation is referred to as *max pooling* (as you are taking the maximum value in each 2×2 subregion of the input image). If the lowest value was used, then the operation would be called *min pooling*. If the mean value was used, then the operation would be called average pooling.

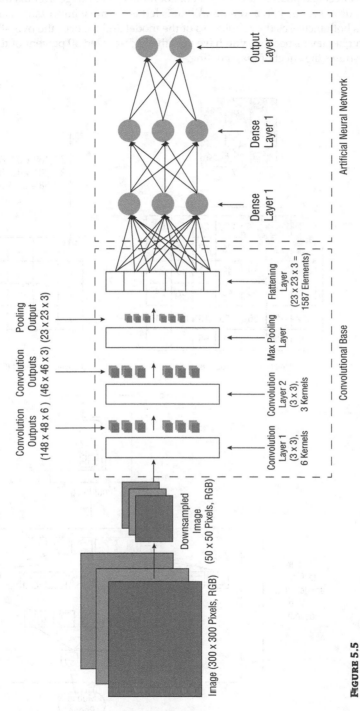

FIGURE 5.5

Architecture of a convolutional neural network

◆ The effect of a pooling layer is that of zooming out of image. Details that are less important disappear as you zoom out. What is left is the most important visual information. This both increases the robustness of the model and reduces the overall computation effort in higher layers because you have effectively discarded 50 percent of the data. Figure 5.8 illustrates the effect of max pooling.

FIGURE 5.6
The convolution operation

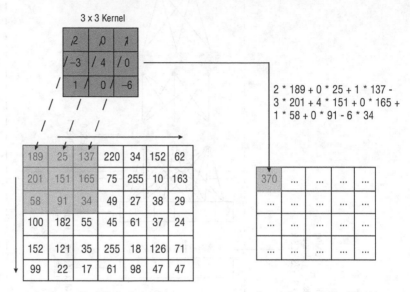

2 * 189 + 0 * 25 + 1 * 137 -
3 * 201 + 4 * 151 + 0 * 165 +
1 * 58 + 0 * 91 - 6 * 34

Image (7 x 6 Pixels, Grayscale)   Convolution Result (5 x 4 Matrix)

FIGURE 5.7
The result of successive convolutions

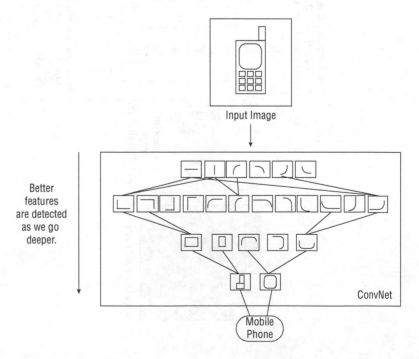

FIGURE 5.8
The effect of
max pooling

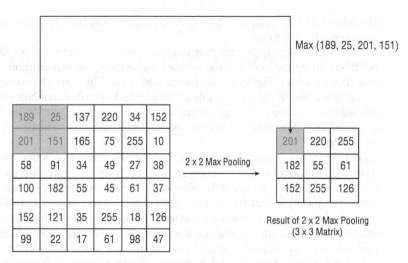

Max (189, 25, 201, 151)

189	25	137	220	34	152
201	151	165	75	255	10
58	91	34	49	27	38
100	182	55	45	61	37
152	121	35	255	18	126
99	22	17	61	98	47

2 x 2 Max Pooling

201	220	255
182	55	61
152	255	126

Result of 2 x 2 Max Pooling
(3 x 3 Matrix)

Convolution Output (6 x 6 Matrix)

◆ **Flattening layer:** This layer is encountered at the boundary of the convolutional base and the dense neural network. It is used to flatten all the two-dimensional convolution results into one long one-dimensional array, which can then be used as an input into the dense layers of the neural network.

If you want to visualize the effects of successive convolutional layers, visit Adam Harley's web page at http://scs.ryerson.ca/~aharley/vis/conv/flat.html. Adam has created a web-based CNN visualization tool that can recognize handwritten digits. Figure 5.9 shows this tool.

FIGURE 5.9
A visualization of CNN
layers by Adam Harley

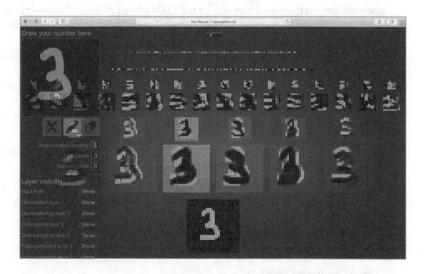

There is no set formula that dictates how many layers of each type you should have in a CNN. There are a number of popular CNN architectures such as VGG16, Inception, VGG19, ResNet50, and MobileNet. In Chapter 10, you will create an Inception deep convolutional neural network from scratch with Keras.

Figure 5.10 depicts the structure of the convolutional base of the VGG16 model, which is a relatively straightforward model with a long sequence of convolution and pooling layers stacked one after the other. The VGG16 network was created by Karen Simonyan and Andrew Zisserman and is discussed in their paper titled "Very Deep Convolutional Networks for Large-Scale Image Recognition." A copy of the paper can be found at https://arxiv.org/abs/1409.1556. Some of the other architectures mentioned here are more complex and involve branches within the model.

After looking at the architecture of the VGG16 network, you may be tempted to stack even more convolutional and pooling layers with the hope of improving the accuracy of the model. While it is generally accepted that deeper networks are capable of learning more complex relationships in the input data, it has been observed in practice that when the number of layers becomes large (several dozens), the effectiveness of the back propagation decreases. To overcome this problem, Kaiming He et al. proposed using the concept of residuals in a deep network. The idea is to feed the output of an earlier layer into the input of a later layer, bypassing a few of the layers in between. Figure 5.11 depicts residual connections in the convolutional base of a CNN.

You can read about residual learning in the paper titled "Deep Residual Learning for Image Recognition" at https://arxiv.org/abs/1512.03385.

ResNet is a popular type of CNN architecture that uses the concept of residuals. In the next section, you will download a pre-trained ResNet model and use it in an app.

Downloading the ResNet50 Model

While it is possible to build a ResNet model from scratch in Python using Keras and then training the model using millions of images, Apple provides a pre-trained ResNet 50-layer model, known as Resnet50, in the Core ML format. The model is trained on the ImageNet competition dataset and can recognize 1,000 object classes. To download this model, navigate to the Core ML model page at https://developer.apple.com/machine-learning/models/ and locate the Resnet50 model (see Figure 5.12).

Click the View Models button and then download the Resnet50.mlmodel file (see Figure 5.13).

You will use this model in the app you will create later in this chapter.

Creating the iOS Project

After downloading a pre-trained Core ML model, launch Xcode on your Mac and create a new project using the Single View App template (see Figure 5.14).

When prompted, use the following project options:

◆ **Product Name:** DominantObjectDetector

◆ **Organization Name:** *Provide a suitable value*

◆ **Organization Identifier:** *Provide a suitable value*

◆ **Language:** Swift

◆ **User Interface:** Storyboard

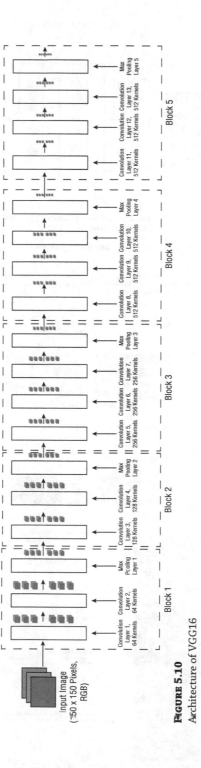

FIGURE 5.10

Architecture of VGG16

FIGURE 5.11
A network that uses
residual learning

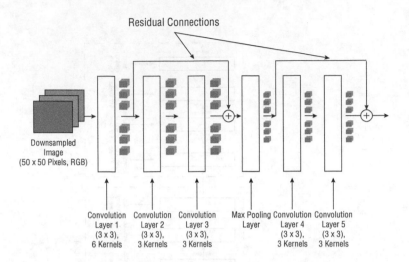

FIGURE 5.12
Pre-trained
Core ML models

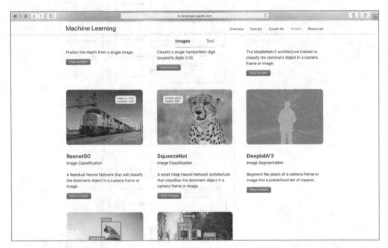

FIGURE 5.13
Downloading the
pre-trained Resnet50
Core ML model

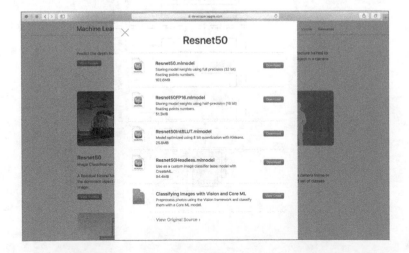

FIGURE 5.14
Creating a new iOS project using the Single View App template

- ◆ **Use Core Data:** Unchecked
- ◆ **Include Unit Tests:** Unchecked
- ◆ **Include UI Tests:** Unchecked

Creating the User Interface

With the project created, set up the user interface of the project using these steps:

1. Open the Main.storyboard file and use the View ➤ Show Library menu item to access the object library window. Drag and drop an image view, two button instances, and a label from the object library onto the default view controller scene.

2. Using the Attributes Inspector, change the caption of one of the buttons to **Select an Image**, and change the caption of the other button to **Capture an Image**. Change the background color of both buttons to a shade of gray to make them easier to see on the storyboard scene. You can access the Attributes Inspector using the View ➤ Inspectors ➤ Show Attributes Inspector menu item.

3. Organize the elements on the default view controller scene to resemble Figure 5.15 and set up appropriate storyboard constraints.

4. Use the Editor ➤ Assistant menu item to access the assistant editor and ensure the ViewController.swift file is open in the assistant editor. Create two outlets in the view controller class called imageView and resultLabel. Associate these outlets with the image view and label object of the storyboard scene (see Figure 5.16).

5. Create two action methods in the ViewController.swift file called onSelectImage-FromPhotoLibrary(_sender: Any) and onSelectImageFromCamera(_sender: Any). Associate these methods with the Touch Up Inside event of the buttons labeled Select an Image and Capture an Image, respectively. The code in your ViewController.swift file should now resemble Listing 5.1.

FIGURE 5.15
Application storyboard
with default view
controller scene

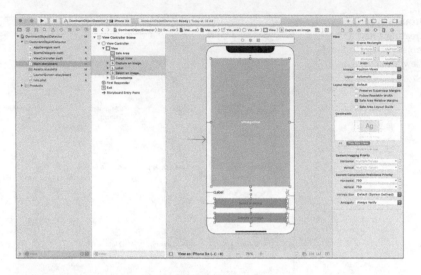

FIGURE 5.16
Using the assistant
editor to create outlets

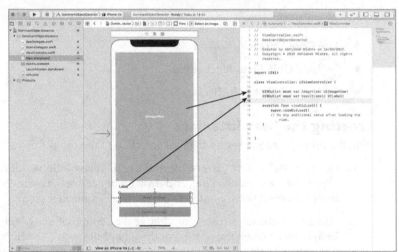

LISTING 5.1:   ViewController.swift File with Outlets and Actions

```swift
import UIKit

class ViewController: UIViewController {

    @IBOutlet weak var imageView: UIImageView!
    @IBOutlet weak var resultLabel: UILabel!
```

```
      override func viewDidLoad() {
          super.viewDidLoad()
          // Do any additional setup after loading the view.
      }

      @IBAction func onSelectImageFromPhotoLibrary(_ sender: Any) {
      }

      @IBAction func onSelectImageFromCamera(_ sender: Any) {
      }

  }
```

6. Add a method called detectDominantImage(in image: UIImage) in your
   ViewController.swift file and implement it as follows:

   ```
   func detectDominantObject(in image: UIImage) {
       // to do: write code to perform object detection with Core ML
   }
   ```

   The implementation of the method will be presented later in this chapter and will use a
   Core ML model to detect the dominant object in the image selected by the user.

7. Update the implementation of the OnSelectImageFromPhotoLibrary(_ sender: Any)
   method to the following:

   ```
   @IBAction func onSelectImageFromPhotoLibrary(_ sender: Any) {
       let picker = UIImagePickerController()
       picker.delegate = self
       picker.sourceType = .photoLibrary
       present(picker, animated: true)
   }
   ```

   This code uses a UIKit UIImagePickerController object to allow the user to select a
   photo from the photo library of the iOS device.

8. Update the implementation of the OnSelectImageFromCamera(_ sender: Any) method
   to the following:

   ```
   @IBAction func onSelectImageFromCamera(_ sender: Any) {
       // ensure camera is available.
       guard UIImagePickerController.isSourceTypeAvailable(.camera) else {

           let alertController = UIAlertController(title: "Error",
                                       message: "Could not access the camera.",
                                       preferredStyle: .alert)
   ```

```
            self.present(alertController, animated: true, completion: nil)
            return
        }

        let picker = UIImagePickerController()
        picker.delegate = self
        picker.sourceType = .camera
        present(picker, animated: true)
    }
```

This code checks to see whether the device has a camera and that the user has granted the app access to the camera. If there is no problem accessing the camera, the code creates a UIKit UIImagePickerController object to allow the user to use the camera to take a picture.

9. Add the following snippet to the bottom of the ViewController.swift file to implement the UIImagePickerControllerDelegate method func imagePickerController (_ picker:, didFinishPickingMediaWithInfo:) in a class extension:

```
extension ViewController: UIImagePickerControllerDelegate,
                          UINavigationControllerDelegate {

    func imagePickerController(_ picker: UIImagePickerController,
        didFinishPickingMediaWithInfo info:
        [UIImagePickerController.InfoKey : Any]) {
        picker.dismiss(animated: true)
        let image = info[UIImagePickerController.InfoKey.originalImage]
                as! UIImage
        imageView.image = image
        detectDominantObject(in: image)
    }
}
```

This code displays the picture selected by the user (or taken with the camera) in the image view object of the application's user interface and calls the detectDominantObject(in:) method to perform object detection. The code in ViewController.swift should resemble Listing 5.2.

LISTING 5.2:   ViewController.swift File with UIImagePicker Integration

```
import UIKit

class ViewController: UIViewController {

    @IBOutlet weak var imageView: UIImageView!
    @IBOutlet weak var resultLabel: UILabel!
```

```swift
    override func viewDidLoad() {
        super.viewDidLoad()
        // Do any additional setup after loading the view.
    }

    @IBAction func onSelectImageFromPhotoLibrary(_ sender: Any) {
        let picker = UIImagePickerController()
        picker.delegate = self
        picker.sourceType = .photoLibrary
        present(picker, animated: true)
    }

    @IBAction func onSelectImageFromCamera(_ sender: Any) {
        // ensure camera is available.
        guard UIImagePickerController.isSourceTypeAvailable(.camera) else {

            let alertController = UIAlertController(title: "Error",
                                    message: "Could not access the camera.",
                                    preferredStyle: .alert)

            alertController.addAction(UIAlertAction(title: "ok",
                                        style: .default, handler: nil))

            self.present(alertController,
                        animated: true, completion: nil)

    return
        }

        let picker = UIImagePickerController()
        picker.delegate = self
        picker.sourceType = .camera
        present(picker, animated: true)
    }

    func detectDominantObject(in image: UIImage) {
        // to do: write code to perform object detection with Core ML
    }
}

extension ViewController: UIImagePickerControllerDelegate,
                        UINavigationControllerDelegate {

    func imagePickerController(_ picker: UIImagePickerController,
        didFinishPickingMediaWithInfo info:
        [UIImagePickerController.InfoKey : Any]) {
        picker.dismiss(animated: true)
```

```
        let image = info[UIImagePickerController.InfoKey.originalImage]
                as! UIImage
        imageView.image = image
        detectDominantObject(in: image)
    }
}
```

Updating Privacy Settings

Before your app can access the camera on the device, you need to ask the user's permission and provide a short description of what your app intends to do with the camera. Asking the user for permission is performed automatically by the `UIImagePickerController` class. All you need to do is add a key to the application's `Info.plist` file and set the value of this key to a user-friendly message that will inform the user what your app intends to do with the camera.

Click the `Info.plist` file in the project navigator to open it in the plist editor. Choose the Editor ➤ Add Item menu to insert a new key into the `Info.plist` file. Select the Privacy – Camera Usage Description key from the list of available keys and provide a short string of text that describes how your app will use the camera (see Figure 5.17).

FIGURE 5.17
Editing the application's info.plist file

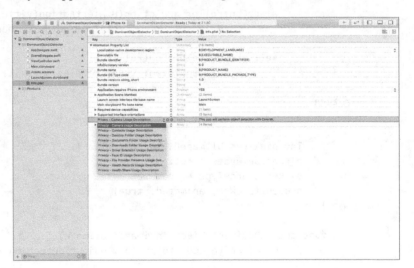

Using the Resnet50 Model in the iOS Project

Now that we have built the app's user interface, it is time to use the Resnet50 model that was downloaded in an earlier section to detect objects on the image selected by the user. Perform the following steps:

1. Control-click the `DominantObjectDetector` folder group in the Project navigator window and select the Add Files to DominantObjectDetector menu item. Navigate to the `Resnet50.mlmodel` file in your Downloads folder and ensure the Copy Items If Needed

option is checked and the `DominantObjectDetector` target is selected in the dialog box (see Figure 5.18).

FIGURE 5.18

Import settings for the `Resnet50.mlmodel` file

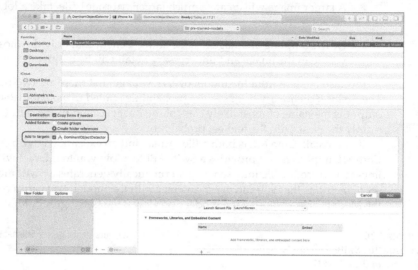

2. Select the `Resnet50.mlmodel` file in the Project navigator to get an overview of the model (see Figure 5.19).

FIGURE 5.19

Overview of the `Resnet50.mlmodel` file

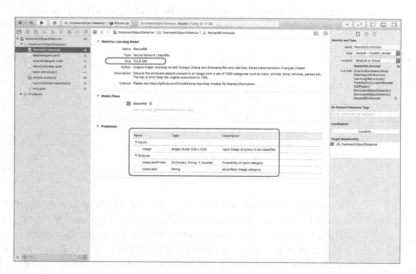

As you can see from the model overview screen, the size of the model is over 100 MB, and the inputs to the model are RGB (color) images of 224×224 pixels. The image that you select from the photo library (or camera) is much larger than this and will need to be downsampled to this size. You may be wondering why the input image size is so small. There are two good reasons for this:

◆ A larger image will create a much larger `.mlmodel` file, take a lot longer to train, and will be slower to use.

◆ Downsampling an image has the added benefit that only the most important objects are visible in the image and unnecessary detail will be removed.

It is also evident from the model overview page that there are two outputs from the model. The first is a dictionary of class-wise probabilities called `classLabelProbs`, and the second output is the name of most likely class of the image, called `classLabel`. The most likely class is simply the class with the highest probability.

If you recall, Core ML is both a file format and an execution environment. The latter aspect of Core ML implies that it provides a Swift API to allow you to interact with the model. When you import a `.mlmodel` file into Xcode, it automatically generates a Swift model class that contains a set of methods that you can use to interact with the model. You can access this Swift class from the Model Class section of the model overview page (see Figure 5.20).

FIGURE 5.20

Accessing the Swift interface to the Core ML model file

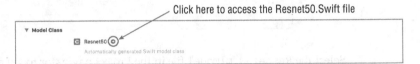

Click here to access the Resnet50.Swift file

Figure 5.21 depicts a section of the model class file. It is worth noting that the input image is expected to be represented as a `CVPixelBuffer` object and not `UIImage`.

FIGURE 5.21

A section of the `Resnet50.Swift` file

Creating a `CVPixelBuffer` object from a `UIImage` is a complex task, and it involves several side activities such as resizing the image and rotating the image to ensure it is the right size up. While it is possible for you to manually create the `CVPixelBuffer`, the most common approach is to convert a `UIImage` into a `CIImage` and then use the Vision framework to convert the `CIImage` instance into a `CVPixelBuffer`. The advantage of using the Vision framework is that not only can it convert `CIImage` instances into `CVPixelBuffer` instances, but it can also resize the `CIImage` to the dimensions expected by the model.

3. Select the `ViewController.swift` file in the Project navigator and add the following import statements to the top of the file to import the Core ML and Vision frameworks.

```
import CoreML
import Vision
```

4. To use the Vision framework to perform object detection with a custom Core ML model, you need to encapsulate your request into a VNCoreMLRequest object and then use a VNImageRequestHandler object to execute the request. Add the following lazy variable to the ViewController.swift file:

```
lazy var classificationRequest: VNCoreMLRequest = {
    do {
        let model = try VNCoreMLModel(for: Resnet50().model)

        let request = VNCoreMLRequest(model: model,
            completionHandler: { [weak self] request, error in
                self?.processResults(for: request, error: error)
        })

        request.imageCropAndScaleOption = .centerCrop
        return request
    } catch {
        fatalError("Failed to load Core ML model")
    }
}()
```

By using a lazy variable, you are ensuring that this code will not be executed when the class is loaded, but instead when you eventually access the classificationRequest variable from your code.

This code creates a VNCoreMLModel instance from the autogenerated Core ML model class Resnet50 and then creates a VNCoreMLRequest instance passing the VNCoreMLModel and a completion handler as parameters.

The VNCoreMLRequest object has a method called perform() that takes care of the heavy lifting of converting the image to a CVPixelBuffer and using the model to perform object detection. You will call the perform() method later in this chapter. The completion handler that you supplied while creating the VNCoreMLRequest object is called when the operation completes, and in this snippet, the completion handler calls the processResults(for:, error:) method, which you will create next.

Before returning the VNCoreMLRequest instance, the imageCropAndScaleOption property is set to centerCrop. This property is used by Vision to determine how it should scale the image down to the dimensions required by the model. Since the image taken by the camera is rectangular, and the image required by the model is a square, some cropping will also occur. There are three potential options you can specify.

◆ centerCrop: This option resizes the image proportionally until the smallest dimension of the image matches the dimensions expected by the model. The resized image (which is still a rectangle) is cropped into a square by using the central portion. This option can end up cropping off parts of the object in the center of the image.

◆ scaleFill: This option resizes the image disproportionally until both dimensions of the image match the dimensions expected by the model. The resized image will appear to be squashed.

◆ scaleFit: This option resizes the image proportionally until the longest dimension of the image matches the dimensions expected by the model. The resized image is converted into a square by padding the shorter dimension with black pixels.

Figure 5.22 depicts the effect of these three scale and crop options. Ideally you should choose the option that matches the choice when the model was trained. This is possible if you have trained the model; however, in the case of a pre-trained model, it is best to choose either center-Crop or scaleFill and ask the user to place the dominant object as close to the center of the image as possible.

FIGURE 5.22
VNCoreMLRequest scale
and crop options

Original   centerCrop   scaleFill   scaleFit

5. Implement the processResults(for:, error:) method in the ViewController.swift file as follows:

```
func processResults(for request: VNRequest, error: Error?) {
    DispatchQueue.main.async {
        guard let results = request.results else {
            print("Unable to classify image.\n\(error!.localizedDescription)")
            self.resultLabel.text = "Unable to classify image."
            return
        }

        let classifications = results as! [VNClassificationObservation]

        if classifications.isEmpty {
            self.resultLabel.text = "Did not recognize anything."
        } else {
            self.resultLabel.text = String(format: " percent@  percent.1f
percent percent",
                            classifications[0].identifier,
                        classifications[0].confidence * 100)
        }
    }
}
```

This method is called from the completion handler of the VNCoreMLRequest object. The method accepts two parameters; the first is a VNRequest instance called request, and the other is an optional error object. You can access the results of the classification by using the results member of the VNRequest object. The results of the classification are returned as an array of VNClassificationObservation objects. Each object has two member variables: identifier, which represents the class of the detected object, and confidence, which represents the probability of that class. The results are sorted in descending order of probability, with the first item in the array being the most probable object class.

It is important to note that this method is not called on the main UI thread, and, therefore, any updates to the user interface must be wrapped in a `DispatchQueue.main.async{}` block.

6. Now that you have written the code to create a VNCoreMLRequest and processed the results of the image classification, all you need to do is write code to create and execute the VNCoreMLRequest when the user selects an image. Earlier in this chapter you have created an empty method called func detectDominantObject(in image: UIImage). Replace the empty method with the following:

```
func detectDominantObject(in image: UIImage) {
    resultLabel.text = "Processing..."

    guard let ciImage = CIImage(image: image),
        let orientation = CGImagePropertyOrientation(rawValue:
                        UInt32(image.imageOrientation.rawValue))
    else {
        print("Unable to create CIImage instance")
        resultLabel.text = "Failed."
        return
    }

    DispatchQueue.global(qos: .userInitiated).async {
        let handler = VNImageRequestHandler(ciImage: ciImage,
                                orientation: orientation)
        do {
            try handler.perform([self.classificationRequest])
        } catch {
            print("Failed to perform
                    classification.\n\(error.localizedDescription)")
        }
    }
}
```

This function is already wired to be called from the UIImagePickerController delegate method. It receives a UIImage instance that represents the image selected by the user from the photo library or captured with the camera. The code in this function converts the UIImage instance into a CIImage instance and then creates a VNImageRequestHandler object with the CIImage instance.

```
guard let ciImage = CIImage(image: image),
    let orientation = CGImagePropertyOrientation(rawValue:
                    UInt32(image.imageOrientation.rawValue))
else {
    print("Unable to create CIImage instance")
    resultLabel.text = "Failed."
    return
}
```

Recall that the VNImageRequestHandler object can be used for executing a VNCoreMLRequest—which is performed by calling perform on the handler object.

```
let handler = VNImageRequestHandler(ciImage: ciImage,
                                    orientation: orientation)
do {
    try handler.perform([self.classificationRequest])
} catch {
    print("Failed to perform
        classification.\n\(error.localizedDescription)")
}
```

Since object detection is a time-consuming operation and you do not want to block your application user-interface while Core ML is executing the model, the call to create the VNImageRequestHandler and execute the VNCoreMLRequest is wrapped in a DispatchQueue .global(qos: .userInitiated).async block. The code in the ViewController.swift file should now resemble Listing 5.3.

LISTING 5.3:   Completed ViewController.swift File

```
import UIKit
import CoreML
import Vision

class ViewController: UIViewController {

    @IBOutlet weak var imageView: UIImageView!
    @IBOutlet weak var resultLabel: UILabel!

    lazy var classificationRequest: VNCoreMLRequest = {
        do {
            let model = try VNCoreMLModel(for: Resnet50().model)

            let request = VNCoreMLRequest(model: model, completionHandler: {
    [weak self] request, error in
                self?.processResults(for: request, error: error)
            })
            request.imageCropAndScaleOption = .centerCrop
            return request
        } catch {
            fatalError("Failed to load Core ML model")
        }
    }()

    override func viewDidLoad() {
        super.viewDidLoad()
        // Do any additional setup after loading the view.
    }
```

```swift
@IBAction func onSelectImageFromPhotoLibrary(_ sender: Any) {
    let picker = UIImagePickerController()
    picker.delegate = self
    picker.sourceType = .photoLibrary
    present(picker, animated: true)
}


@IBAction func onSelectImageFromCamera(_ sender: Any) {
    // ensure camera is available.
    guard UIImagePickerController.isSourceTypeAvailable(.camera) else {

        let alertController = UIAlertController(title: "Error",
                                message: "Could not access the camera.",
                                preferredStyle: .alert)
        alertController.addAction(UIAlertAction(title: "ok",
                                    style: .default, handler: nil))

        self.present(alertController, animated: true, completion: nil)
        return
    }

    let picker = UIImagePickerController()
    picker.delegate = self
    picker.sourceType = .camera
    present(picker, animated: true)
}

func detectDominantObject(in image: UIImage) {
    resultLabel.text = "Processing..."

    guard let ciImage = CIImage(image: image),
        let orientation = CGImagePropertyOrientation(rawValue:
    UInt32(image.imageOrientation.rawValue))
        else {
        print("Unable to create CIImage instance")
        resultLabel.text = "Failed."
        return
    }

    DispatchQueue.global(qos: .userInitiated).async {
        let handler = VNImageRequestHandler(ciImage: ciImage, orientation:
    orientation)
        do {
            try handler.perform([self.classificationRequest])
        } catch {
            print("Failed to perform classification.\n\(error.localizedDe
scription)")
        }
    }
}
```

```
func processResults(for request: VNRequest, error: Error?) {
    DispatchQueue.main.async {
        guard let results = request.results else {
            print("Unable to classify image.\n\(error!.localizedDes
cription)")
            self.resultLabel.text = "Unable to classify image."
            return
        }

        let classifications = results as! [VNClassificationObservation]

        if classifications.isEmpty {
            self.resultLabel.text = "Did not recognize anything."
        } else {
            self.resultLabel.text = String(format: " percent@  percent.1f
percent percent", classifications[0].identifier, classifications[0].
confidence * 100)
        }
    }
}


extension ViewController: UIImagePickerControllerDelegate,
    UINavigationControllerDelegate {

    func imagePickerController(_ picker: UIImagePickerController,
        didFinishPickingMediaWithInfo info: [UIImagePickerController
        .InfoKey : Any]) {
        picker.dismiss(animated: true)
        let image = info[UIImagePickerController.InfoKey.originalImage]
        as! UIImage
        imageView.image = image
        detectDominantObject(in: image)
    }
}
```

Save your project and run the app on an iOS device. Use the camera to take a picture of an object. You should see the results of the object detection process on the screen. Figure 5.23 depicts the results of running the app on a device and taking a picture of a flowerpot.

Keep in mind that you have set the value of the imageCropAndScale option of the VNCoreMLRequest object to .centerCrop. Therefore, you need to frame the object in the center of the image, and at a little distance from the camera, so that most of the object is present in the center-cropped version. You can try different imageCropAndScale values to gauge the performance of the model with these values.

FIGURE 5.23
Results of running the
app with the picture of
a flowerpot

NOTE You can download the code files for this chapter from wrox.com or from GitHub using the following URL:

https://github.com/asmtechnology/iosmlbook-chapter5.git

Summary

- ◆ Computer vision is a discipline within artificial intelligence that deals with the development of algorithms that can be applied to the domain of digital images and video.
- ◆ Object detection is an application of computer vision techniques to detect one or more objects in an image.
- ◆ Artificial neural networks (ANNs) are computing tools that were developed by Warren McCulloch and Walter Pitts in 1943; their design is inspired by biological neural networks.
- ◆ ANNs are made up of units called neurons and are organized into a series of layers.

◆ During the training process, a set of training samples (for which you know the outcome) is fed into the network one at a time, and the predictions made by the network are compared with expected results. A mathematical error function (such as mean squared error) is used to capture the overall error in prediction, and the weights of the neural network are adjusted to reduce the value of this error function.

◆ When the neural network has encountered all the training samples, one training epoch is said to have elapsed. Networks are typically trained for several epochs until the error in predictions has stopped reducing.

◆ A convolutional neural network architecture consists of two parts, a convolutional base and a regular dense neural network on top of the base. The purpose of the convolutional base is to extract useful features from the input image, and the purpose of the dense network is to use the outputs of the convolutional base to solve a typical binary or multiclass classification problem.

◆ Apple provides several pre-trained models in the Core ML format that you can download and use in your app.

Chapter 6

Creating an Image Classifier with the Create ML App

WHAT'S IN THIS CHAPTER

♦ Training an image classifier with the Create ML app

♦ Using the model generated by the Create ML app in an iOS application

In this chapter, you will use the Create ML app to train a machine learning model that can detect the dominant object in an image and classify the image as containing a dog or a cat. The model will be trained on a subset of the Kaggle Dogs vs. Cats dataset. After the model is trained, you will use the model in an iOS app that allows users to take a picture and determine whether the picture contains a dog or a cat. The full version of this dataset contains 25,000 images and is available on Kaggle.com at https://www.kaggle.com/c/dogs-vs-cats/data.

Training an image classification model can take a long time, and, therefore, the downloads that accompany this chapter include a reduced version of the Kaggle dataset, containing only 404 images instead of the original 25,000. The reduced dataset consists of two folders.

♦ Train: Contains 202 images. There are 101 images of dogs located within the train/dog folder. The remaining images are images of cats located within the train/cat folder.

♦ Test: Contains an additional 202 images, using a similar folder hierarchy as the train folder.

If you decide to use the full version of the Dogs vs. Cats dataset, you will need to download it from Kaggle.com and reorganize its contents to ensure that each object category in the training data is in its own subfolder.

NOTE You can download the code files for this chapter from wrox.com or from GitHub using the following URL:

https://github.com/asmtechnology/iosmlbook-chapter6.git

Introduction to the Create ML App

The Create ML app is a macOS application that allows you to build machine learning models using a wizard-style user interface. The Create ML app was introduced in WWDC 2019 and is a successor to the Create ML framework.

The similarly named Create ML framework is a Swift framework that allows you to use Xcode and Create ML models using Swift code. The Create ML app, on the other hand, does not require you to write any code at all. The Create ML app is included with Xcode 11 and requires macOS Catalina or higher. If you are using Xcode 11 on an earlier version of macOS, then you cannot use the Create ML app.

Besides not requiring you to write any code, the Create ML app also provides a task-oriented approach to machine learning. As you have learned in previous chapters of this book, there are many different types of models, and some of them can be used for different types of problems with varying degrees of success. Libraries like Scikit-learn require that you choose the algorithm for a particular problem and then proceed to build your model. Create ML (both the Swift library and the App) takes a different approach to model building. Instead of choosing the algorithm, you choose the problem you are trying to solve from a list of options, and Create ML will choose the best algorithm for the job. At the time this book was written, the following tasks were supported:

- Image classification and object detection
- Sound classification
- Activity classification
- Text classification
- Tabular classification and regression

While a task-oriented high-level interface does simplify model building, it comes with a few limitations, some of which may be lifted by Apple in future releases of the Create ML app.

- Depending on the task at hand, you may not have any control over the algorithm that was chosen or why it was chosen.
- You may have limited control over hyperparameters.
- You can only use Precision and Recall as the performance metrics. It is not possible to define custom metrics.
- For tabular data, you will need to perform feature engineering before you import the data into the Create ML app.

For image classification and object detection models, the Create ML app uses transfer learning to speed up the training process. The output of the Create ML app is a model in the Core ML format, ready to be used in your iOS applications. The size of the model is generally small (a few kilobytes). This is because the model exported by Create ML does not include the convolutional base. The convolution base, which is the bigger part of the machine learning model, is already included with iOS and macOS.

Creating the Image Classification Model with the Create ML App

At the time this book was written, the Create ML app required that you use macOS Catalina and Xcode 11.0 or higher. Launch Xcode on your Mac and then launch the Create ML app by using the Xcode ➤ Open Developer Tool ➤ Create ML menu item (see Figure 6.1).

FIGURE 6.1
Launching the
Create ML app

When the Create ML app has launched, use the File ➤ New Project menu item to create a new Create ML app project. You will be prompted to select a task. Select Image from the list of task categories and Image Classifier from the options that are available (see Figure 6.2) and click the Next button.

FIGURE 6.2
Selecting the Image
Classifier template

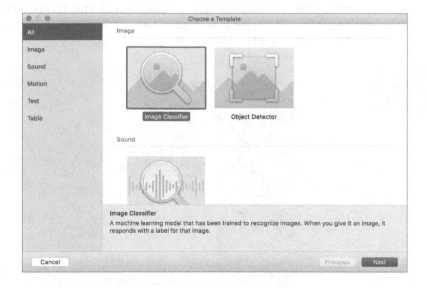

You will be presented with a dialog box that will allow you to specify the name of the new Create ML project and some metadata associated with the project (see Figure 6.3). Name the new project DogsCatsTransferLearningClassifier, provide a suitable project description, and click the Next button.

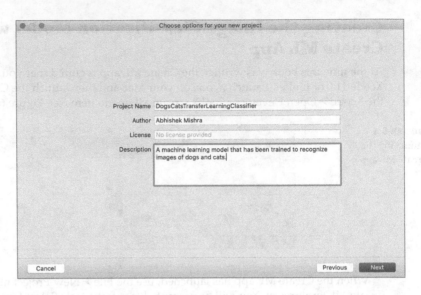

After specifying the project metadata, you will be prompted to specify a location for the new Create ML project. Select a location on your hard disk and click the Create button to finish creating the new project.

After the project is created, it will be loaded into Create ML. Locate the Training Data section in the Inputs tab and use the Select Files dropdown menu item to navigate to the `train` folder of the Dogs vs. Cats dataset (see Figure 6.4).

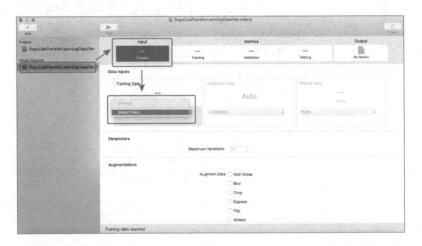

After specifying the location of the input data, scroll down to the Augmentations section of the screen and check all the data augmentation options (see Figure 6.5).

FIGURE 6.5
Training data
augmentation options

Data augmentation is a technique that is used to make a deep-learning convolutional neural network model more robust to changes in the pose of the dominant object and to changes in lighting conditions between images. Specifically, the technique involves creating augmented copies of the original data, with a selection of geometric transformation and brightness/contrast enhancements. The augmented images are included with the original training data, and the larger dataset is used for the training process. Click the Train button in the toolbar to begin training the classification model (see Figure 6.6).

FIGURE 6.6
Beginning the model
training process

Depending on the hardware configuration of your computer, the training process can take a considerable amount of time. Even with a reduced dataset, the training process took about four hours on a MacBook. When the training process is complete, you will be presented with information on the performance of the model on the training and validation datasets (see Figure 6.7). The Create ML app automatically reserves a portion of the training data for model validation.

The only performance metrics available in Create ML for a multiclass classification model at the time of writing were Precision and Recall. In the future, Apple may decide to add metrics or allow you to define your own custom metrics. As you can see from Figure 6.7, the model has an 88 percent precision on the validation set, which is not bad considering the small size of the dataset. You will get better accuracy if you use the entire Dogs vs. Cats dataset of 25,000 images. However, this will significantly increase the model training time.

FIGURE 6.7
Model performance
statistics

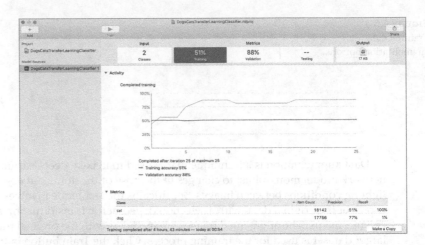

To test the predictions of the model, click the Testing tab and use the Choose Files drop-down menu to navigate to the `test` folder of the dataset (see Figure 6.8).

FIGURE 6.8
Navigating to the
test dataset

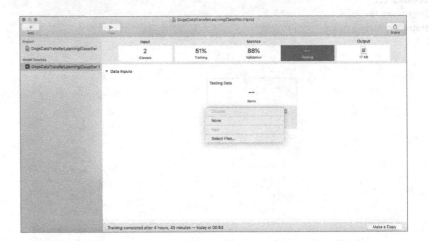

The test dataset included with the downloads that accompany this chapter contains 202 images, and it should take a few minutes for the Create ML app to make predictions on the entire set. While making predictions, data augmentation is not performed. You should see the results of the prediction process when the predictions are ready (see Figure 6.9).

The average precision of the model on the test dataset is 86 percent, which is slightly lower than the 88 percent precision on the validation dataset. This indicates that the model may be overfitting the training data. However, since you do not have control over the hyperparameters or the algorithm, there is little you can do to remedy this except try to increase the size of the training data. The Output tab contains your trained Core ML model, which you can drag and drop onto the macOS desktop or a Finder window to access the `.mlmodel` file. The output Core ML model file generated by the Create ML app will be called `DogsCatsTransferLearning-Classifier 1.mlmodel`. Rename the file to `DogsCatsTransferLearningClassifier.mlmodel` before proceeding to the next section.

FIGURE 6.9
Predictions on the
test dataset

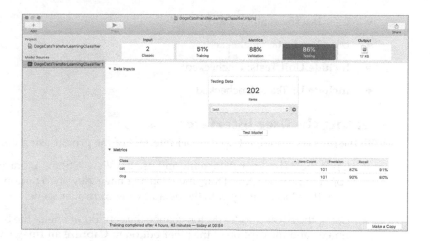

Creating the iOS Project

After saving the Core ML model on your computer, launch Xcode on your Mac and create a new project using the Single View App template (see Figure 6.10).

FIGURE 6.10
Creating a new iOS
project using the Single
View App template

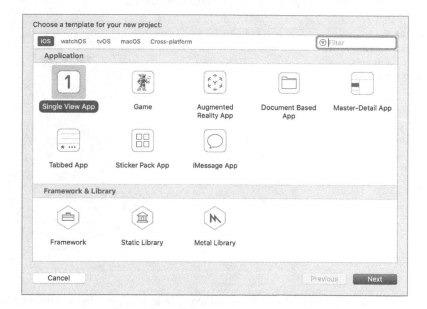

When prompted, use the following project options:

- **Product Name:** PetDetectorTL
- **Organization Name:** *Provide a suitable value*
- **Organization Identifier:** *Provide a suitable value*
- **Language:** Swift

◆ **User Interface:** Storyboard

◆ **Use Core Data:** Unchecked

◆ **Include Unit Tests:** Unchecked

◆ **Include UI Tests:** Unchecked

Creating the User Interface

With the project created, set up the user interface of the project using these steps:

1. Open the `Main.storyboard` file and use the View ➤ Show Library menu item to access the object library window. Drag and drop an image view, two button instances, and a label from the object library onto the default view controller scene.

2. Using the Attributes Inspector, change the caption of one of the buttons to **Select an Image**, and the caption of the other button to **Capture an Image**. Change the background color of both buttons to a shade of gray to make them easier to see on the storyboard scene. You can access the Attributes Inspector using the View ➤ Inspectors ➤ Show Attributes Inspector menu item.

3. Organize the elements on the default view controller scene to resemble Figure 6.11 and set up the appropriate storyboard constraints.

FIGURE 6.11
Application storyboard with default view controller scene

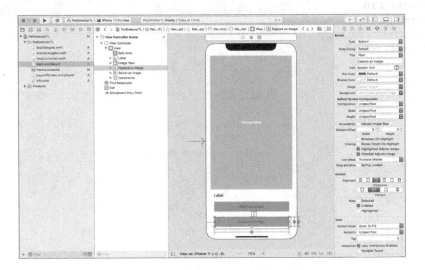

4. Use the Editor ➤ Assistant menu item to access the Assistant Editor and ensure the `ViewController.swift` file is open in the Assistant Editor. Create two outlets in the view controller class called `imageView` and `resultLabel`. Associate these outlets with the image view and label object of the storyboard scene (see Figure 6.12).

FIGURE 6.12
Using the Assistant
Editor to create outlets

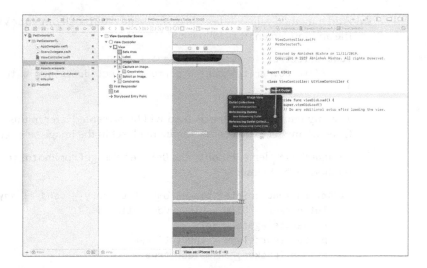

5. Create two action methods in the `ViewController.swift` file called onSelectImage-
FromPhotoLibrary(_ sender: Any) and onSelectImageFromCamera(_ sender: Any.
Associate these methods with the Touch Up Inside event of the buttons labeled Select an
Image and Capture an Image, respectively. The code in your `ViewController.swift` file
should now resemble Listing 6.1.

LISTING 6.1:   ViewController.swift File with Outlets and Actions

```swift
import UIKit

class ViewController: UIViewController {

    @IBOutlet weak var imageView: UIImageView!
    @IBOutlet weak var resultLabel: UILabel!

    override func viewDidLoad() {
        super.viewDidLoad()
        // Do any additional setup after loading the view.
    }

    @IBAction func onSelectImageFromPhotoLibrary(_ sender: Any) {
    }

    @IBAction func onSelectImageFromCamera(_ sender: Any) {
    }

}
```

6. Add a method called detectPet(in image: UIImage) in your ViewController.swift file and implement it as follows:

```
func detectPet(in image: UIImage) {
    // to do: write code to perform object detection with Core ML
}
```

The implementation of the method will be presented later in this chapter and will use a Core ML model to detect the dominant object in the image selected by the user.

7. Update the implementation of the OnSelectImageFromPhotoLibrary(_ sender: Any) method to the following:

```
@IBAction func onSelectImageFromPhotoLibrary(_ sender: Any) {
    let picker = UIImagePickerController()
    picker.delegate = self
    picker.sourceType = .photoLibrary
    present(picker, animated: true)
}
```

This code uses a UIKit UIImagePickerController object to allow the user to select a photo from the photo library of the iOS device.

8. Update the implementation of the OnSelectImageFromCamera(_ sender: Any) method to the following:

```
@IBAction func onSelectImageFromCamera(_ sender: Any) {
    // ensure camera is available.
    guard UIImagePickerController.isSourceTypeAvailable(.camera) else {

        let alertController = UIAlertController(title: "Error",
                            message: "Could not access the camera.",
                            preferredStyle: .alert)

        self.present(alertController, animated: true, completion: nil)
        return
    }

    let picker = UIImagePickerController()
    picker.delegate = self
    picker.sourceType = .camera
    present(picker, animated: true)
}
```

This code checks to see whether the device has a camera and that the user has granted the app access to the camera. If there is no problem accessing the camera, the code creates a UIKit UIImagePickerController object to allow the user to use the camera to take a picture.

9. Add the following snippet to the bottom of `ViewController.swift` to implement the `UIImagePickerControllerDelegate` method func `imagePickerController` (_ `picker:`, `didFinishPickingMediaWithInfo:`) in a class extension:

```swift
extension ViewController: UIImagePickerControllerDelegate,
                          UINavigationControllerDelegate {

    func imagePickerController(_ picker: UIImagePickerController,
        didFinishPickingMediaWithInfo info:
        [UIImagePickerController.InfoKey : Any]) {
        picker.dismiss(animated: true)
        let image = info[UIImagePickerController.InfoKey.originalImage]
                    as! UIImage
        imageView.image = image
        detectPet(in: image)
    }
}
```

This code displays the picture selected by the user (or taken with the camera) in the image view object of the application's user interface and calls the `detectPet(in:)` method to perform object detection. The code in `ViewController.swift` should resemble Listing 6.2.

LISTING 6.2:   ViewController.swift file with UIImagePicker Integration

```swift
import UIKit

class ViewController: UIViewController {

    @IBOutlet weak var imageView: UIImageView!
    @IBOutlet weak var resultLabel: UILabel!

    override func viewDidLoad() {
        super.viewDidLoad()
        // Do any additional setup after loading the view.
    }

    @IBAction func onSelectImageFromPhotoLibrary(_ sender: Any) {
        let picker = UIImagePickerController()
        picker.delegate = self
        picker.sourceType = .photoLibrary
        present(picker, animated: true)
    }
```

```
@IBAction func onSelectImageFromCamera(_ sender: Any) {
    // ensure camera is available.
    guard UIImagePickerController.isSourceTypeAvailable(.camera) else {

        let alertController = UIAlertController(title: "Error",
                                message: "Could not access the camera.",
                                preferredStyle: .alert)

        self.present(alertController,
                    animated: true, completion: nil)
        return
    }

    let picker = UIImagePickerController()
    picker.delegate = self
    picker.sourceType = .camera
    present(picker, animated: true)
}

func detectPet(in image: UIImage) {
    // to do: write code to perform object detection with Core ML
}
}

extension ViewController: UIImagePickerControllerDelegate,
                        UINavigationControllerDelegate {

    func imagePickerController(_ picker: UIImagePickerController,
        didFinishPickingMediaWithInfo info:
        [UIImagePickerController.InfoKey : Any]) {
        picker.dismiss(animated: true)
        let image = info[UIImagePickerController.InfoKey.originalImage]
                    as! UIImage
        imageView.image = image
        detectPet (in: image)
    }
}
```

Updating Privacy Settings

Before your app can access the camera on the device, you need to ask the user's permission and provide a short description of what your app intends to do with the camera. Asking the user for permission is performed automatically by the UIImagePickerController class; all you need to do is add a key to the application's Info.plist file and set the value of this key to a user-friendly message that will inform the user what your app intends to do with the camera.

Click the `Info.plist` file in the Project Navigator to open it in the plist editor. Click the Editor ➢ Add Item menu to insert a new key into the `Info.plist` file. Select the Privacy – Camera Usage Description key from the list of available keys and provide a short string of text that describes how your app will use the camera (see Figure 6.13).

FIGURE 6.13
Editing the application's
`Info.plist` file

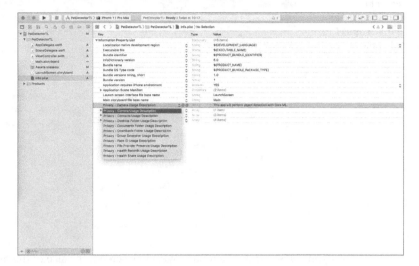

Using the Core ML Model in the iOS Project

Now that you have built the app's user interface, it is time to use the machine learning model that was built with the Create ML app to detect whether the image selected by the user contains a dog or a cat. Perform the following steps:

1. Control-click the `PetDetectorTL` folder group in the Project navigator window and select the Add Files to PetDetectorTL menu item. Navigate to the `DogsCatsTransfer-LearningClassifier.mlmodel` file on your computer and ensure that the Copy Items if Needed option is checked and the `PetDetector` target is selected in the dialog box (see Figure 6.14).

FIGURE 6.14
Import settings for the
`DogsCatsTransfer-`
`LearningClassifier`
`.mlmodel` file

2. Select the DogsCatsTransferLearningClassifier.mlmodel file in the Project navigator to get an overview of the model (see Figure 6.15).

FIGURE 6.15
Overview of the
DogsCatsTransfer-
LearningClassifier
.mlmodel file

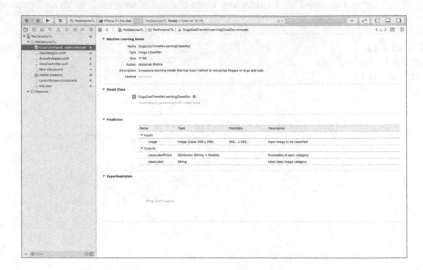

As you can see from the model overview screen, the size of the model is just 17KB, and the inputs to the model are RGB (color) images of 229x229 pixels. The image that you select from the photo library (or camera) is much larger than this and will need to be downsampled to this size. Keep in mind that this 17KB model does not include the convolutional base and will work only on iOS and macOS versions that were introduced after WWDC 2019.

It is also evident from the model overview page that there are two outputs from the model. The first is a dictionary of class-wise probabilities called classLabelProbs, and the second output is the name of most likely class of the image, called classLabel. The most likely class is simply the class with the highest probability. You can access this Swift class from the Model Class section of the model overview page (see Figure 6.16).

FIGURE 6.16
Accessing the Swift
interface to the Core ML
model file

Figure 6.17 depicts a section of the model class file. It is worth noting that the input image is expected to be represented as a CVPixelBuffer object and not a UIImage.

Creating a CVPixelBuffer object from a UIImage is a complex task, and it involves several side activities such as resizing the image and rotating the image to ensure it is right-side up. While it is possible for you to manually create the CVPixelBuffer, the most common approach is to convert a `UIImage` into a `CIImage` and then use the Vision framework to convert the `CIImage` instance into a `CVPixelBuffer`. The advantage of using the Vision framework is that not only can it convert `CIImage` instances into `CVPixelBuffer` instances, it can also resize the `CIImage` to the dimensions expected by the model.

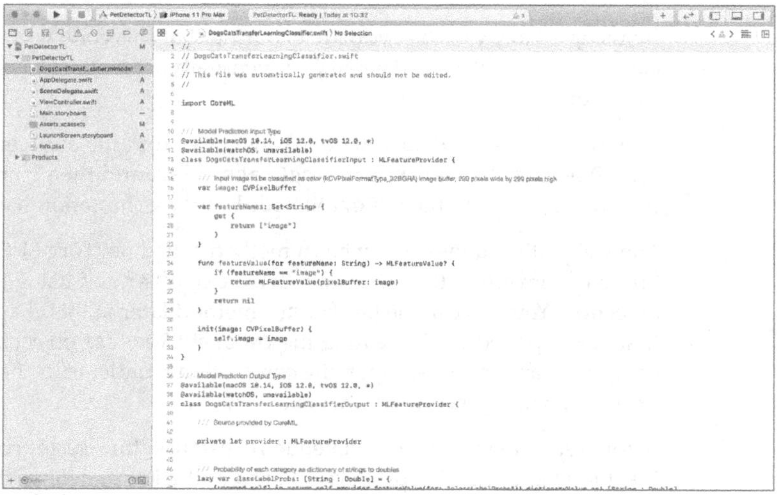

FIGURE 6.17
A section of the `DogsCatsTransfer-LearningClassifier.Swift` file

3. Select the `ViewController.swift` file in the Project navigator and add the following import statements to the top of the file to import the Core ML and Vision frameworks.

```swift
import CoreML
import Vision
```

4. To use the Vision framework to perform object detection with a custom Core ML model, you need to encapsulate your request into a `VNCoreMLRequest` object and then use a `VNImageRequestHandler` object to execute the request. Add the following `lazy` variable to the `ViewController.swift` file:

```swift
lazy var classificationRequest: VNCoreMLRequest = {
    do {
        let model = try VNCoreMLModel(for: DogsCatsTransferLearningClassifie
r().model)

        let request = VNCoreMLRequest(model: model,
            completionHandler: { [weak self] request, error in
                self?.processResults(for: request, error: error)
        })
```

```
            request.imageCropAndScaleOption = .scaleFit
            return request
        } catch {
            fatalError("Failed to load Core ML model")
        }
    }()
```

By using a lazy variable, you are ensuring that this code will not be executed when the class is loaded, but instead when you eventually access the classificationRequest variable from your code.

This code creates a VNCoreMLModel instance from the autogenerated Core ML model class DogsCatsTransferLearningClassifier, and then it creates a VNCoreMLRequest instance by passing the VNCoreMLModel and a completion handler as parameters.

The VNCoreMLRequest object has a method called perform() that takes care of the heavy lifting of converting the image to a CVPixelBuffer and using the model to perform object detection. You will call the perform() method later in this chapter. The completion handler that you supplied while creating the VNCoreMLRequest object is called when the operation completes, and in this snippet, the completion handler calls the processResults(for:, error:), which you will create next.

Before returning the VNCoreMLRequest instance, the imageCropAndScaleOption property is set to scaleFit. This property is used by Vision to determine how it should scale the image down to the dimensions required by the model. Since the image taken by the camera is rectangular and the image required by the model is a square, some cropping will also occur. There are three potential options you can specify.

◆ centerCrop: This option resizes the image proportionally until the smallest dimension of the image matches the dimensions expected by the model. The resized image (which is still a rectangle) is cropped into a square by using the central portion. This option can end up cropping off parts of the object in the center of the image.

◆ scaleFill: This option resizes the image disproportionally until both dimensions of the image match the dimensions expected by the model. The resized image will appear to be squashed.

◆ scaleFit: This option resizes the image proportionally until the longest dimension of the image matches the dimensions expected by the model. The resized image is converted into a square by padding the shorter dimension with black pixels.

5. Implement the processResults(for:, error:) method in the ViewController.swift file as follows:

```
func processResults(for request: VNRequest, error: Error?) {
    DispatchQueue.main.async {
        guard let results = request.results else {
            print("Unable to classify image.\n\(error!.localizedDescription)")
            self.resultLabel.text = "Unable to classify image."
```

```
            return
        }

        let classifications = results as! [VNClassificationObservation]

        if classifications.isEmpty {
            self.resultLabel.text = "Did not recognize anything."
        } else {

            self.resultLabel.text = String(format: " percent@
percent.1f percent",
                                    classifications[0].identifier,
                                    classifications[0].confidence * 100)

        }
    }
}
```

This method is called from the completion handler of the VNCoreMLRequest object. The method accepts two parameters; the first is a VNRequest instance called request, and the other is an optional error object. You can access the results of the classification by using the results member of the VNRequest object. The results of the classification are returned as an array of VNClassificationObservation objects. Each object has two member variables: identifier, which represents the class of the detected object, and confidence, which represents the probability of that class. The results are sorted in descending order of probability, with the first item in the array being the most probable object class.

It is important to note that this method is not called on the main UI thread, and, therefore, any updates to the user interface must be wrapped in a DispatchQueue.main.async {} block.

6. Now that you have written the code to create a VNCoreMLRequest and processed the results of the image classification, all you need to do is write code to create and execute the VNCoreMLRequest when the user selects an image. Earlier in this chapter, you created an empty method called func detectPet(in image: UIImage). Replace the empty method with the following:

```
func detectPet(in image: UIImage) {
    resultLabel.text = "Processing..."

    guard let ciImage = CIImage(image: image),
        let orientation = CGImagePropertyOrientation(rawValue:
                    UInt32(image.imageOrientation.rawValue))
    else {
        print("Unable to create CIImage instance")
        resultLabel.text = "Failed."
        return
    }
```

```
DispatchQueue.global(qos: .userInitiated).async {
    let handler = VNImageRequestHandler(ciImage: ciImage,
                                    orientation: orientation)
    do {
        try handler.perform([self.classificationRequest])
    } catch {
        print("Failed to perform
                classification.\n\(error.localizedDescription)")
    }
}
}
```

This function is already wired to be called from the UIImagePickerController delegate method. It receives a UIImage instance that represents the image selected by the user from the photo library or captured with the camera. The code in this function converts the UIImage instance into a CIImage instance and then creates a VNImageRequestHandler object with the CIImage instance.

```
guard let ciImage = CIImage(image: image),
    let orientation = CGImagePropertyOrientation(rawValue:
                        UInt32(image.imageOrientation.rawValue))
else {
    print("Unable to create CIImage instance")
    resultLabel.text = "Failed."
    return
}
```

Recall that the VNImageRequestHandler object can be used to execute a VNCoreMLRequest, which is performed by calling perform on the handler object.

```
let handler = VNImageRequestHandler(ciImage: ciImage,
                                orientation: orientation)
do {
    try handler.perform([self.classificationRequest])
} catch {
    print("Failed to perform
            classification.\n\(error.localizedDescription)")
}
```

Since object detection is a time-consuming operation and you do not want to block your application user interface while Core ML is executing the model, the call to create the VNImageRequestHandler and execute the VNCoreMLRequest is wrapped in a DispatchQueue.global(qos: .userInitiated).async block. The code in the ViewController.swift file should now resemble Listing 6.3.

LISTING 6.3:   Completed ViewController.swift File

```swift
import UIKit
import CoreML
import Vision

class ViewController: UIViewController {

    @IBOutlet weak var imageView: UIImageView!
    @IBOutlet weak var resultLabel: UILabel!

    lazy var classificationRequest: VNCoreMLRequest = {
        do {
            let model = try VNCoreMLModel(for: DogsCatsTransferLearningClassi
    fier().model)

            let request = VNCoreMLRequest(model: model,
                completionHandler: { [weak self] request, error in
                    self?.processResults(for: request, error: error)
            })

            request.imageCropAndScaleOption = .scaleFit
            return request
        } catch {
            fatalError("Failed to load Core ML model")
        }
    }()


    override func viewDidLoad() {
        super.viewDidLoad()
        // Do any additional setup after loading the view.
    }

    @IBAction func onSelectImageFromPhotoLibrary(_ sender: Any) {
        let picker = UIImagePickerController()
        picker.delegate = self
        picker.sourceType = .photoLibrary
        present(picker, animated: true)
    }

    @IBAction func onSelectImageFromCamera(_ sender: Any) {
        // ensure camera is available.
        guard UIImagePickerController.isSourceTypeAvailable(.camera) else {
```

```swift
                let alertController = UIAlertController(title: "Error",
                                    message: "Could not access the camera.",
                                    preferredStyle: .alert)

            alertController.addAction(UIAlertAction(title: "ok",
                                    style: .default, handler: nil))
    self.present(alertController, animated: true, completion: nil)
            return
        }

        let picker = UIImagePickerController()
        picker.delegate = self
        picker.sourceType = .camera
        present(picker, animated: true)

    }

    func detectPet(in image: UIImage) {
        resultLabel.text = "Processing..."

        guard let ciImage = CIImage(image: image),
            let orientation = CGImagePropertyOrientation(rawValue:
                        UInt32(image.imageOrientation.rawValue))
        else {
            print("Unable to create CIImage instance")
            resultLabel.text = "Failed."
            return
        }

        DispatchQueue.global(qos: .userInitiated).async {
            let handler = VNImageRequestHandler(ciImage: ciImage,
                                    orientation: orientation)
            do {
                try handler.perform([self.classificationRequest])
            } catch {
                print("Failed to perform
                        classification.\n\(error.localizedDescription)")
            }
        }

    }

    func processResults(for request: VNRequest, error: Error?) {
        DispatchQueue.main.async {
            guard let results = request.results else {
```

```
                    print("Unable to classify image.\n\(error!.localizedDes
        cription)")
                self.resultLabel.text = "Unable to classify image."
                return
            }

            let classifications = results as! [VNClassificationObservation]

            if classifications.isEmpty {
                self.resultLabel.text = "Did not recognize anything."
            } else {

                self.resultLabel.text = String(format: " percent@
        percent.1f percent",

                                        classifications[0].identifier,
                                    classifications[0].confidence * 100)
            }
        }
    }

}

extension ViewController: UIImagePickerControllerDelegate,
                        UINavigationControllerDelegate {

    func imagePickerController(_ picker: UIImagePickerController,
        didFinishPickingMediaWithInfo info:
        [UIImagePickerController.InfoKey : Any]) {
        picker.dismiss(animated: true)
        let image = info[UIImagePickerController.InfoKey.originalImage]
                as! UIImage
        imageView.image = image
        detectPet(in: image)
    }
}
```

Save your project and run the app on an iOS device. Use the camera to take a picture of a dog or a cat. You should see the results of the object detection process on the screen. Figure 6.18 depicts the results of running the app on a device and selecting the picture of a dog from the photo library.

NOTE If you do not want to test this app on a real phone, launch Safari on the iOS Simulator and drag a few images of dogs and cats from your macOS finder into Safari on the iOS Simulator.

You can now run the app on the iOS Simulator and select these images from the photo library on the simulator.

FIGURE 6.18
Results of running the
app with the picture
of a dog

As you can see, the result indicates that the model has successfully detected the image as that of a dog, with a 67.8 percent confidence. Keep in mind that you have set the value of the image-CropAndScale option of the VNCoreMLRequest object to .scaleFit. You can try different imageCropAndScale values to gauge the performance of the model with these values.

NOTE You can download the code files for this chapter from wrox.com or from GitHub using the following URL:

https://github.com/asmtechnology/iosmlbook-chapter6.git

Summary

◆ The Create ML app is a macOS application that allows you to build machine learning models using a wizard-style user interface.

◆ The Create ML app was introduced in WWDC 2019 and is a successor to the Create ML framework. It provides a task-oriented approach to model building.

◆ The Create ML framework is a Swift framework that allows you to use Xcode and create machine learning models using Swift code. The Create ML app, on the other hand, does not require you to write any code at all.

◆ The Create ML app is included with Xcode 11 and requires macOS Catalina or higher.

◆ The Create ML app allows you to create image classification, object detection, sound classification, activity classification, text classification, tabular classification, and tabular regression models.

◆ Depending on the task at hand, the Create ML app may not provide any control on the algorithm that was chosen or on the hyperparameters.

Chapter 7

Creating a Tabular Classifier with Create ML

WHAT'S IN THIS CHAPTER

- ◆ Preparing training and test datasets using a Jupyter Notebook instance
- ◆ Training a tabular classifier with the Create ML app
- ◆ Using the model generated by the Create ML app in an iOS application

In this chapter, you will create a classification model that can be used to classify the quality of wines based on their chemical composition. The model will be trained on the popular UCI ML wine dataset using the Create ML app.

If you recall from Chapter 6, the Create ML app is a new model-building tool provided by Apple in Xcode 11. It runs on macOS Catalina and provides a high-level task-oriented interface. It allows you to use a GUI to train and export models into the Core ML file format. Being a task-oriented interface, the Create ML app asks you to specify what you want to do and attempts to choose the best model for your task. Depending on the task you want to perform, you may be able to select the type of model that should be generated.

After the model is trained, you will use the model in an iOS app that allows users to input the chemical characteristics of a wine and learn the quality of the beverage.

NOTE You can download the code files for this chapter from wrox.com or from GitHub using the following URL:

https://github.com/asmtechnology/iosmlbook-chapter7.git

Preparing the Dataset for the Create ML App

This chapter uses the wines dataset hosted at the UCI Machine Learning repository. A copy of the dataset is included with the resources that accompany this lesson. The original dataset can also be downloaded from https://archive.ics.uci.edu/ml/machine-learning-databases/wine/. Scikit-learn also includes this dataset as part of its toy datasets module.

The dataset consists of 178 rows that represent the results of chemical analysis on wines grown by three different cultivators in the same region in Italy. Each row consists of 13 features that represent a measurement for the concentration of a constituent chemical in the wine, and a single target attribute that can take one of three values—0, 1, and 2. The value of the target attribute represents the quality of the wine, with 0 representing the poorest quality and 2 representing the highest quality. The 13 features are as follows:

- **Alcohol:** Percentage of alcohol in the wine. Alcohol is created as a direct result of the fermentation process and can be used as an indicator of the sugar content of the wine.

- **Malic acid:** Percentage of malic acid in the wine. This is an acid found in grapes and can influence the taste of the wine.

- **Ash:** Percentage of ash in the wine.

- **Alkalinity of the ash:** A measure of the alkalinity of the ash.

- **Magnesium**: Amount of magnesium (in milligrams) in a serving of wine (assuming one serving = 100 grams).

- **Total phenols:** Phenol content of the wine, measured in ml/100g. A phenol is a class of molecules that are involved in the taste and smell of a wine. There are two types of phenols in wine—flavonoids and nonflavonoids.

- **Flavanoids:** Flavanoid phenol content of the wine, measured in ml/100g. A flavonoid is a phenol that has a major impact on the taste of red wine.

- **Nonflavanoid phenols:** Nonflavanoid content of the wine, measured in ml/100g.

- **Proanthocyanins:** Proanthocyanin content of the wine, measured in mg/100g.

- **Color intensity:** A measure of how dark the wine is.

- **Hue**: Indicates the hue of the wine.

- **OD280/OD315 of diluted wine:** A measure of the concentration of proteins OD280 and OD315 in the wine sample.

- **Proline:** A measure of the proline content of the wine (mg/100g). Proline is an amino acid commonly found in grape juice.

At the time this book was written, the Create ML app did not allow you to perform feature engineering or data preprocessing. The Create ML app expects the dataset to be preprocessed and split into separate training and validation sets beforehand. In this section, you will load the Scikit-learn toy version of the UCI ML dataset, prepare the dataset to make it compatible with Create ML, and export the dataset to CSV files.

To get started, launch the macOS Terminal application and type the following command to start a new Jupyter Notebook instance:

```
$ cd <your directory>
$ jupyter notebook
```

When Jupyter Notebook has finished loading in your web browser, create a new notebook file using the IOS_ML_BOOK kernel (see Figure 7.1) and name the file dataset_preprocessing.ipnyb.

FIGURE 7.1
Creating a new
notebook file

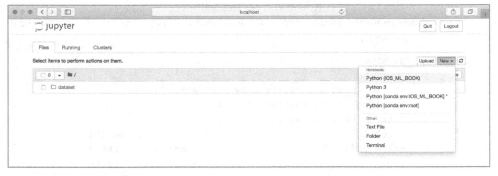

Type the following code in a notebook cell to load the Scikit-learn version of the dataset into a Pandas dataframe called df_wine:

```
# load wine dataset
import numpy as np
import pandas as pd

from sklearn import datasets
wine_dataset = datasets.load_wine()

df_wine = pd.DataFrame(data= np.c_[wine_dataset['data'],
                       wine_dataset['target']],
                       columns= wine_dataset['feature_names'] + ['target'])
```

The UCI ML wine dataset consists of 178 rows, and each row has 14 attributes (columns), one of which is the target attribute. You can verify the shape of the dataset using the following snippet:

```
# examine the shape of the dataset.
print ('df_wine has ' +
       str(df_wine.shape[0]) + ' rows and ' +
       str(df_wine.shape[1]) + ' columns')

>> df_wine has 178 rows and 14 columns
```

Figure 7.2 depicts the results of using the dataframe's head() method to inspect the first few rows of the dataframe.

FIGURE 7.2
Inspecting the first five
rows of the UCI ML
wine dataset

	al_phenols	flavanoids	nonflavanoid_phenols	proanthocyanins	color_intensity	hue	od280/od315_of_diluted_wines	proline	target
	2.80	3.06	0.28	2.29	5.64	1.04	3.92	1065.0	0.0
	2.65	2.76	0.26	1.28	4.38	1.05	3.40	1050.0	0.0
	2.80	3.24	0.30	2.81	5.68	1.03	3.17	1185.0	0.0
	3.85	3.49	0.24	2.18	7.80	0.86	3.45	1480.0	0.0
	2.80	2.69	0.39	1.82	4.32	1.04	2.93	735.0	0.0

In [2]: df_wine.head()
Out[2]:

If you look closely, you will see that values in the target column are floating-point numbers. You can verify the data types of the columns by using the `info()` method of the dataframe object.

```
df_wine.info()

<class 'pandas.core.frame.DataFrame'>
RangeIndex: 178 entries, 0 to 177
Data columns (total 14 columns):
alcohol                       178 non-null float64
malic_acid                    178 non-null float64
ash                           178 non-null float64
alcalinity_of_ash             178 non-null float64
magnesium                     178 non-null float64
total_phenols                 178 non-null float64
flavanoids                    178 non-null float64
nonflavanoid_phenols          178 non-null float64
proanthocyanins               178 non-null float64
color_intensity               178 non-null float64
hue                           178 non-null float64
od280/od315_of_diluted_wines  178 non-null float64
proline                       178 non-null float64
target                        178 non-null float64
dtypes: float64(14)
memory usage: 19.5 KB
```

If you recall, the dataset consists of data on three classes of wines. The `target` attribute is categorical and has only one of three values 0, 1, and 2. Create ML can only create tabular classifiers for data in which the target attribute is either an integer or a string. Therefore, let's change the data type of the `target` attribute to consist of the integers. Type the following code in an empty notebook cell and execute it:

```
# change the datatype of the target column to unsigned int8
df_wine[['target']] = df_wine[['target']].astype(np.uint8)
```

You can either use the `info()` method to inspect the data types of the columns of the `df_wine` dataframe after executing the previous statements, or use the `head()` method to sample the first five rows. Figure 7.3 depicts the results of using the dataframe's `head()` method to inspect the first few rows of the dataframe after the data type of the target attribute has been converted to string.

FIGURE 7.3
Inspecting the first five rows of the UCI ML wine dataset after converting the data type of the target attribute

	al_phenols	flavanoids	nonflavanoid_phenols	proanthocyanins	color_intensity	hue	od280/od315_of_diluted_wines	proline	target
	2.80	3.06	0.28	2.29	5.64	1.04	3.92	1065.0	0
	2.65	2.76	0.26	1.28	4.38	1.05	3.40	1050.0	0
	2.80	3.24	0.30	2.81	5.68	1.03	3.17	1185.0	0
	3.85	3.49	0.24	2.18	7.80	0.86	3.45	1480.0	0
	2.80	2.69	0.39	1.82	4.32	1.04	2.93	735.0	0

Next, let's find out whether any of the columns contain missing values, and the statistical characteristics of the data in the columns. The following snippet can be used to determine whether any of the columns of the dataset has missing values:

```
# how many missing values?
df_wine.isnull().sum()


alcohol                       0
malic_acid                    0
ash                           0
alcalinity_of_ash             0
magnesium                     0
total_phenols                 0
flavanoids                    0
nonflavanoid_phenols          0
proanthocyanins               0
color_intensity               0
hue                           0
od280/od315_of_diluted_wines  0
proline                       0
target                        0
dtype: int64
```

As you can see, none of the 178 rows contains missing data. Let's now examine the statistical characteristics of the 14 columns using the Pandas `describe()` function. The results are depicted in Figure 7.4.

FIGURE 7.4
Inspecting the statistical characteristics of the numeric columns of the UCI ML wine dataset

```
In [8]:  # examine the statistical characteristics of the dataframe.
         df_wine.describe()

Out[8]:
              alcohol    malic_acid    ash      alcalinity_of_ash  magnesium   total_phenols  flavanoids  nonflavanoid_phenols  proar
     count  178.000000  178.000000  178.000000    178.000000      178.000000   178.000000   178.000000      178.000000
     mean    13.000618    2.336348    2.366517     19.494944        99.741573    2.295112     2.029270        0.361854
     std      0.811827    1.117146    0.274344      3.339564        14.282484    0.625851     0.998859        0.124453
     min     11.030000    0.740000    1.360000     10.600000        70.000000    0.980000     0.340000        0.130000
     25%     12.362500    1.602000    2.210000     17.200000        88.000000    1.742500     1.205000        0.270000
     50%     13.050000    1.865000    2.360000     19.500000        98.000000    2.355000     2.135000        0.340000
     75%     13.677500    3.082500    2.557500     21.500000       107.000000    2.800000     2.875000        0.437500
     max     14.830000    5.800000    3.230000     30.000000       162.000000    3.880000     5.080000        0.660000
```

As you can see, the values in the 13 feature columns do not have similar scales. Later in this section we will standardize the values in the 13 columns to bring them into the range [0, 1]. For now, it is important to make a note of the minimum and maximum values of each of the features. You will need these in the iOS app that you create later in this chapter. This information is summarized in Table 7.1.

TABLE 7.1:   Minimum and Maximum Values of the Features of the UCI ML Wine Dataset

FEATURE	MINIMUM	MAXIMUM
alcohol	11.030000	14.830000
malic_acid	0.740000	5.800000
ash	1.360000	3.230000
alcalinity_of_ash	10.600000	30.000000
magnesium	70.000000	162.000000
total_phenols	0.980000	3.880000
flavanoids	0.340000	5.080000
nonflavanoid_phenols	0.130000	0.660000
proanthocyanins	0.410000	3.580000
color_intensity	1.280000	13.000000
hue	0.480000	1.710000
od280/od315_of_diluted_wines	1.270000	4.000000
proline	278.000000	1680.000000

Let's examine the distribution of the data in the target attribute using a histogram. Type the following code in an empty notebook cell and execute it. The resulting histogram is depicted in Figure 7.5.

```
# histogram of columns
import matplotlib
df_wine['target'].hist(figsize=(7,4))
```

FIGURE 7.5
Histogram of the data in the target attribute of the Iris dataset

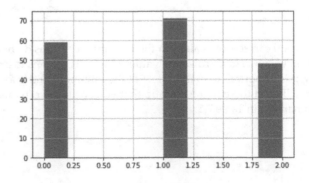

As you can see, the dataset is imbalanced, and there is more data for class 1 than the others. Let's now split the 178 observations of the dataset into a training and test set using a Scikit-learn function called `train_test_split()`. This function is defined in the `model_selection` submodule and can be used to split a Pandas dataframe into two dataframes, one for model building and the other for model evaluation.

The `test_train_split()` function has several parameters, most of which have default values. The most commonly used parameters are the following:

- `test_size`: This value can be an integer or floating-point number. When the value is an integer, it specifies the number of elements that should be retained for the test set. When the value is a floating-point number, it specifies the percentage of the original dataset to include in the test set.

- `random_state`: This is an integer value that is used to seed the random number generator used to shuffle the samples. It is a good idea to specify a value for this parameter so that each time you execute the notebook, you arrive at the same results.

- `stratify`: The default value of this parameter is `None`, which implies stratified sampling must not be used. Since you want to enable stratified sampling, the value of this parameter will be set to the name of the column that you want to stratify on.

The output of the `train_test_split()` function is a list of four arrays in the following order:

- The first item of the list is an array that contains the training set features.

- The second item of the list is an array that contains the test set features.

- The third item of the list is an array that contains the training set labels (the target variable).

- The fourth item of the list is an array that contains the test set labels.

You can find detailed information on the parameters of the `train_test_split()` function at `https://scikit-learn.org/stable/modules/generated/sklearn.model_selection .train_test_split.html`.

Type the following snippet in an empty notebook cell to split the 14-column dataframe `df_wine` into two dataframes—a 13-column dataframe called `df_wine_features` that contains all the feature attributes, and a 1-column dataframe called `df_wine_target` that contains the target variable.

```
# split the df_iris dataframe into two,
# one with the features and the other with the target
df_wine_target = df_wine.loc[:,['target']]
df_wine_features = df_wine.drop(['target'], axis=1)
```

After separating the `df_wine` dataframe into two dataframes, type the following code in an empty notebook cell to standardize the values in the 13 columns of the `df_wine_features` dataset. Standardization is a process that converts the values in each column to lie in the range [0, 1] by subtracting the minimum value of the corresponding column from each value and then dividing the result by the range of values in the column.

```
# standardize the columns of df_wine_features.
df_wine_features=(df_wine_features-df_wine_features.min())/(df_wine_features
.max()-df_wine_features.min())
```

You can examine the results of the standardization process by examining the first few rows of the dataframe using the head() method. The results are depicted in Figure 7.6.

FIGURE 7.6
Inspecting the first five rows of the UCI ML wine dataset after standardization

		alcohol	malic_acid	ash	alcalinity_of_ash	magnesium	total_phenols	flavanoids	nonflavanoid_phenols	proanthocyanin
In [11]:	df_wine_features.head()									
Out[11]:	0	0.842105	0.191700	0.572193	0.257732	0.619565	0.627586	0.573840	0.283019	0.59306
	1	0.571053	0.205534	0.417112	0.030928	0.326087	0.575862	0.510649	0.245283	0.27444
	2	0.560526	0.320158	0.700535	0.412371	0.336957	0.627586	0.611814	0.320755	0.75709
	3	0.878947	0.239130	0.609626	0.319588	0.467391	0.989655	0.664557	0.207547	0.55836
	4	0.581579	0.365613	0.807487	0.536082	0.521739	0.627586	0.495781	0.490566	0.44479

With the data in the df_wine_features dataframe standardized, execute the following code in an empty notebook cell to create the training and test datasets:

```
# create a training set and a test set.
from sklearn.model_selection import train_test_split

wine_split = train_test_split(df_wine_features, df_wine_target,
                              test_size=0.25, random_state=17,
                              stratify = df_wine_target['target'])

df_wine_features_train = wine_split[0]
df_wine_features_test = wine_split[1]
df_wine_target_train = wine_split[2]
df_wine_target_test = wine_split[3]
```

The results of executing the train_test_split() function will give you four dataframes, two of which contain the features and target variable for the training set, and the other two for the test set.

The Create ML app requires that the features and target variable are present in the same CSV file, and, therefore, you need to combine the features and target variables for each of the train and test data. Execute the following code in an empty notebook cell to combine df_wine_features_train and df_wine_target_train into a single dataframe and save the dataframe to a CSV file called wine_train.csv.

The code assumes that the ./datasets/sklearnexport folder structure exists in the same directory as your notebook file. If you want to export the file to a different location, update the code snippet accordingly and substitute references to the ./datasets/sklearnexport folder with your chosen location.

```
# combine df_wine_features_train and df_wine_target_train into a single
# dataframe and export the combined dataset to a CSV file.
df_wine_train = pd.concat([df_wine_features_train, df_wine_target_train], axis=1)
df_wine_train.to_csv('./datasets/sklearnexport/wine_train.csv', header=True,
index=None)
```

Similarly, execute the following code in an empty notebook cell to combine df_wine_features_test and df_wine_target_test into a single dataframe and save the dataframe to a CSV file called wine_test.csv. Remember to substitute the value of the path to the CSV file with something that is appropriate for your computer.

```
# combine df_wine_features_test and df_wine_target_test into a single
# dataframe and export the combined dataset to a CSV file.
df_wine_test = pd.concat([df_wine_features_test, df_wine_target_test], axis=1)
df_wine_test.to_csv('./datasets/sklearnexport/wine_test.csv', header=True,
index=None)
```

With the `wine_train.csv` and `wine_test.csv` files ready, it is time to use the Create ML app to create the classification model.

Creating the Tabular Classification Model with the Create ML App

At the time this book was written, the Create ML app required that you use macOS Catalina and Xcode 11.0 or higher. Launch Xcode on your Mac and then launch the Create ML app by using the Xcode ➤ Open Developer Tool ➤ Create ML menu item (see Figure 7.7).

FIGURE 7.7
Launching the
Create ML app

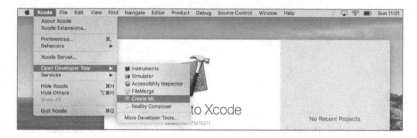

When the Create ML app has launched, use the File ➤ New Project menu item to create a new Create ML app project. You will be prompted to select a task; select Table from the list of task categories and Tabular Classifier from the options that are available (see Figure 7.8) and click the Next button.

FIGURE 7.8
Selecting the Tabular
Classifier template

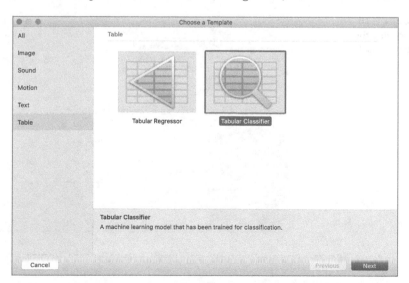

You will be presented with a dialog box that will allow you to specify the name of the new Create ML project, and some metadata associated with the project (see Figure 7.9). Name the new project `WineClassifier`, provide a suitable project description, and click the Next button.

FIGURE 7.9
Create ML project
options dialog

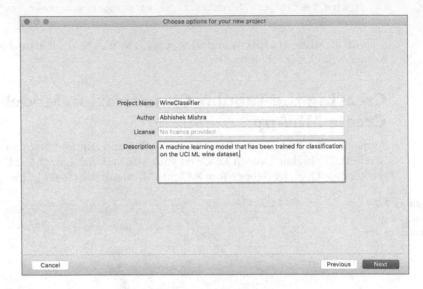

After specifying project metadata, you will be prompted to specify a location for the new Create ML project. Select a location on your hard disk and click the Create button to finish creating the new project.

After the project is created, it will be loaded into Create ML. Locate the Training Data section in the Inputs tab and use the Select Files drop-down menu item to navigate to the `wine_train` `.csv` file that you created in the previous section (see Figure 7.10).

FIGURE 7.10
Specifying the
input dataset

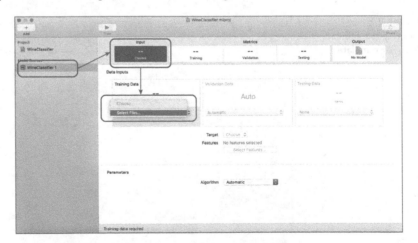

The wine_train.csv file contains 14 columns, 13 of which are features, and the remaining column (called *target*) is the target attribute. Since Create ML does not know the name of the target attribute in your CSV file, you will need to select it from the Target drop-down (see Figure 7.11).

After selecting the name of the target attribute, you will need to specify the features (columns) that should be used to train the model. By default, none of the features are selected. Click the Select Features button below the target attribute drop-down menu to access the feature selection dialog box (see Figure 7.12).

FIGURE 7.12
Accessing the feature selection dialog box

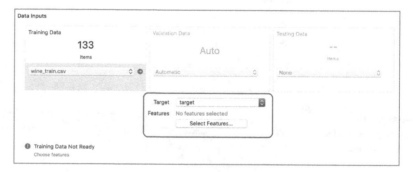

When the feature selection dialog box appears, ensure you have checked all 13 features and click the Select button (see Figure 7.13).

After specifying the names of the features and target attribute, use the Select Files option in the Testing Data section to specify the name of the test dataset. Choose the wine_test.csv file that you created in the previous section (see Figure 7.14).

Your screen should now resemble Figure 7.15. At the bottom of the screen, in the parameters section, Create ML provides a drop-down menu that allows you to select the algorithm that will be used to create the classification model. The default selection is Automatic, which means Create ML will pick the best algorithm for your data. Click the Train button in the toolbar to begin training the classification model.

FIGURE 7.13
Selecting the names of
the columns of the
dataset that repre-
sent features

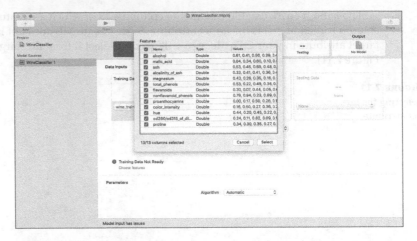

FIGURE 7.14
Specifying the
test dataset

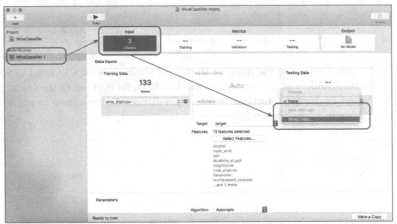

FIGURE 7.15
Beginning the model
training process

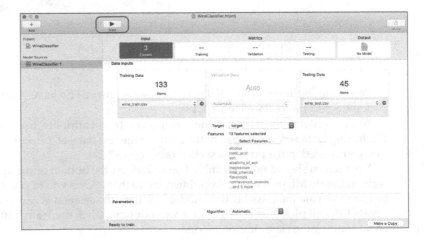

The training process will complete in a few seconds, and you will be presented with information on the performance of the model on the training and test datasets (see Figure 7.16).

FIGURE 7.16
Beginning the model
training process

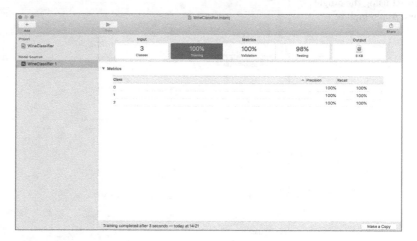

The only performance metrics available in Create ML for a multiclass classification model at the time this book was written were Precision and Recall; in the future, Apple may decide to add additional metrics or allow you to define your own custom metrics.

The Output tab contains your trained Core ML model, which you can drag and drop onto the macOS desktop or a Finder window to access the .mlmodel file. The output Core ML model file generated by the Create ML app will be called WineClassifier 1.mlmodel. Rename the file to WineClassifier.mlmodel before proceeding to the next section.

Creating the iOS Project

After exporting the model to the Core ML format, launch Xcode on your Mac and create a new project using the *Single View App* template (see Figure 7.17).

When prompted, use the following project options:

- **Product Name:** WineClassifierApp
- **Organization Name:** *Provide a suitable value*
- **Organization Identifier:** *Provide a suitable value*
- **Language:** Swift
- **User Interface:** Storyboard
- **Use Core Data:** Unchecked
- **Include Unit Tests:** Unchecked
- **Include UI Tests:** Unchecked

FIGURE 7.17
Creating a new iOS
project using the Single
View App template

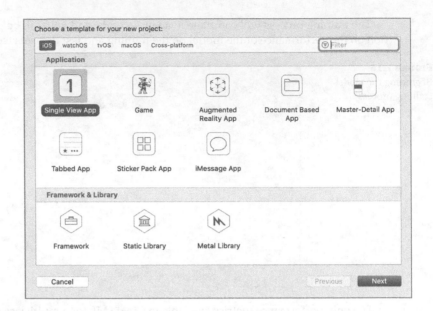

FIGURE 7.17
Creating a new iOS
project using the Single
View App template

Creating the User Interface

With the project created, set up the user interface of the project using these steps:

1. Open the Main.storyboard file and use the View ➤ Show Library menu item to access the object library window. Drag and drop 13 label instances from the object library onto the default view controller scene.

2. Place these labels one below the other and use the Attributes Inspector to change the captions of these labels according to the following list. You can access the Attributes Inspector using the View ➤ Inspectors ➤ Show Attributes Inspector menu item.

    ◆ Alcohol content:

    ◆ Malic acid content:

    ◆ Ash content:

    ◆ Alkalinity of Ash:

    ◆ Magnesium content:

    ◆ Total phenol content:

    ◆ Flavanoid content:

    ◆ Non-flavanoid content:

    ◆ Proanthocyanin content:

    ◆ Color intensity:

    ◆ Hue:

- ◆ OD280/OD315 content:
- ◆ Proline content:

3. Drag and drop 13 text field instances from the object library onto the default view controller scene and arrange them one below the other, to the right of the labels you have created in the previous step. To make the text fields easily visible, use the Attributes Inspector to change the border style of each of the text fields to Line (see Figure 7.18).

NOTE The scene layout described in this section is designed to support devices with larger screen sizes (iPhone X and above). Because of the large number of text fields, this app may not work correctly on devices with smaller screens. On such screens, you will need to use a scroll view to ensure the user can scroll through the fields.

FIGURE 7.18
Using the Attributes Inspector to change the border style of the text fields

4. Drag and drop a button from the object library onto the default view controller scene, and place the button at the bottom of the scene, below all the text fields and labels. Use the Attributes Inspector to change the caption of the button to *Get Wine Quality*. Change the background color of the buttons to a shade of gray to make it easier to see on the storyboard scene.

5. Drag and drop a tap gesture recognizer object from the object library onto the default view controller.

6. Organize the elements on the default view controller scene to resemble Figure 7.19 and set up the appropriate storyboard constraints.

FIGURE 7.19
Application storyboard with default view controller scene

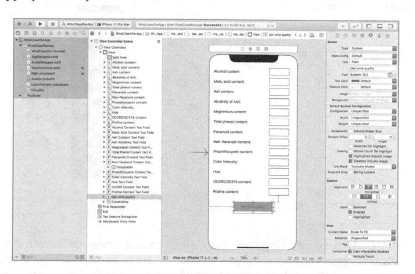

7. Use the Editor ➤ Assistant menu item to access the assistant editor and ensure the `ViewController.swift` file is open in the assistant editor. Create 13 outlets in the view controller class per the following list:

- ◆ `alcoholContentTextField`
- ◆ `malicAcidContentTextField`
- ◆ `ashContentTextField`
- ◆ `ashAlkalinityTextField`
- ◆ `magnesiumContentTextField`
- ◆ `totalPhenolContentTextField`
- ◆ `flavanoidContentTextField`
- ◆ `nonFlavanoidContentTextField`
- ◆ `proanthocyaninContentTextField`
- ◆ `colorIntensityTextField`
- ◆ `hueTextField`
- ◆ `od280ContentTextField`
- ◆ `prolineContentTextField`

Associate these outlets with the corresponding text fields of the storyboard scene (see Figure 7.20).

FIGURE 7.20
Using the assistant
editor to create outlets

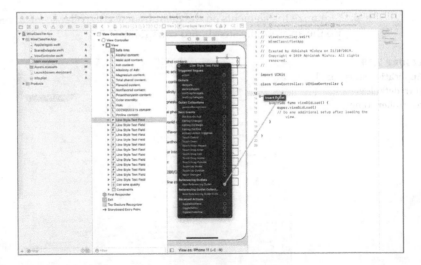

8. Set up the view controller class to act as the delegate for each of the text fields in the storyboard scene. There are many ways to do this; one way is to Ctrl-click a text field in the storyboard and connect the delegate outlet to the View Controller object (see Figure 7.21).

2222

FIGURE 7.21
Setting up the text field delegate

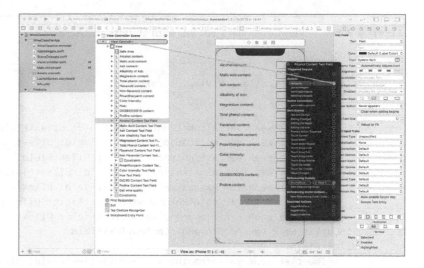

9. Create an action method in the `ViewController.swift` file called `onGetWineQuality` (_ sender: Any) and associate this method with the Touch Up Inside event of the button.

10. Create an action method in the `ViewController.swift` file called `onBackgroundTapped` (_ sender: Any) and associate this method with the `selector` property of the tap gesture recognizer (see Figure 7.22).

FIGURE 7.22
Setting up the selector property of the tap gesture recognizer

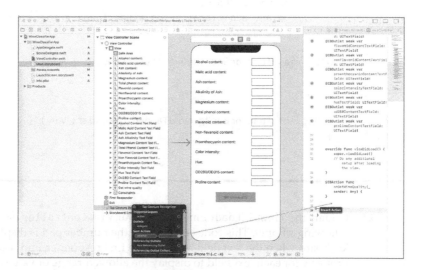

The code in your `ViewController.swift` file should now resemble Listing 7.1.

LISTING 7.1: ViewController.swift File with Outlets and Actions

```swift
import UIKit

class ViewController: UIViewController {


    @IBOutlet weak var alcoholContentTextField: UITextField!
    @IBOutlet weak var malicAcidContentTextField: UITextField!
    @IBOutlet weak var ashContentTextField: UITextField!
    @IBOutlet weak var ashAlkalinityTextField: UITextField!
    @IBOutlet weak var magnesiumContentTextField: UITextField!
    @IBOutlet weak var totalPhenolContentTextField: UITextField!
    @IBOutlet weak var flavanoidContentTextField: UITextField!
@IBOutlet weak var nonFlavanoidContentTextField
UITextField!
    @IBOutlet weak var proanthocyaninContentTextField: UITextField!
    @IBOutlet weak var colorIntensityTextField: UITextField!
    @IBOutlet weak var hueTextField: UITextField!
    @IBOutlet weak var od280ContentTextField: UITextField!
    @IBOutlet weak var prolineContentTextField: UITextField!


    override func viewDidLoad() {
        super.viewDidLoad()
        // Do any additional setup after loading the view.
    }

    @IBAction func onGetWineQuality(_ sender: Any) {
    }


    @IBAction func onBackgroundTapped(_ sender: Any) {
    }

}
```

---

11. Update the `viewDidLoad()` method in your `ViewController.swift` file to resemble the following snippet. This code ensures that the number pad is displayed as the default keyboard when the text field becomes the first responder, and it sets up the placeholder property for each text field to display the allowed range of values.

```swift
override func viewDidLoad() {
  super.viewDidLoad()

  alcoholContentTextField.keyboardType = .decimalPad
```

```
    malicAcidContentTextField.keyboardType = .decimalPad
    ashContentTextField.keyboardType = .decimalPad
    ashAlkalinityTextField.keyboardType = .decimalPad
    magnesiumContentTextField.keyboardType = .decimalPad
    totalPhenolContentTextField.keyboardType = .decimalPad
    flavanoidContentTextField.keyboardType = .decimalPad
    nonFlavanoidContentTextField.keyboardType = .decimalPad
    proanthocyaninContentTextField.keyboardType = .decimalPad
    colorIntensityTextField.keyboardType = .decimalPad
    hueTextField.keyboardType = .decimalPad
    od280ContentTextField.keyboardType = .decimalPad
    prolineContentTextField.keyboardType = .decimalPad

    alcoholContentTextField.placeholder = "11.03 - 14.83"
    malicAcidContentTextField.placeholder = "0.74 - 5.8"
    ashContentTextField.placeholder = "1.36 - 3.23"
    ashAlkalinityTextField.placeholder = "10.6 - 30.0"
    magnesiumContentTextField.placeholder = "70 - 162"
    totalPhenolContentTextField.placeholder = "0.98 - 3.88"
    flavanoidContentTextField.placeholder = "0.34 - 5.0"
    nonFlavanoidContentTextField.placeholder = "0.13 - 0.66"
    proanthocyaninContentTextField.placeholder = "0.41 - 3.58"
    colorIntensityTextField.placeholder = "1.28 - 13.0"
    hueTextField.placeholder = "0.48 - 1.71"
    od280ContentTextField.placeholder = "1.27 - 4.0"
    prolineContentTextField.placeholder = "278 - 1680"
}
```

12. Update the implementation of the onBackgroundTapped(_ sender: Any) method to the following:

```
@IBAction func onBackgroundTapped(_ sender: Any) {
    alcoholContentTextField.resignFirstResponder()
    malicAcidContentTextField.resignFirstResponder()
    ashContentTextField.resignFirstResponder()
    ashAlkalinityTextField.resignFirstResponder()
    magnesiumContentTextField.resignFirstResponder()
    totalPhenolContentTextField.resignFirstResponder()
    flavanoidContentTextField.resignFirstResponder()
    nonFlavanoidContentTextField.resignFirstResponder()
    proanthocyaninContentTextField.resignFirstResponder()
    colorIntensityTextField.resignFirstResponder()
    hueTextField.resignFirstResponder()
    od280ContentTextField.resignFirstResponder()
    prolineContentTextField.resignFirstResponder()
}
```

This code dismisses the keyboard when a tap is detected in the background areas of the screen.

13. Implement the `UITextFieldDelegate` method `textFieldDidEndEditing(_, reason)` in a class extension as follows:

```
extension UIViewController : UITextFieldDelegate {
    public func textFieldDidEndEditing(_ textField: UITextField, reason:
UITextField.DidEndEditingReason) {
        textField.resignFirstResponder()
    }
}
```

The code in `ViewController.swift` should resemble Listing 7.2.

LISTING 7.2:   ViewController.swift File with Code to Dismiss the Keypad

```
import UIKit

class ViewController: UIViewController {

    @IBOutlet weak var alcoholContentTextField: UITextField!
    @IBOutlet weak var malicAcidContentTextField: UITextField!
    @IBOutlet weak var ashContentTextField: UITextField!
    @IBOutlet weak var ashAlkalinityTextField: UITextField!
    @IBOutlet weak var magnesiumContentTextField: UITextField!
    @IBOutlet weak var totalPhenolContentTextField: UITextField!
    @IBOutlet weak var flavanoidContentTextField: UITextField!
    @IBOutlet weak var nonFlavanoidContentTextField: UITextField!
    @IBOutlet weak var proanthocyaninContentTextField: UITextField!
    @IBOutlet weak var colorIntensityTextField: UITextField!
    @IBOutlet weak var hueTextField: UITextField!
    @IBOutlet weak var od280ContentTextField: UITextField!
    @IBOutlet weak var prolineContentTextField: UITextField!


    override func viewDidLoad() {
        super.viewDidLoad()

        alcoholContentTextField.keyboardType = .decimalPad
        malicAcidContentTextField.keyboardType = .decimalPad
        ashContentTextField.keyboardType = .decimalPad
        ashAlkalinityTextField.keyboardType = .decimalPad
        magnesiumContentTextField.keyboardType = .decimalPad
        totalPhenolContentTextField.keyboardType = .decimalPad
        flavanoidContentTextField.keyboardType = .decimalPad
        nonFlavanoidContentTextField.keyboardType = .decimalPad
        proanthocyaninContentTextField.keyboardType = .decimalPad
        colorIntensityTextField.keyboardType = .decimalPad
```

```swift
        hueTextField.keyboardType = .decimalPad
        od280ContentTextField.keyboardType = .decimalPad
        prolineContentTextField.keyboardType = .decimalPad

        alcoholContentTextField.placeholder = "11.03 - 14.83"
        malicAcidContentTextField.placeholder = "0.74 - 5.8"
        ashContentTextField.placeholder = "1.36 - 3.23"
        ashAlkalinityTextField.placeholder = "10.6 - 30.0"
        magnesiumContentTextField.placeholder = "70 - 162"
        totalPhenolContentTextField.placeholder = "0.98 - 3.88"
        flavanoidContentTextField.placeholder = "0.34 - 5.0"
        nonFlavanoidContentTextField.placeholder = "0.13 - 0.66"
        proanthocyaninContentTextField.placeholder = "0.41 - 3.58"
        colorIntensityTextField.placeholder = "1.28 - 13.0"
        hueTextField.placeholder = "0.48 - 1.71"
        od280ContentTextField.placeholder = "1.27 - 4.0"
        prolineContentTextField.placeholder = "278 - 1680"

    }

    @IBAction func onGetWineQuality(_ sender: Any) {
    }


    @IBAction func onBackgroundTapped(_ sender: Any) {
        alcoholContentTextField.resignFirstResponder()
        malicAcidContentTextField.resignFirstResponder()
        ashContentTextField.resignFirstResponder()
        ashAlkalinityTextField.resignFirstResponder()
        magnesiumContentTextField.resignFirstResponder()
        totalPhenolContentTextField.resignFirstResponder()
        flavanoidContentTextField.resignFirstResponder()
        nonFlavanoidContentTextField.resignFirstResponder()
        proanthocyaninContentTextField.resignFirstResponder()
        colorIntensityTextField.resignFirstResponder()
        hueTextField.resignFirstResponder()
        od280ContentTextField.resignFirstResponder()
        prolineContentTextField.resignFirstResponder()
    }

}

extension UIViewController : UITextFieldDelegate {
    public func textFieldDidEndEditing(_ textField: UITextField, reason:
      UITextField.DidEndEditingReason) {
        textField.resignFirstResponder()
    }
}
```

Using the Classification Model in the iOS Project

Now that you have built the app's user interface, it is time to use the classification model that was created in an earlier section to predict the class of wine from its chemical composition. Perform the following steps:

1. Control-click the `WineClassifierApp` folder group in the Project Navigator window and select the Add Files to IrisPredictor menu item. Navigate to the `WineClassifier.mlmodel` file on your computer and ensure the Copy Items If Needed option is checked and the `WineClassifierApp` target is selected in the dialog box (see Figure 7.23).

FIGURE 7.23
Import settings for the
`WineClassifier`
`.mlmodel` file

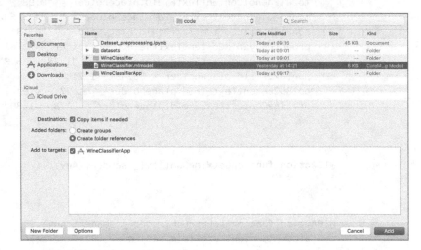

2. Select the `WineClassifier.mlmodel` file in the Project Navigator to get an overview of the model (see Figure 7.24).

FIGURE 7.24
Overview of the
`WineClassifier`
`.mlmodel` file

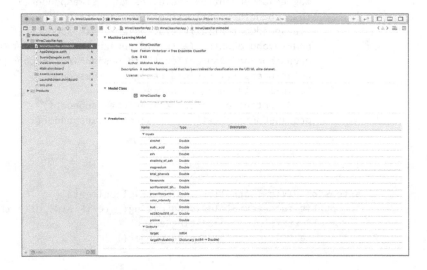

As you can see from the model overview screen, the size of the model is 8 KB, and the inputs to the model are 13 double-precision numbers, with the same names that were present in the .csv files used to train the model.

3. Access the autogenerated Swift class from the Model Class section of the model overview page (see Figure 7.25).

FIGURE 7.25

Accessing the Swift interface to the Core ML model file

Locate the definition of a class called WineClassifierInput in the autogenerated WineClassifier.swift file. This class represents the input for the Core ML model; the initializer for this class is listed here. Your four individual input variables (which you will collect from the text fields) will need to be wrapped into a WineClassifierInput instance, before being passed along as the input to the Core ML model.

```
init(alcohol: Double, malic_acid: Double, ash: Double,
    alcalinity_of_ash: Double, magnesium: Double,
    total_phenols: Double, flavanoids: Double,
    nonflavanoid_phenols: Double, proanthocyanins: Double,
    color_intensity: Double, hue: Double,
    od280_od315_of_diluted_wines: Double, proline: Double) {
        self.alcohol = alcohol
        self.malic_acid = malic_acid
        self.ash = ash
        self.alcalinity_of_ash = alcalinity_of_ash
        self.magnesium = magnesium
        self.total_phenols = total_phenols
        self.flavanoids = flavanoids
        self.nonflavanoid_phenols = nonflavanoid_phenols
        self.proanthocyanins = proanthocyanins
        self.color_intensity = color_intensity
        self.hue = hue
        self.od280_od315_of_diluted_wines = od280_od315_of_diluted_wines
        self.proline = proline
    }
```

4. Select the ViewController.swift file in the Project Navigator and add the following import statement to the top of the file to import the Core ML framework.

```
import CoreML
```

5. Modify the onGetWineQuality(_ sender:Any) method in the ViewController.swift file to resemble the following:

```swift
@IBAction func onGetWineQuality(_ sender: Any) {

    // read data from text fields
    guard let alcoholContent = Double(alcoholContentTextField.text ?? "0.0"),
        let malicAcidContent = Double(malicAcidContentTextField.text ?? "0.0"),
        let ashContent = Double(ashContentTextField.text ?? "0.0"),
        let ashAlkalinity = Double(ashAlkalinityTextField.text ?? "0.0"),
        let magnesiumContent = Double(magnesiumContentTextField.text ?? "0.0"),
        let totalPhenolContent = Double(totalPhenolContentTextField.text ??
"0.0"),
        let flavanidContent = Double(flavanoidContentTextField.text ?? "0.0"),
        let nonFlavanoidContent = Double(nonFlavanoidContentTextField.text ??
"0.0"),
        let proanthocyaninContent = Double(proanthocyaninContentTextField.text
?? "0.0"),
        let colorIntensity = Double(colorIntensityTextField.text ?? "0.0"),
        let hue = Double(hueTextField.text ?? "0.0"),
        let od280Content = Double(od280ContentTextField.text ?? "0.0"),
        let prolineContent = Double(prolineContentTextField.text ?? "0.0") else
    {

            let alertController = UIAlertController(title: "Error",
                message: "One or more fields contain non-numeric data.",
                preferredStyle: .alert)

            alertController.addAction(UIAlertAction(title: "Ok",
                                        style: .cancel, handler: nil))
            self.present(alertController, animated: true, completion: nil)
            return

    }

    // ensure the values entered by the user are within the ranges of
    // the data that was used to create the decision-tree model.
    //
    // refer to table 7.1 in the chapter for the ranges.
    if (alcoholContent < 11.03 || alcoholContent > 14.83) {
        let alertController = UIAlertController(title: "Error",
        message: "Alcohol content must be within the interval [11.03, 14.83].",
        preferredStyle: .alert)

        alertController.addAction(UIAlertAction(title: "Ok",
                                    style: .cancel, handler: nil))
        self.present(alertController, animated: true, completion: nil)
        return
    }
```

```swift
if (malicAcidContent < 0.74 || malicAcidContent > 5.8) {
    let alertController = UIAlertController(title: "Error",
    message: "Malic acid content must be within the interval [0.74, 5.8].",
    preferredStyle: .alert)

    alertController.addAction(UIAlertAction(title: "Ok",
                             style: .cancel, handler: nil))
    self.present(alertController, animated: true, completion: nil)
    return
}

if (ashContent < 1.36 || ashContent > 3.23) {
    let alertController = UIAlertController(title: "Error",
    message: "Ash content must be within the interval [1.36, 3.23].",
    preferredStyle: .alert)

    alertController.addAction(UIAlertAction(title: "Ok",
                             style: .cancel, handler: nil))
    self.present(alertController, animated: true, completion: nil)
    return
}

if (ashAlkalinity < 10.6 || ashAlkalinity > 30.0) {
    let alertController = UIAlertController(title: "Error",
    message: "Alkalinity of ash must be within the interval [10.6, 30.0].",
    preferredStyle: .alert)

    alertController.addAction(UIAlertAction(title: "Ok",
                             style: .cancel, handler: nil))
    self.present(alertController, animated: true, completion: nil)
    return
}

if (magnesiumContent < 70.0 || magnesiumContent > 162.0) {
    let alertController = UIAlertController(title: "Error",
    message: "Magnesium content must be within the interval [70.0,
            162.0].",
    preferredStyle: .alert)

    alertController.addAction(UIAlertAction(title: "Ok",
                             style: .cancel, handler: nil))
    self.present(alertController, animated: true, completion: nil)
    return
}

if (totalPhenolContent < 0.98 || totalPhenolContent > 3.88) {
    let alertController = UIAlertController(title: "Error",
```

```swift
            message: "Total phenol content must be within the interval [0.98,
                    3.88].",
            preferredStyle: .alert)

        alertController.addAction(UIAlertAction(title: "Ok",
                                    style: .cancel, handler: nil))
        self.present(alertController, animated: true, completion: nil)
        return
    }

    if (flavanoidContent < 0.34 || flavanoidContent > 5.08) {
let alertController = UIAlertController(title: "Error",
        message: "Flavanoid content must be within the interval [0.34, 5.08].",
        preferredStyle: .alert)

        alertController.addAction(UIAlertAction(title: "Ok",
                                    style: .cancel, handler: nil))
        self.present(alertController, animated: true, completion: nil)
        return
    }

    if (nonFlavonidContent < 0.13 || nonFlavonidContent > 0.66) {
        let alertController = UIAlertController(title: "Error",
        message: "Nonflavanoid content must be within the interval [0.13,
                0.66].",
        preferredStyle: .alert)

        alertController.addAction(UIAlertAction(title: "Ok",
                                    style: .cancel, handler: nil))
        self.present(alertController, animated: true, completion: nil)
        return
    }

    if (proanthocyaninContent < 0.41 || proanthocyaninContent > 3.58) {
        let alertController = UIAlertController(title: "Error",
        message: "Proanthocyanin content must be within the interval [0.41,
                3.58].",
        preferredStyle: .alert)

        alertController.addAction(UIAlertAction(title: "Ok",
                                    style: .cancel, handler: nil))
        self.present(alertController, animated: true, completion: nil)
        return
    }

    if (colorIntensity < 1.28 || colorIntensity > 13.0) {
        let alertController = UIAlertController(title: "Error",
        message: "Color intensity must be within the interval [1.28, 13.0].",
        preferredStyle: .alert)
```

```
            alertController.addAction(UIAlertAction(title: "Ok",
                                    style: .cancel, handler: nil))
        self.present(alertController, animated: true, completion: nil)
        return
    }

    if (hue < 0.48 || hue > 1.71) {
        let alertController = UIAlertController(title: "Error",
            message: "Hue must be within the interval [0.48, 1.71].",
            preferredStyle: .alert)

        alertController.addAction(UIAlertAction(title: "Ok",
                                    style: .cancel, handler: nil))
        self.present(alertController, animated: true, completion: nil)
        return
    }

    if (od280Content < 1.27 || od280Content > 4.0) {
        let alertController = UIAlertController(title: "Error",
        message: "OD280/OD315 content must be within the interval [1.27,
                4.0].",
        preferredStyle: .alert)

        alertController.addAction(UIAlertAction(title: "Ok",
                                    style: .cancel, handler: nil))
        self.present(alertController, animated: true, completion: nil)
        return
    }

    if (prolineContent < 278.0 || prolineContent > 1680.0) {
        let alertController = UIAlertController(title: "Error",
        message: "Proline content must be within the interval [278.0,
                1680.0].",
        preferredStyle: .alert)

        alertController.addAction(UIAlertAction(title: "Ok",
                                    style: .cancel, handler: nil))
        self.present(alertController, animated: true, completion: nil)
        return
    }

    // standardize the values supplied by the user to lie within the range
    // [0, 1].
    // Note: The minimum and maximum values for each feature are taken
    // from table 7.1.
    let standardizedAlcoholContent = (alcoholContent - 11.03) / (14.83 - 11.03)
    let standardizedMalicAcidContent = (malicAcidContent - 0.74) / (5.8 - 0.74)
```

```swift
let standardizedAshContent = (ashContent - 1.36) / (3.23 - 1.36)
let standardizedAshAlkalinity = (ashAlkalinity - 10.6) / (30.0 - 10.6)
let standardizedMagnesiumContent = (magnesiumContent - 70.0) /
                                   (162.0 - 70.0)
let standardizedTotalPhenolContent = (totalPhenolContent - 0.98) /
                                       (3.88 - 0.98)
let standardizedFlavanoidContent = (flavanoidContent - 0.34) / (5.08 - 0.34)
let standardizedNonFlavanoidContent = (nonFlavanoidContent - 0.13) /
                                       (0.66 - 0.13)
let standardizedProanthocyaninContent = (proanthocyaninContent - 0.41) /
                                          (3.58 - 0.41)
let standardizedColorIntensity = (colorIntensity - 1.28) / (13.0 - 1.28)
let standardizedHue = (hue - 0.48) / (1.71 - 0.48)
let standardizedOd280Content = (od280Content - 1.27) / (4.0 - 1.27)
let standardizedProlineContent = (prolineContent - 278.0) /
                                  (1680.0 - 278.0)

// prepare inputs to Core ML model.
let input = WineClassifierInput(alcohol: standardizedAlcoholContent,
                malic_acid: standardizedMalicAcidContent,
                ash: standardizedAshContent,
                alcalinity_of_ash: standardizedAshAlkalinity,
                magnesium: standardizedMagnesiumContent,
                total_phenols: standardizedTotalPhenolContent,
                flavanoids: standardizedFlavonidContent,
                nonflavanoid_phenols: standardizedNonFlavonidContent,
                proanthocyanins: standardizedProanthocyaninContent,
                color_intensity: standardizedColorIntensity,
                hue: standardizedHue,
                od280_od315_of_diluted_wines: standardizedOd280Content,
                proline: standardizedProlineContent)

// use the model to determine the quality of the wine.
let model = WineClassifier()

guard let result = try? model.prediction(input: input) else {

    let alertController = UIAlertController(title: "Core ML Error",
                        message: "An unexpected error occurred.",
                        preferredStyle: .alert)

    alertController.addAction(UIAlertAction(title: "Ok",
                                    style: .cancel, handler: nil))
    self.present(alertController, animated: true, completion: nil)
    return
}

var wineQuality:String?
```

```
    if result.target == 0 {
        wineQuality = "Category 0 (low)"
    } else if result.target == 1 {
        wineQuality = "Category 1 (medium)"
    } else if result.target == 2 {
        wineQuality = "Category 2 (high)"     }



    guard let quality = wineQuality else {
        return
    }

    let alertController = UIAlertController(title: "Prediction result",
                        message: "Wine quality is: " + quality,
                        preferredStyle: .alert)

    alertController.addAction(UIAlertAction(title: "Ok",
                                        style: .cancel, handler: nil))
    self.present(alertController, animated: true, completion: nil)
}
```

This method is called when the Get Wine Quality button is tapped. It reads all the values from the text fields and attempts to convert the values to double-precision numbers. If the conversion fails, then an error message is displayed to the user. If the conversion is successful, the code performs some basic checks on the values provided by the user to ensure they lie in the ranges of the corresponding features of the training dataset.

If the inputs provided by the user lie in appropriate numeric ranges, the code first standardizes the values typed by the user and then creates a WineClassifierInput instance from the standardized values. Since the model was built using a standardized dataset, it is important that the user input is also brought into the range [0, 1], using the same feature-wise standardization factors (minimum value, and maximum value) as the code in the Jupyter Notebook.

```
// standardize the values supplied by the user to lie within the range
// [0, 1].
// Note: The minimum and maximum values for each feature are taken
// from table 7.1.
let standardizedAlcoholContent = (alcoholContent - 11.03) / (14.83 - 11.03)
let standardizedMalicAcidContent = (malicAcidContent - 0.74) / (5.8 - 0.74)
let standardizedAshContent = (ashContent - 1.36) / (3.23 - 1.36)
let standardizedAshAlkalinity = (ashAlkalinity - 10.6) / (30.0 - 10.6)
let standardizedMagnesiumContent = (magnesiumContent - 70.0) /
                            (162.0 - 70.0)
let standardizedTotalPhenolContent = (totalPhenolContent - 0.98) /
                            (3.88 - 0.98)
```

```
let standardizedFlavanoidContent = (flavanoidContent - 0.34) / (5.08 - 0.34)
let standardizedNonFlavanoidContent = (nonFlavanoidContent - 0.13) /
                              (0.66 - 0.13)
let standardizedProanthocyaninContent = (proanthocyaninContent - 0.41) /
                              (3.58 - 0.41)
let standardizedColorIntensity = (colorIntensity - 1.28) / (13.0 - 1.28)
let standardizedHue = (hue - 0.48) / (1.71 - 0.48)
let standardizedOd280Content = (od280Content - 1.27) / (4.0 - 1.27)
let standardizedProlineContent = (prolineContent - 278.0) /
                              (1680.0 - 278.0)

// prepare inputs to Core ML model.
let input = WineClassifierInput(alcohol: standardizedAlcoholContent,
                   malic_acid: standardizedMalicAcidContent,
                   ash: standardizedAshContent,
                   alcalinity_of_ash: standardizedAshAlkalinity,
                   magnesium: standardizedMagnesiumContent,
                   total_phenols: standardizedTotalPhenolContent,
                   flavanoids: standardizedFlavonidContent,
                   nonflavanoid_phenols: standardizedNonFlavonidContent,
                   proanthocyanins: standardizedProanthocyaninContent,
                   color_intensity: standardizedColorIntensity,
                   hue: standardizedHue,
                   od280_od315_of_diluted_wines: standardizedOd280Content,
                   proline: standardizedProlineContent)
```

An instance of the Core ML model wrapper class `WineClassifier` is created next, and the `prediction()` method is called on the instance. The prediction method can throw an exception. The code that is presented in this chapter displays a generic error to the user if an exception is detected.

```
let model = WineClassifier()

guard let result = try? model.prediction(input: input) else {

    let alertController = UIAlertController(title: "Core ML Error",
                          message: "An unexpected error occurred.",
                          preferredStyle: .alert)

    alertController.addAction(UIAlertAction(title: "Ok",
                                    style: .cancel, handler: nil))
    self.present(alertController, animated: true, completion: nil)
    return
}
```

If no exceptions occurred, the result of the prediction is an object of type `wineClassifierOutput`, which is also declared in the autogenerated Core ML wrapper class. The `WineClassifierOutput` class contains a member variable called `target`, which corresponds to the target variable of the machine learning model.

The complete code in the `ViewController.swift` file is presented in Listing 7.3.

LISTING 7.3:   Complete ViewController.swift File

```swift
import UIKit
import CoreML

class ViewController: UIViewController {

    @IBOutlet weak var alcoholContentTextField: UITextField!
    @IBOutlet weak var malicAcidContentTextField: UITextField!
    @IBOutlet weak var ashContentTextField: UITextField!
    @IBOutlet weak var ashAlkalinityTextField: UITextField!
    @IBOutlet weak var magnesiumContentTextField: UITextField!
    @IBOutlet weak var totalPhenolContentTextField: UITextField!
    @IBOutlet weak var flavanoidContentTextField: UITextField!
    @IBOutlet weak var nonFlavanoidContentTextField: UITextField!
    @IBOutlet weak var proanthocyaninContentTextField: UITextField!
    @IBOutlet weak var colorIntensityTextField: UITextField!
    @IBOutlet weak var hueTextField: UITextField!
    @IBOutlet weak var od280ContentTextField: UITextField!
    @IBOutlet weak var prolineContentTextField: UITextField!


    override func viewDidLoad() {
        super.viewDidLoad()

        alcoholContentTextField.keyboardType = .decimalPad
        malicAcidContentTextField.keyboardType = .decimalPad
        ashContentTextField.keyboardType = .decimalPad
        ashAlkalinityTextField.keyboardType = .decimalPad
        magnesiumContentTextField.keyboardType = .decimalPad
        totalPhenolContentTextField.keyboardType = .decimalPad
        flavanoidContentTextField.keyboardType = .decimalPad
        nonFlavanoidContentTextField.keyboardType = .decimalPad
        proanthocyaninContentTextField.keyboardType = .decimalPad
        colorIntensityTextField.keyboardType = .decimalPad
        hueTextField.keyboardType = .decimalPad
        od280ContentTextField.keyboardType = .decimalPad
        prolineContentTextField.keyboardType = .decimalPad

        alcoholContentTextField.placeholder = "11.03 - 14.83"
        malicAcidContentTextField.placeholder = "0.74 - 5.8"
        ashContentTextField.placeholder = "1.36 - 3.23"
```

```swift
        ashAlkalinityTextField.placeholder = "10.6 - 30.0"
        magnesiumContentTextField.placeholder = "70 - 162"
        totalPhenolContentTextField.placeholder = "0.98 - 3.88"
        flavanoidContentTextField.placeholder = "0.34 - 5.08 "
        nonFlavanoidContentTextField.placeholder = "0.13 - 0.66"
        proanthocyaninContentTextField.placeholder = "0.41 - 3.58"
        colorIntensityTextField.placeholder = "1.28 - 13.0"
        hueTextField.placeholder = "0.48 - 1.71"
        od280ContentTextField.placeholder = "1.27 - 4.0"
        prolineContentTextField.placeholder = "278 - 1680"
    }

    @IBAction func onGetWineQuality(_ sender: Any) {
        // read data from text fields
        guard let alcoholContent = Double(alcoholContentTextField.text ??
                                    "0.0"),
            let malicAcidContent = Double(malicAcidContentTextField.text ??
                                    "0.0"),
            let ashContent = Double(ashContentTextField.text ?? "0.0"),
            let ashAlkalinity = Double(ashAlkalinityTextField.text ?? "0.0"),
            let magnesiumContent = Double(magnesiumContentTextField.text ??
                                    "0.0"),
            let totalPhenolContent = Double(totalPhenolContentTextField
    .text ??
                                            "0.0"),
            let flavanoidContent = Double(flavanoidContentTextField.text ??
                                    "0.0"),
            let nonFlavanoidContent = Double(nonFlavanoidContentTextField
    .text ??
                                            "0.0"),
            let proanthocyaninContent =
                        Double(proanthocyaninContentTextField.text
    ?? "0.0"),
            let colorIntensity = Double(colorIntensityTextField.text
    ?? "0.0"),
            let hue = Double(hueTextField.text ?? "0.0"),
            let od280Content = Double(od280ContentTextField.text ?? "0.0"),
            let prolineContent = Double(prolineContentTextField.text
    ?? "0.0")
        else {

                let alertController = UIAlertController(title: "Error",
                    message: "One or more fields contain non-numeric data.",
                    preferredStyle: .alert)

                alertController.addAction(UIAlertAction(title: "Ok",
                                            style: .cancel, handler: nil))
                self.present(alertController, animated: true, completion: nil)
                return

        }
```

```
// ensure the values entered by the user are within the ranges of
// the data that was used to create the decision-tree model.
//
// refer to table 7.1 in the chapter for the ranges.
if (alcoholContent < 11.03 || alcoholContent > 14.83) {
    let alertController = UIAlertController(title: "Error",
        message: "Alcohol content must be within the interval [11.03,
                14.83].",
        preferredStyle: .alert)

    alertController.addAction(UIAlertAction(title: "Ok",
                            style: .cancel, handler: nil))
    self.present(alertController, animated: true, completion: nil)
    return
}

if (malicAcidContent < 0.74 || malicAcidContent > 5.8) {
    let alertController = UIAlertController(title: "Error",
        message: "Malic acid content must be within the interval [0.74,
                5.8].",
        preferredStyle: .alert)

    alertController.addAction(UIAlertAction(title: "Ok",
                        style: .cancel, handler: nil))
    self.present(alertController, animated: true, completion: nil)
    return
}

if (ashContent < 1.36 || ashContent > 3.23) {
    let alertController = UIAlertController(title: "Error",
        message: "Ash content must be within the interval [1.36,
                3.23].",
        preferredStyle: .alert)

    alertController.addAction(UIAlertAction(title: "Ok",
                            style: .cancel, handler: nil))
    self.present(alertController, animated: true, completion: nil)
    return
}

if (ashAlkalinity < 10.6 || ashAlkalinity > 30.0) {
    let alertController = UIAlertController(title: "Error",
        message: "Alkalinity of ash must be within the interval [10.6,
                30.0].",
        preferredStyle: .alert)
```

```
                        alertController.addAction(UIAlertAction(title: "Ok",
                                              style: .cancel, handler: nil))
            self.present(alertController, animated: true, completion: nil)
            return
    }

    if (magnesiumContent < 70.0 || magnesiumContent > 162.0) {
        let alertController = UIAlertController(title: "Error",
            message: "Magnesium content must be within the interval [70.0,
                    162.0].",
            preferredStyle: .alert)

        alertController.addAction(UIAlertAction(title: "Ok",
                                  style: .cancel, handler: nil))
        self.present(alertController, animated: true, completion: nil)
        return
    }

    if (totalPhenolContent < 0.98 || totalPhenolContent > 3.88) {
        let alertController = UIAlertController(title: "Error",
            message: "Total phenol content must be within the interval
                    [0.98, 3.88].",
            preferredStyle: .alert)

        alertController.addAction(UIAlertAction(title: "Ok",
                                    style: .cancel, handler: nil))
        self.present(alertController, animated: true, completion: nil)
        return
    }

    if (flavanoidContent < 0.34 || flavanoidContent > 5.08) {
        let alertController = UIAlertController(title: "Error",
            message: "Flavanoid content must be within the
    interval [0.34,
                    5.08].",
            preferredStyle: .alert)

        alertController.addAction(UIAlertAction(title: "Ok",
                                    style: .cancel, handler: nil))
        self.present(alertController, animated: true, completion: nil)
        return
    }

    if (nonFlavanoidContent < 0.13 || nonFlavanoidContent > 0.66) {
        let alertController = UIAlertController(title: "Error",
            message: "Nonflavanoid content must be within the interval
```

```
                        [0.13, 0.66].",
                preferredStyle: .alert)

        alertController.addAction(UIAlertAction(title: "Ok",
                                    style: .cancel, handler: nil))
        self.present(alertController, animated: true, completion: nil)
        return
}

if (proanthocyaninContent < 0.41 || proanthocyaninContent > 3.58) {
    let alertController = UIAlertController(title: "Error",
        message: "Proanthocyanin content must be within the interval
                    [0.41, 3.58].",
        preferredStyle: .alert)

    alertController.addAction(UIAlertAction(title: "Ok",
                                style: .cancel, handler: nil))
    self.present(alertController, animated: true, completion: nil)
    return
}

if (colorIntensity < 1.28 || colorIntensity > 13.0) {
    let alertController = UIAlertController(title: "Error",
        message: "Color intensity must be within the interval [1.28,
                    13.0].",
        preferredStyle: .alert)

    alertController.addAction(UIAlertAction(title: "Ok",
                                style: .cancel, handler: nil))
    self.present(alertController, animated: true, completion: nil)
    return
}

if (hue < 0.48 || hue > 1.71) {
    let alertController = UIAlertController(title: "Error",
        message: "Hue must be within the interval [0.48, 1.71].",
        preferredStyle: .alert)

    alertController.addAction(UIAlertAction(title: "Ok",
                                style: .cancel, handler: nil))
    self.present(alertController, animated: true, completion: nil)
    return
}

if (od280Content < 1.27 || od280Content > 4.0) {
    let alertController = UIAlertController(title: "Error",
        message: "OD280/OD315 content must be within the interval
```

```
                                      [1.27, 4.0].",
                    preferredStyle: .alert)

                alertController.addAction(UIAlertAction(title: "Ok",
                                        style: .cancel, handler: nil))
                self.present(alertController, animated: true, completion: nil)
                return
            }

            if (prolineContent < 278.0 || prolineContent > 1680.0) {
                let alertController = UIAlertController(title: "Error",
                    message: "Proline content must be within the interval [278.0,
                            1680.0].",
                    preferredStyle: .alert)

                alertController.addAction(UIAlertAction(title: "Ok",
                                        style: .cancel, handler: nil))
                self.present(alertController, animated: true, completion: nil)
                return
            }

            // standardize the values supplied by the user to lie within
        the range
            // [0, 1].
            // Note: The minimum and maximum values for each feature are
        taken from
            // table 7.1.
            let standardizedAlcoholContent = (alcoholContent - 11.03) /
                                        (14.83 - 11.03)
            let standardizedMalicAcidContent = (malicAcidContent - 0.74) /
                                        (5.8 - 0.74)
            let standardizedAshContent = (ashContent - 1.36) / (3.23 - 1.36)
            let standardizedAshAlkalinity = (ashAlkalinity - 10.6) / (30.0 - 10.6)
            let standardizedMagnesiumContent = (magnesiumContent - 70.0) /
                                        (162.0 - 70.0)
            let standardizedTotalPhenolContent = (totalPhenolContent - 0.98) /
                                        (3.88 - 0.98)
            let standardizedFlavanoidContent = (flavanoidContent - 0.34) / (5.08
            let standardizedNonFlavanoidContent = (nonFlavanoidContent - 0.13) /
                                        (0.66 - 0.13)
            let standardizedProanthocyaninContent = (proanthocyaninContent - 0.41)
                                        / (3.58 - 0.41)
            let standardizedColorIntensity = (colorIntensity - 1.28) / (13.0 - 1.28)
            let standardizedHue = (hue - 0.48) / (1.71 - 0.48)
            let standardizedOd280Content = (od280Content - 1.27) / (4.0 - 1.27)
            let standardizedProlineContent = (prolineContent - 278.0) /
                                        (1680.0 - 278.0)
```

```swift
// prepare inputs to Core ML model.
let input = WineClassifierInput(alcohol: standardizedAlcoholContent,
             malic_acid: standardizedMalicAcidContent,
             ash: standardizedAshContent,
             alcalinity_of_ash: standardizedAshAlkalinity,
             magnesium: standardizedMagnesiumContent,
             total_phenols: standardizedTotalPhenolContent,
                   flavanoids: standardizedFlavanoidContent,
             nonflavanoid_phenols: standardizedNonFlavanoidContent,
             proanthocyanins: standardizedProanthocyaninContent,
             color_intensity: standardizedColorIntensity,
             hue: standardizedHue,
             od280_od315_of_diluted_wines: standardizedOd280Content,
             proline: standardizedProlineContent)

// use the model to determine the quality of the wine.
let model = WineClassifier()

guard let result = try? model.prediction(input: input) else {

    let alertController = UIAlertController(title: "Core ML Error",
                          message: "An unexpected error occurred.",
                          preferredStyle: .alert)

    alertController.addAction(UIAlertAction(title: "Ok",
                         style: .cancel, handler: nil))
    self.present(alertController, animated: true, completion: nil)
    return
}


var wineQuality:String?

if result.target == 0 {
    wineQuality = "Category 0 (low)"
} else if result.target == 1 {
    wineQuality = "Category 1 (medium)"
} else if result.target == 2 {
    wineQuality = "Category 2 (high)"
}


guard let quality = wineQuality else {
    return
}

let alertController = UIAlertController(title: "Prediction result",
                    message: "Wine quality is: " + quality,
                    preferredStyle: .alert)
```

```
                    alertController.addAction(UIAlertAction(title: "Ok",
                                            style: .cancel, handler: nil))
            self.present(alertController, animated: true, completion: nil)
        }


        @IBAction func onBackgroundTapped(_ sender: Any) {
            alcoholContentTextField.resignFirstResponder()
            malicAcidContentTextField.resignFirstResponder()
            ashContentTextField.resignFirstResponder()
            ashAlkalinityTextField.resignFirstResponder()
            magnesiumContentTextField.resignFirstResponder()
            totalPhenolContentTextField.resignFirstResponder()
            flavanoidContentTextField.resignFirstResponder()
            nonFlavanoidContentTextField.resignFirstResponder()
            proanthocyaninContentTextField.resignFirstResponder()
            colorIntensityTextField.resignFirstResponder()
            hueTextField.resignFirstResponder()
            od280ContentTextField.resignFirstResponder()
            prolineContentTextField.resignFirstResponder()
        }

    }

    extension UIViewController : UITextFieldDelegate {
        public func textFieldDidEndEditing(_ textField: UITextField, reason:
            UITextField.DidEndEditingReason) {
            textField.resignFirstResponder()
        }
    }
```

Testing the App

Save your project and run the app on the iOS simulator. Specify values for the feature variables and then tap on the background area of the screen to dismiss the keyboard. Tap the Get Wine Quality button and observe the results. Figure 7.26 depicts the results of running the app on the simulator.

NOTE   You can download the code files for this chapter from wrox.com or from GitHub using the following URL:

https://github.com/asmtechnology/iosmlbook-chapter7.git

FIGURE 7.26
Results of running the
app on the iOS simulator

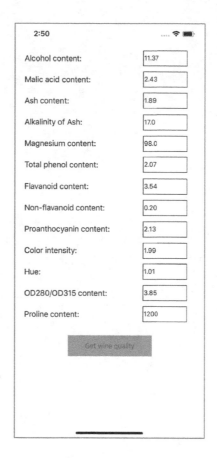

Summary

◆ The Create ML app provides a high-level task-oriented interface and can be used to create a Core ML–compatible model.

◆ The Create ML app does not provide any feature engineering, data preprocessing, or hyperparameter selection capabilities.

◆ At the time this book was written, the only metrics supported for classification models were Precision and Recall.

◆ A Jupyter Notebook was used to preprocess the UCI ML wines dataset and save it in a format that the Create ML app can use.

◆ The dataset was the popular Iris flowers dataset, consisting of 178 rows, each with 13 numeric features and one categorical target variable.

◆ The Create ML app requires that the target variable be either an integer or a string data type.

◆ If you standardize the inputs to the model during the training stage, you must also standardize the inputs to the model during the inferencing stage.

Chapter 8

Creating a Decision Tree Classifier

WHAT'S IN THIS CHAPTER

- ◆ Training a decision tree classifier with Scikit-learn
- ◆ Examining the decision tree generated by the classifier
- ◆ Using the decision tree to find out the relative importance of each feature in the dataset
- ◆ Using Core ML tools to convert a Scikit-learn model into the Core ML format
- ◆ Using the decision tree model in an iOS application

In this chapter, you will create a decision tree classification model that can be used to classify Iris flowers. The model will be trained on the popular Iris flowers dataset. After the model is trained, you will use Core ML tools to export the model into the Core ML file format and finally use the model in an iOS app that allows users to input the characteristics of an Iris flower and learn what species it is likely to represent.

NOTE   You can download the code files for this chapter from wrox.com or from GitHub using the following URL:

https://github.com/asmtechnology/iosmlbook-chapter8.git

Decision Tree Recap

Decision trees were introduced briefly in Chapter 1, and as their name suggests, they are tree-like structures where each node represents a decision boundary and where leaves represent outcomes of the decision. Tree-based algorithms such as decision trees, random forests, and boosted trees are commonly used with real-world classification problems and are often the winning algorithms behind several Kaggle.com competitions based on tabular data.

The following are some of the key reasons for the success of tree-based algorithms:

- ◆ Many tree-based algorithms do not require input data to be normalized. They are not sensitive to the difference in ranges in the values of the feature variables.

- ◆ Unlike mathematical algorithms such as logistic regression and neural networks, tree-based algorithms do not try to transform the input values into an abstract space where the values are likely to be easily separable. Instead, tree-based algorithms partition the input space of the problem into smaller subspaces and try to arrive at a partitioning strategy that neatly splits the input data into distinct classes.

- ◆ The results of a decision tree algorithm are easy to explain. You need only traverse the decision tree to explain the output of the classifier.

The shape (and predictive power) of a decision tree is heavily influenced by the nodes at the root of the tree, and tree-based algorithms can be used for both classification and regression tasks. When used for regression tasks, a decision tree is in effect acting as a clustering algorithm, and predicting a value that is closest to the values it has been trained on.

The main disadvantage of a tree-based model is that it is prone to overfitting. You can easily make a very deep tree in which each data point sits in exactly one leaf node of the tree. There are several strategies used to prevent overfitting; the main one is called *pruning* and involves deleting one or more nodes of the tree that do not satisfy some statistical criteria.

Creating a decision tree involves choosing one of the feature variables as the root node, selecting a threshold value as the decision boundary, and building two branches from the root node. One branch corresponds to values less than or equal to the threshold value, and the other corresponds to values greater than the threshold. The process then recursively examines the child node at the end of each branch and attempts to further split the child node based on the value of some other feature in the dataset, until some termination criteria is met. Common termination criteria are as follows:

◆ The maximum depth of the tree has exceeded a set value.

◆ The number of data points in each leaf node is within a set maximum.

The key question when building a decision tree is which feature to pick in order to partition the current level of the tree and what threshold value to use. A naïve implementation could use the mean value of the feature as the threshold, but this is not guaranteed to provide a better overall split because it is not considering the other features of the data point. Some of the more commonly used splitting techniques involve computing a statistical metric on the resulting partitions and selecting the value that results in a purer split. The purity of a node is a measure of the number of target classes captured by that node. A node that has 10 data points all belonging to the same class is 100 percent pure. A node that has 10 data points, 8 of which belong to class A and 2 of which belong to class B, is only 80 percent pure.

As you may have come to expect, you do not need to code the decision-tree building algorithm from scratch. Instead, you can use a library such as Scikit-learn to build the decision tree. You will build the decision tree model later in this chapter, but first let's examine the dataset on which the model is to be built.

Examining the Dataset

This chapter uses the Iris flowers dataset hosted at the UCI Machine Learning repository. A copy of the dataset is included with the resources that accompany this lesson. The original dataset can also be downloaded from http://archive.ics.uci.edu/ml/datasets/Iris. Scikit-learn also includes this dataset as part of its toy datasets module.

The dataset consists of 150 samples that represent Iris flowers from three classes—Iris Setosa, Iris Virginica, and Iris Versicolor—with 50 samples each. Each row of the dataset contains the following attributes:

◆ **Sepal length:** Length of the sepal in cm

◆ **Sepal width:** Width of the sepal in cm

◆ **Petal length:** Length of the petal in cm

◆ **Petal width:** Length of the petal in cm

◆ **Class:** A string that identifies the class of the flower

Launch the macOS Terminal application and type the following command to start a new Jupyter Notebook instance:

```
$ cd <your directory>
$ jupyter notebook
```

When Jupyter Notebook has finished loading in your web browser, create a new notebook file using the IOS_ML_BOOK kernel (see Figure 8.1) and name the file decision_tree_model.ipnyb.

FIGURE 8.1
Creating a new
notebook file

Type the following code in a notebook cell to load the Scikit-learn version of the dataset into a Pandas dataframe called df_iris:

```
import numpy as np
import pandas as pd

from sklearn import datasets
iris_dataset = datasets.load_iris()

df_iris = pd.DataFrame(data= np.c_[iris_dataset['data'],
                                   iris_dataset['target']],
columns= iris_dataset['feature_names'] + ['target'])
```

The Iris flowers dataset consists of 150 rows, and each row has five attributes (columns), one of which is the target attribute. You can verify the shape of the dataset using the following snippet:

```
# examine the shape of the dataset.
print ('df_iris has ' +
        str(df_iris.shape[0]) + ' rows and ' +
        str(df_iris.shape[1]) + ' columns')

>> df_iris has 150 rows and 5 columns
```

Figure 8.2 depicts the results of using the dataframe's head() method to inspect the first few rows of the dataframe.

FIGURE 8.2
Inspecting the first five
rows of the Iris
flowers dataset

```
In [2]:  # view the first 5 rows of the dataframe
         pd.set_option('display.max_columns', None)
         df_iris.head()
```

Out[2]:

	sepal length (cm)	sepal width (cm)	petal length (cm)	petal width (cm)	target
0	5.1	3.5	1.4	0.2	0.0
1	4.9	3.0	1.4	0.2	0.0
2	4.7	3.2	1.3	0.2	0.0
3	4.6	3.1	1.5	0.2	0.0
4	5.0	3.6	1.4	0.2	0.0

If you look closely, you will see that values in the target column are floating-point numbers. You can verify the data types of the columns by using the info() method of the data-frame object.

```
df_iris.info()

<class 'pandas.core.frame.DataFrame'>
RangeIndex: 150 entries, 0 to 149
Data columns (total 5 columns):
sepal length (cm)     150 non-null float64
sepal width (cm)      150 non-null float64
petal length (cm)     150 non-null float64
petal width (cm)      150 non-null float64
target                150 non-null float64
dtypes: float64(5)
memory usage: 6.0 KB
```

Let's now examine the distribution of values in the target column. Execute the following code in an empty notebook cell. The resulting histogram of target values is presented in Figure 8.3.

```
# histogram of columns
import matplotlib
df_iris.hist(figsize=(12,12))
```

FIGURE 8.3
Histogram of the data in
the target attribute of
the Iris flowers dataset

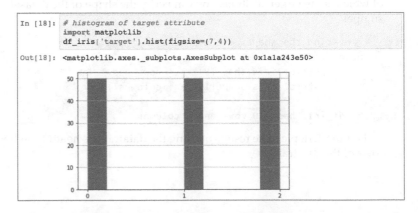

As you can see, there is absolutely no class imbalance in this dataset; there are 50 data points of each class of the Iris flower. The `target` attribute is clearly categorical, with only one of three values 0, 1, and 2, yet the data type of the `target` attribute of the `df_iris` dataframe has been determined earlier in this chapter to be `float64`. While Scikit-learn can easily train a decision tree model for a continuous numeric target attribute, Core ML tools will not be able to export a decision tree model unless the target attribute is discrete and of the `String` data type. Let's therefore, change the data type of the `target` attribute to consist of the strings '0', '1', and '2'.

Type the following code in an empty notebook cell and execute it:

```
# change the data type of the target column to string
df_iris[['target']] = df_iris[['target']].astype(np.uint8)
df_iris['target'] = df_iris['target'].apply(str)
```

You can either use the `info()` method to inspect the data types of the columns of the `df_iris` dataframe after executing these statements or use the `head()` method to sample the first five rows. Figure 8.4 depicts the results of using the dataframe's `head()` method to inspect the first few rows of the dataframe after the data type of the `target` attribute has been converted to `string`.

FIGURE 8.4

Inspecting the first five rows of the Iris flowers dataset after converting the data type of the target attribute

```
In [4]:  # change the datatype of the target column to string
         df_iris[['target']] = df_iris[['target']].astype(np.uint8)
         df_iris['target'] = df_iris['target'].apply(str)

In [13]: df_iris.head()

Out[13]:
```

	sepal length (cm)	sepal width (cm)	petal length (cm)	petal width (cm)	target
0	5.1	3.5	1.4	0.2	0
1	4.9	3.0	1.4	0.2	0
2	4.7	3.2	1.3	0.2	0
3	4.6	3.1	1.5	0.2	0
4	5.0	3.6	1.4	0.2	0

Next, let's find out whether any of the columns contain missing values, and the statistical characteristics of the data in the columns. The following snippet can be used to determine whether any of the columns of the dataset has missing values:

```
# how many missing values?
df_iris.isnull().sum()


sepal length (cm)    0
sepal width (cm)     0
petal length (cm)    0
petal width (cm)     0
target               0
dtype: int64
```

As you can see, none of the 150 rows contains missing data. Let's now examine the statistical characteristics of the five columns using the Pandas `describe()` function. The results are depicted in Figure 8.5.

FIGURE 8.5

FIGURE 8.5

Inspecting the statistical characteristics of the numeric columns of the Iris flowers dataset

```
In [7]:  # examine the statistical characteristics of the dataframe.
         df_iris.describe()

Out[7]:
```

	sepal length (cm)	sepal width (cm)	petal length (cm)	petal width (cm)
count	150.000000	150.000000	150.000000	150.000000
mean	5.843333	3.057333	3.758000	1.199333
std	0.828066	0.435866	1.765298	0.762238
min	4.300000	2.000000	1.000000	0.100000
25%	5.100000	2.800000	1.600000	0.300000
50%	5.800000	3.000000	4.350000	1.300000
75%	6.400000	3.300000	5.100000	1.800000
max	7.900000	4.400000	6.900000	2.500000

As you can see, the four feature columns have values of similar scales. Note that the target attribute has been excluded from the results of the describe() function because it is no longer a numeric attribute. Let's examine the distribution of the data in the target attribute using a histogram. Type the following code in an empty notebook cell and execute it. The resulting histogram is depicted in Figure 8.5.

Let's now split the 150 observations of the dataset into a training and test set. In this chapter, you will not perform any hyperparameter optimization and, therefore, will not create separate training, test, and validation sets. Furthermore, the Iris flowers dataset is a small dataset with just 150 rows and as such does not contain enough samples to allow you to create a separate validation set. Therefore, if you decide to perform hyperparameter optimization, you will need to use the same set for both testing and validation. This is not the best practice, but with such a small dataset, you do not have much choice in the matter.

Creating Training and Test Datasets

In the previous section, you examined the dataset to understand the distribution and ranges of the values taken by the feature and target variables. In this section, you will split your 150-row dataset into a training and test set. The training set will be used to train the model, and the test set will be used to evaluate the model. Scikit-learn provides a function called train_test_split() in the model_selection submodule that can be used to split a Pandas dataframe into two dataframes, one for model building and the other for model evaluation.

The test_train_split() function has several parameters, most of which have default values. The most commonly used parameters are the following:

◆ test_size: This value can be an integer or floating-point number. When the value is an integer, it specifies the number of elements that should be retained for the test set. When the value is a floating-point number, it specifies the percentage of the original dataset to include in the test set.

◆ random_state: This is an integer value that is used to seed the random number generator used to shuffle the samples. It is a good idea to specify a value for this parameter so that each time you execute the notebook, you arrive at the same results.

◆ stratify: The default value of this parameter is None, which implies stratified sampling must not be used. Since stratified sampling is not needed in the current dataset, you will use the default value for this parameter.

The output of the train_test_split() function is a list of four arrays in the following order:

◆ The first item of the list is an array that contains the training set features.

◆ The second item of the list is an array that contains the test set features.

◆ The third item of the list is an array that contains the training set labels (target variable).

◆ The fourth item of the list is an array that contains the test set labels.

You can find detailed information on the parameters of the train_test_split() function at https://scikit-learn.org/stable/modules/generated/sklearn.model_selection.train_test_split.html.

Type the following snippet in a empty notebook cell to split the five-column dataframe df_iris into two dataframes—a four-column dataframe called df_iris_features that contains all the feature attributes, and a one-column dataframe called df_iris_target that contains the target variable.

```
# split the df_iris dataframe into two,
# one with the features and the other with the target
df_iris_target = df_iris.loc[:,['target']]
df_iris_features = df_iris.drop(['target'], axis=1)
```

After separating the df_iris dataframe into two dataframes, type the following code in an empty notebook cell to create the training and test datasets:

```
# create a training set and a test set.
from sklearn.model_selection import train_test_split

iris_split = train_test_split(df_iris_features, df_iris_target,
                             test_size=0.25, random_state=17,
                             stratify = df_iris_target['target'])

df_iris_features_train = iris_split[0]
df_iris_features_test = iris_split[1]
df_iris_target_train = iris_split[2]
df_iris_target_test = iris_split[3]
```

With the test and training datasets created, you will create a decision tree classification model in the next section.

NOTE Both the training and test datasets contain two dataframes each, one with the features and the other with the target attribute.

Creating the Decision Tree Classification Model with Scikit-learn

Scikit-learn provides the DecisionTreeClassifier class as part of the tree module, and it can be used to build a decision tree classification model. The documentation for the DecisionTreeClassifier class can be found at https://scikit-learn.org/stable/modules/generated/sklearn.tree.DecisionTreeClassifier.html.

When instantiating a `DecisionTreeClassifier` instance, you can provide a number of arguments that control the manner in which the tree is built. These arguments are the hyperparameters of the decision tree model and control the manner in which nodes are split, as well as the mechanism to constrain the overall depth of the tree. All the parameters have default values, which will work fine for the small dataset we are using. In a real-world scenario, you would build a baseline model using the default values and then attempt to build a model that outperforms the baseline version by trying different hyperparameter combinations.

Type the following code snippet into an empty notebook cell to create a decision tree classifier on the training set:

```
# train a decision tree model
from sklearn.tree import DecisionTreeClassifier

model = DecisionTreeClassifier(random_state=17)
model.fit(df_iris_features_train, df_iris_target_train.values.ravel())
```

Executing this code should result in output similar to the following:

```
DecisionTreeClassifier(class_weight=None, criterion='gini', max_depth=None,
                       max_features=None, max_leaf_nodes=None,
                       min_impurity_decrease=0.0, min_impurity_split=None,
                       min_samples_leaf=1, min_samples_split=2,
                       min_weight_fraction_leaf=0.0, presort=False,
                       random_state=17, splitter='best')
```

You can see the default values used for the hyperparameters. Of particular interest is the `criterion='gini'` hyperparameter, which indicates that the Gini impurity metric is used to determine the optimal threshold at which to split a node.

With the model created, you can use the model to make predictions on the test set using the `predict()` method provided by the `DecisionTreeClassifier` class. Type the following snippet in an empty notebook cell to make predictions and print the predicted values:

```
# get predictions from model, compute accuracy.
predictions = model.predict(df_iris_features_test)
print (predictions)

['2' '2' '2' '2' '1' '1' '1' '0' '2' '1' '0' '0' '1' '2' '0' '0' '1' '0'
 '1' '0' '1' '0' '1' '0' '2' '2' '0' '2' '0' '1' '2' '2' '1' '0' '2' '2'
 '2' '1']
```

Let's now compute the value of a performance metric that we can use to evaluate the classifier. The metric being used in this chapter is accuracy, and while it can be computed from the confusion matrix for the classifier, we will use Scikit-learn's `accuracy_score` function, which is part of the `metrics` module. The following snippet demonstrates the use of this function:

```
from sklearn.metrics import accuracy_score
accuracy = accuracy_score(df_iris_target_test, predictions)
print (accuracy)

0.9210526315789473
```

As you can see, the accuracy of this decision tree classifier is 92.15 percent on the predictions made on the test set, which is pretty good considering we have not performed any feature engineering or hyperparameter optimization at all.

If you recall, earlier in the lesson, it was mentioned that one of the advantages of a decision tree model is that it is easy to explain the predictions by simply traversing the structure of the decision tree. You can access the decision tree itself using the `tree_` attribute of the trained model; however, the decision tree is represented by an object of type `sklearn.tree._tree.Tree`. You can convert this `Tree` object into an image using the `graphviz` and `pydotplus` Python packages. These packages are not covered in this book, and if you want to execute the snippet to visualize the decision tree, you will need to install these packages in your `IOS_ML_BOOK` Conda environment.

To install the `graphviz` and `pydotplus` packages, perform the following steps:

1. Save your notebook and close the Jupyter Notebook web pages in your browser.

2. Close the macOS Terminal window to shut down the Jupyter Notebook server.

3. Relaunch a new macOS Terminal window and type the following commands, pressing the Enter key after each command:

```
$ conda activate IOS_ML_BOOK
$ conda install pydotplus
$ conda install graphviz
```

These commands make the `IOS_ML_BOOK` environment the active Python environment on your computer and install the `pydotplus` and `graphviz` packages along with their dependencies. When the installation is complete, the output in your Terminal window should resemble the following:

```
Downloading and Extracting Packages
fontconfig-2.13.0    | 202 KB  | #################################### | 100%
graphite2-1.3.13     | 80 KB   | #################################### | 100%
pixman-0.38.0        | 341 KB  | #################################### | 100%
cairo-1.14.12        | 860 KB  | #################################### | 100%
graphviz-2.40.1      | 6.3 MB  | #################################### | 100%
fribidi-1.0.5        | 60 KB   | #################################### | 100%
pango-1.42.4         | 455 KB  | #################################### | 100%
harfbuzz-1.8.8       | 414 KB  | #################################### | 100%
Preparing transaction: done
Verifying transaction: done
Executing transaction: done
```

4. Using the Terminal app, navigate to the directory in which you saved your Jupyter Notebook in step 1.

5. Restart the Jupyter Notebook server by typing the following and pressing the Enter key:

```
$ jupyter notebook
```

A new web browser window (or tab) will be opened for you with the Jupyter Notebook web interface visible in it. Open the `decision_tree_model.ipnyb` notebook file by clicking it from the list of available files.

6. When the notebook is open, click the Cell ➤ Run All menu item to execute the code in all the cells of the notebook (see Figure 8.6).

FIGURE 8.6
Executing the code in all
the cells of the
Jupyter Notebook

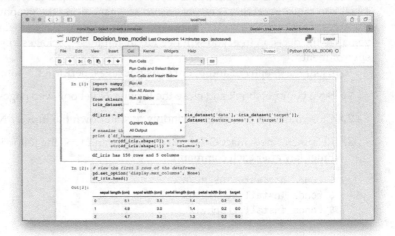

You should now be at the same point before you shut down the notebook to install the additional libraries.

Type the following code in a new notebook cell and execute it to visualize the decision tree graphically. The result of executing this snippet is depicted in Figure 8.7.

```
# visualize the decision tree
from sklearn.externals.six import StringIO
from IPython.display import Image
from sklearn.tree import export_graphviz
import pydotplus

dot_data = StringIO()
export_graphviz(model, out_file=dot_data,
                filled=True, rounded=True,
                special_characters=True,
                feature_names=df_iris_features.columns)

graph = pydotplus.graph_from_dot_data(dot_data.getvalue())
Image(graph.create_png())
```

FIGURE 8.7
Graphical representation
of the decision
tree model

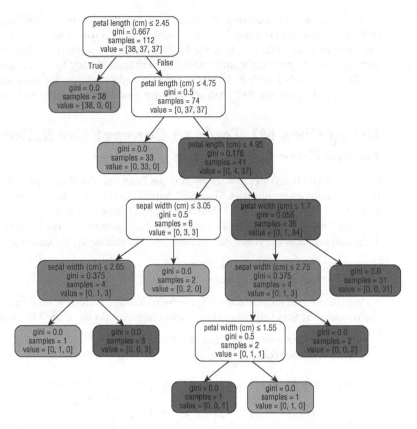

The tree consists of nodes and leaves, as you would expect. Each node and leaf is represented by a rounded rectangle, and within the node you will see some information about the node. For instance, at the top of the tree you should see the root node, which contains the following information:

◆ **Petal length (cm) <= 2.45:** This represents the third feature column (petal length), and the threshold value is 2.45 cm.

◆ **gini = 0.667:** This represents the Gini impurity score for the node.

◆ **samples = 112:** This represents the total number of datapoints in the node.

◆ **value = [38, 37, 37]:** This represents the total number of samples of each of the three classes in the node. There are 38 datapoints of class 0 (Iris Setosa), 37 datapoints of class 1 (Iris Versicolor), and 37 datapoints of class 2 (Iris Virginica) in this node.

Another extremely useful property of tree-based classifiers is that it is possible to get information on the relative importance (or contributions) of the individual features in the output of the model. This can be helpful to find out which features are more important than others. Type the following code into an empty notebook cell and execute it:

```
print (model.feature_importances_)
[0.        0.04687874 0.93379574 0.01932552]
```

The results are interesting. It appears that the first feature (sepal length) has no importance in this model and that the third feature (petal length) is the most important feature. As a side exercise, you may want to drop the first feature and train a second decision tree model based on just the three remaining features and compare its accuracy to the original model. The notebook file that is included with this chapter's downloads contains the code for this side exercise. For the rest of this chapter, we will proceed with the model we have trained on four features.

Using Core ML Tools to Convert the Scikit-learn Model to the Core ML Format

Core ML tools is an open source Python package provided by Apple that can be used to convert models made using libraries like Scikit-learn into the Core ML format. You can learn more about Core ML tools at https://github.com/apple/coremltools.

Installing Core ML tools is a straightforward process. If you haven't already done so, launch a Terminal window on your Mac and execute the following statements:

```
$ conda activate IOS_ML_BOOK
$ pip install coremltools
```

With Core ML tools installed, type the following code into an empty notebook cell to export the model that was trained earlier in this chapter, into the Core ML format:

```
# export the model to Core ML format
import coremltools

coreml_model = coremltools.converters.sklearn.convert(model,
                                ["sepal length (cm)", "sepal width (cm)",
"petal length (cm)", "petal width (cm)"],
                                "target")

coreml_model.author = 'Abhishek Mishra'
coreml_model.short_description = 'Decision tree model trained on the
Iris dataset.'

# feature descriptions
coreml_model.input_description['sepal length (cm)'] = 'Sepal length in cm.'
coreml_model.input_description['sepal width (cm)'] = 'Sepal width in cm.'
coreml_model.input_description['petal length (cm)'] = 'Petal length in cm.'
coreml_model.input_description['petal width (cm)'] = 'Petal width in cm.'

# description of target variable
coreml_model.output_description['target'] = 'A categorical value value, 0 =
Iris-Setosa, 1 = Iris-Versicolour, 3= Iris-Virginica'
coreml_model.save('iris_dtree.mlmodel')
```

The `coremltools.converters` package provides a converter class called `sklearn` that can be used to convert Scikit-learn models into the Core ML format. The `sklearn` class exposes a method named `convert()` that performs the bulk of the work. The `convert()` method requires three arguments—the model to convert, an array of feature names, and the name of the target variable. The `convert()` method returns a Core ML–compatible Python object that can be saved to the Core ML file format using the `save()` method.

Prior to saving the model to a disk file, it is a good idea to set up some metadata about the model. This data will be visible in Xcode when you import the `.mlmodel` file. You can use the `author` and `short_description` attributes of the Core ML Python object to specify the name of the author and a general description of the type of model. You can also use the `input_descrip-tion` and `output_description` dictionaries to specify descriptions for each of the features and the target attribute, respectively. After executing this snippet, you should find a model file called `iris_dtree.mlmodel` in the same folder as the Jupyter Notebook file.

Creating the iOS Project

After exporting the Scikit-learn model to the Core ML format, launch Xcode on your Mac and create a new project using the *Single View App* template (see Figure 8.8).

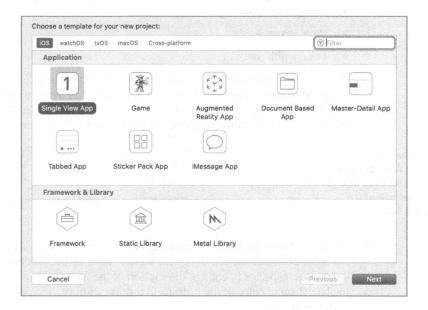

When prompted, use the following project options:

◆ **Product Name:** `IrisClassifier`

◆ **Organization Name:** *Provide a suitable value*

◆ **Organization Identifier:** *Provide a suitable value*

◆ **Language:** Swift

◆ **User Interface:** Storyboard

◆ **Use Core Data:** Unchecked

◆ **Include Unit Tests:** Unchecked

◆ **Include UI Tests:** Unchecked

Creating the User Interface

With the project created, set up the user interface of the project using these steps:

1. Open the `Main.storyboard` file and use the View ➤ Show Library menu item to access the object library window. Drag and drop four label instances object library onto the default view controller scene.

2. Place these labels one below the other, and use the Attributes Inspector to change the captions of these labels according to the following list. You can access the Attributes Inspector using the View ➤ Inspectors ➤ Show Attributes Inspector menu item.

   ◆ Sepal length (cm):

   ◆ Sepal width (cm):

   ◆ Petal length (cm):

   ◆ Petal width (cm):

3. Drag and drop four text field instances from the object library onto the default view controller scene and arrange them one below the other, to the right of the labels you created in the previous step. To make the text fields easily visible, use the Attributes Inspector to set the border style of each of the text fields to Line (see Figure 8.9).

FIGURE 8.9
Using the Attributes
Inspector to change the
border style of the
text fields

4. Drag and drop a button from the object library onto the default view controller scene, and place the button at the bottom of the scene, below all the text fields and labels. Use the Attributes Inspector to change the caption of the button to Get Iris Flower Species. Change the background color of the buttons to a shade of gray to make it easier to see on the storyboard scene.

5. Drag and drop a tap gesture recognizer object from the object library onto the default view controller.

6. Organize the elements on the default view controller scene to resemble Figure 8.10 and set up the appropriate storyboard constraints.

FIGURE 8.10
Application storyboard
with default view
controller scene

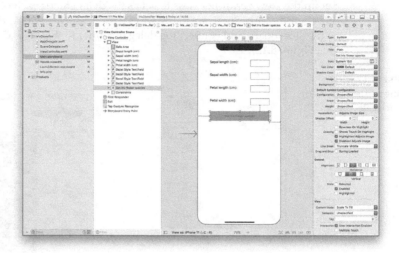

7. Use the Editor ➤ Assistant menu item to access the Assistant Editor and ensure the `ViewController.swift` file is open in the Assistant Editor. Create four outlets in the view controller class per the following list:

- `sepalLengthTextField`

- `sepalWidthTextField`

- `petalLengthTextField`

- `petalWidthTextField`

Associate these outlets with the corresponding text fields of the storyboard scene (see Figure 8.11).

FIGURE 8.11
Using the Assistant
Editor to create outlets

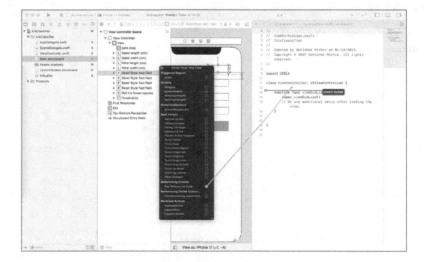

8. Set up the view controller class to act as the delegate for each of the text fields in the storyboard scene. There are many ways to do this. One way is to Ctrl-click a text field in the storyboard and connect the delegate outlet to the View Controller object (see Figure 8.12).

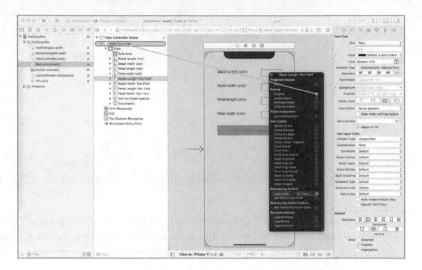

9. Create an action method in the `ViewController.swift` file called `onGetIrisSpecies (_ sender: Any)` and associate this method with the `Touch Up Inside` event of the button.

10. Create an action method in the `ViewController.swift` file called `onBackground-Tapped(_ sender: Any)` and associate this method with the `selector` property of the tap gesture recognizer (see Figure 8.13).

The code in your `ViewController.swift` file should now resemble Listing 8.1.

LISTING 8.1: ViewController.swift File with Outlets and Actions

```swift
import UIKit

class ViewController: UIViewController {

    @IBOutlet weak var sepalLengthTextField: UITextField!
    @IBOutlet weak var sepalWidthTextField: UITextField!
    @IBOutlet weak var petalLengthTextField: UITextField!
    @IBOutlet weak var petalWidthTextField: UITextField!

    override func viewDidLoad() {
        super.viewDidLoad()
        // Do any additional setup after loading the view.
    }

    @IBAction func onGetIrisSpecies(_ sender: Any) {
    }

    @IBAction func onBackgroundTapped(_ sender: Any) {
    }

}
```

---

11. Update the `viewDidLoad()` method in your `ViewController.swift` file to resemble the following snippet. This code ensures that the number pad is displayed as the default keyboard when the text field becomes the first responder.

```swift
override func viewDidLoad() {
    super.viewDidLoad()

    sepalLengthTextField.keyboardType = .decimalPad
    sepalWidthTextField.keyboardType = .decimalPad
    petalLengthTextField.keyboardType = .decimalPad
    petalWidthTextField.keyboardType = .decimalPad
}
```

12. Update the implementation of the `onBackgroundTapped(_ sender: Any)` method to the following:

```swift
@IBAction func onBackgroundTapped(_ sender: Any) {
    sepalLengthTextField.resignFirstResponder()
    sepalWidthTextField.resignFirstResponder()
    petalLengthTextField.resignFirstResponder()
    petalWidthTextField.resignFirstResponder()
}
```

This code uses dismisses the keyboard when a tap is detected in the background areas of the screen.

13. Implement the `UITextFieldDelegate` method `textFieldDidEndEditing(_, reason)` in a class extension as follows:

```
extension UIViewController : UITextFieldDelegate {
    public func textFieldDidEndEditing(_ textField: UITextField, reason:
UITextField.DidEndEditingReason) {
        textField.resignFirstResponder()
    }
}
```

The code in `ViewController.swift` should resemble Listing 8.2.

LISTING 8.2:   ViewController.swift File with Code to Dismiss the Keypad

```
import UIKit

class ViewController: UIViewController {

    @IBOutlet weak var sepalLengthTextField: UITextField!
    @IBOutlet weak var sepalWidthTextField: UITextField!
    @IBOutlet weak var petalLengthTextField: UITextField!
    @IBOutlet weak var petalWidthTextField: UITextField!

    override func viewDidLoad() {
        super.viewDidLoad()

        sepalLengthTextField.keyboardType = .decimalPad
        sepalWidthTextField.keyboardType = .decimalPad
        petalLengthTextField.keyboardType = .decimalPad
        petalWidthTextField.keyboardType = .decimalPad
    }

    @IBAction func onGetIrisSpecies(_ sender: Any) {
    }

    @IBAction func onBackgroundTapped(_ sender: Any) {
        sepalLengthTextField.resignFirstResponder()
        sepalWidthTextField.resignFirstResponder()
        petalLengthTextField.resignFirstResponder()
        petalWidthTextField.resignFirstResponder()
    }
}
```

```
extension UIViewController : UITextFieldDelegate {
    public func textFieldDidEndEditing(_ textField: UITextField, reason:
      UITextField.DidEndEditingReason) {
        textField.resignFirstResponder()
    }
}
```

Using the Scikit-learn DecisionTreeClassifier Model in the iOS Project

Now that we have built the app's user interface, it is time to use the logistic regression model that was created in an earlier section to predict the onset of diabetes. Perform the following steps:

1. Control-click on the IrisPredictor folder group in the Project Navigator window and select the Add Files To IrisPredictor menu item. Navigate to the iris_dtree.mlmodel file in your Jupyter Notebook folder and ensure that the Copy Items If Needed option is checked and the IrisPredictor target is selected in the dialog box (see Figure 8.14).

FIGURE 8.14
Import settings for the
iris_dtree.
mlmodel file

2. Select the iris_dtree.mlmodel file in the Project Navigator to get an overview of the model (see Figure 8.15).

   As you can see from the model overview screen, the size of the model is just 1 KB, and the inputs to the model are four double-precision numbers, with the same names that you specified while exporting the model using Core ML tools.

3. Access the autogenerated Swift class from the Model Class section of the model overview page (see Figure 8.16).

   Locate the definition of a class call iris_dtreeInput in the autogenerated iris_dtree. swift file. This class represents the input for the Core ML model; the initializer for this class is listed here. Your four individual input variables (which you will collect from the text fields) will need to be wrapped into an iris_dtreeInput instance, before being passed along as the input to the Core ML model.

FIGURE 8.15
Overview of the
iris_dtree.
mlmodel file

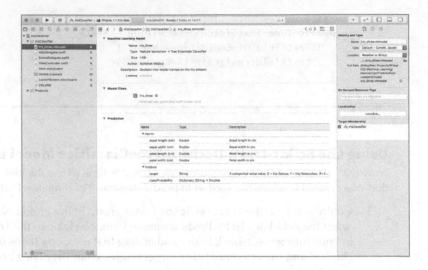

FIGURE 8.16
Accessing the Swift
interface to the Core ML
model file

```
init(sepal_length__cm_: Double, sepal_width__cm_: Double, petal_length__cm_:
Double, petal_width__cm_: Double) {
    self.sepal_length__cm_ = sepal_length__cm_
    self.sepal_width__cm_ = sepal_width__cm_
    self.petal_length__cm_ = petal_length__cm_
    self.petal_width__cm_ = petal_width__cm_
}
```

4. Select the `ViewController.swift` file in the Project Navigator and add the following `import` statement to the top of the file to import the Core ML framework:

```
import CoreML
```

5. Modify the `onGetIrisSpecies(_ sender:Any)` method in the `ViewController.swift` file to resemble the following:

```
@IBAction func onGetIrisSpecies(_ sender: Any) {

    // read data from text fields
    guard let sepalLength = Double(sepalLengthTextField.text ?? "0.0"),
        let sepalWidth = Double(sepalWidthTextField.text ?? "0.0"),
        let petalLength = Double(petalLengthTextField.text ?? "0.0"),
        let petalWidth = Double(petalWidthTextField.text ?? "0.0") else {
```

```swift
        let alertController = UIAlertController(title: "Error",
            message: "One or more fields contain non-numeric data.",
            preferredStyle: .alert)

        alertController.addAction(UIAlertAction(title: "Ok",
                                     style: .cancel, handler: nil))
        self.present(alertController, animated: true, completion: nil)
        return

    }


    // ensure the values entered by the user are within the ranges of
    // the data that was used to create the decision-tree model.
    //
    // refer to figure 8.4 in the chapter for the ranges.
    if (sepalLength < 4.3 || sepalLength > 7.9) {
        let alertController = UIAlertController(title: "Error",
            message: "Sepal length must be within the interval [4.3, 7.9].",
            preferredStyle: .alert)

        alertController.addAction(UIAlertAction(title: "Ok",
                                     style: .cancel, handler: nil))
        self.present(alertController, animated: true, completion: nil)
        return
    }

    if (sepalWidth < 2.0 || sepalWidth > 4.4) {
        let alertController = UIAlertController(title: "Error",
            message: "Sepal width must be within the interval [2.0, 4.4].",
            preferredStyle: .alert)

        alertController.addAction(UIAlertAction(title: "Ok",
                                     style: .cancel, handler: nil))
        self.present(alertController, animated: true, completion: nil)
        return
    }

    if (petalLength < 1.0 || petalLength > 6.9) {
        let alertController = UIAlertController(title: "Error",
            message: "Petal length must be within the interval [1.0, 6.9].",
            preferredStyle: .alert)

        alertController.addAction(UIAlertAction(title: "Ok",
                                     style: .cancel, handler: nil))
        self.present(alertController, animated: true, completion: nil)
        return
    }
```

```swift
if (petalWidth < 0.01 || petalWidth > 2.5) {
    let alertController = UIAlertController(title: "Error",
        message: "Petal width must be within the interval [0.01, 2.5].",
        preferredStyle: .alert)

    alertController.addAction(UIAlertAction(title: "Ok",
                            style: .cancel, handler: nil))
    self.present(alertController, animated: true, completion: nil)
    return
}



// prepare inputs to Core ML model.
let input = iris_dtreeInput(sepal_length__cm: sepalLength,
                        sepal_width__cm: sepalWidth,
                        petal_length__cm: petalLength,
                        petal_width__cm : petalWidth)

// use the model to determine the species of the flower.
let model = iris_dtree()

guard let result = try? model.prediction(input: input) else {

    let alertController = UIAlertController(title: "Core ML Error",
                            message: "An unexpected error occurred.",
                            preferredStyle: .alert)

    alertController.addAction(UIAlertAction(title: "Ok",
                                style: .cancel, handler: nil))
    self.present(alertController, animated: true, completion: nil)
    return
}

var flowerSpecies:String?

if result.target.compare("1") == .orderedSame  {
    flowerSpecies = "Iris Setosa"
} else if result.target.compare("2") == .orderedSame {
    flowerSpecies = "Iris Virginica"
} else if result.target.compare("3") == .orderedSame {
    flowerSpecies = "Iris Versicolor"
}

guard let species = flowerSpecies else {
    return
}
```

```
let alertController = UIAlertController(title: "Prediction result",
                      message: "Flower Species is: " + species,
                      preferredStyle: .alert)

    alertController.addAction(UIAlertAction(title: "Ok",
                                            style: .cancel, handler: nil))
    self.present(alertController, animated: true, completion: nil)
}
```

This method is called when the Get Iris Flower Species button is tapped. It reads all the values from the text fields and attempts to convert the values to double-precision numbers. If the conversion fails, then an error message is displayed to the user.

```
guard let sepalLength = Double(sepalLengthTextField.text ?? "0.0"),
    let sepalWidth = Double(sepalWidthTextField.text ?? "0.0"),
    let petalLength = Double(petalLengthTextField.text ?? "0.0"),
    let petalWidth = Double(petalWidthTextField.text ?? "0.0") else {

        let alertController = UIAlertController(title: "Error",
            message: "One or more fields contain non-numeric data.",
            preferredStyle: .alert)

        alertController.addAction(UIAlertAction(title: "Ok",
                                                style: .cancel, handler: nil))
        self.present(alertController, animated: true, completion: nil)
        return
}
```

If the conversion is successful, the code performs some basic checks on the values provided by the user to ensure they lie in the ranges of the corresponding features of the training dataset. Unlike a logistic regression model, a tree-based classification model works best with data that is similar to the training data. The ranges of values were obtained earlier in the chapter using the describe() function of the Pandas dataframe (refer to Figure 8.4). If the values provided by the user lie within the appropriate numeric ranges, the code creates an instance of an iris_dtreeInput object from the values typed by the user.

```
let input = iris_dtreeInput(sepal_length__cm_: sepalLength,
                        sepal_width__cm_: sepalWidth,
                        petal_length__cm_: petalLength,
                        petal_width__cm_ : petalWidth)
```

An instance of the Core ML model wrapper class iris_dtree is created next, and the prediction() method is called on the instance. The prediction method can throw an exception. The code presented in this chapter displays a generic error to the user if an exception is detected:

```
let model - iris_dtree()

guard let result = try? model.prediction(input: input) else {
```

```
        let alertController = UIAlertController(title: "Core ML Error",
                                 message: "An unexpected error occurred.",
                                 preferredStyle: .alert)

        alertController.addAction(UIAlertAction(title: "Ok",
                                              style: .cancel, handler: nil))
        self.present(alertController, animated: true, completion: nil)
        return
    }
```

If no exceptions occurred, the result of the prediction is an object of type `iris_dtreeOutput`, which is also declared in the autogenerated Core ML wrapper class. The `iris_dtreeOutput` class contains a member variable called `target`, which corresponds to the target variable of the machine learning model.

The complete code in the `ViewController.swift` file is presented in Listing 8.3.

LISTING 8.3: Completed ViewController.swift File

```
import UIKit
import CoreML

class ViewController: UIViewController {

    @IBOutlet weak var sepalLengthTextField: UITextField!
    @IBOutlet weak var sepalWidthTextField: UITextField!
    @IBOutlet weak var petalLengthTextField: UITextField!
    @IBOutlet weak var petalWidthTextField: UITextField!

    override func viewDidLoad() {
        super.viewDidLoad()

        sepalLengthTextField.keyboardType = .decimalPad
        sepalWidthTextField.keyboardType = .decimalPad
        petalLengthTextField.keyboardType = .decimalPad
        petalWidthTextField.keyboardType = .decimalPad
    }

    @IBAction func onGetIrisSpecies(_ sender: Any) {

        // read data from text fields
        guard let sepalLength = Double(sepalLengthTextField.text ?? "0.0"),
            let sepalWidth = Double(sepalWidthTextField.text ?? "0.0"),
            let petalLength = Double(petalLengthTextField.text ?? "0.0"),
            let petalWidth = Double(petalWidthTextField.text ?? "0.0") else {
```

```swift
        let alertController = UIAlertController(title: "Error",
            message: "One or more fields contain non-numeric data.",
            preferredStyle: .alert)

        alertController.addAction(UIAlertAction(title: "Ok",
                            style: .cancel, handler: nil))
        self.present(alertController, animated: true, completion: nil)
        return

}

// ensure the values entered by the user are within the ranges of
// the data that was used to create the decision-tree model.
//
// refer to figure 8-4 in the chapter for the ranges.
if (sepalLength < 4.3 || sepalLength > 7.9) {
    let alertController = UIAlertController(title: "Error",
        message: "Sepal length must be within the interval [4.3, 7.9].",
            preferredStyle: .alert)

    alertController.addAction(UIAlertAction(title: "Ok",
                        style: .cancel, handler: nil))
    self.present(alertController, animated: true, completion: nil)
    return
}

if (sepalWidth < 2.0 || sepalWidth > 4.4) {
    let alertController = UIAlertController(title: "Error",
        message: "Sepal width must be within the interval [2.0, 4.4].",
            preferredStyle: .alert)

    alertController.addAction(UIAlertAction(title: "Ok",
                        style: .cancel, handler: nil))
    self.present(alertController, animated: true, completion: nil)
    return
}

if (petalLength < 1.0 || petalLength > 6.9) {
    let alertController = UIAlertController(title: "Error",
        message: "Petal length must be within the interval [1.0, 6.9].",
            preferredStyle: .alert)

    alertController.addAction(UIAlertAction(title: "Ok",
                        style: .cancel, handler: nil))
    self.present(alertController, animated: true, completion: nil)
```

```swift
            return
        }

        if (petalWidth < 0.01 || petalWidth > 2.5) {
            let alertController = UIAlertController(title: "Error",
                message: "Petal width must be within the interval [0.01, 2.5].",
                preferredStyle: .alert)

            alertController.addAction(UIAlertAction(title: "Ok",
                                    style: .cancel, handler: nil))
            self.present(alertController, animated: true, completion: nil)
            return
        }


        // prepare inputs to Core ML model.
        let input = iris_dtreeInput(sepal_length__cm_: sepalLength,
                            sepal_width__cm_: sepalWidth,
                            petal_length__cm_: petalLength,
                            petal_width__cm_ : petalWidth)

        // use the model to determine the species of the flower.
        let model = iris_dtree()

        guard let result = try? model.prediction(input: input) else {

            let alertController = UIAlertController(title: "Core ML Error",
                            message: "An unexpected error occurred.",
                            preferredStyle: .alert)

            alertController.addAction(UIAlertAction(title: "Ok",
                                        style: .cancel, handler: nil))
            self.present(alertController, animated: true, completion: nil)
            return
        }

        var flowerSpecies:String?

        if result.target.compare("1") == .orderedSame  {
            flowerSpecies = "Iris Setosa"
        } else if result.target.compare("2") == .orderedSame {
            flowerSpecies = "Iris Virginica"
        } else if result.target.compare("3") == .orderedSame {
            flowerSpecies = "Iris Versicolor"
```

```
        }

        guard let species = flowerSpecies else {
            return
        }

        let alertController = UIAlertController(title: "Prediction result",
                            message: "Flower Species is: " + species,
                            preferredStyle: .alert)

        alertController.addAction(UIAlertAction(title: "Ok",
                                    style: .cancel, handler: nil))
        self.present(alertController, animated: true, completion: nil)
    }


    @IBAction func onBackgroundTapped(_ sender: Any) {
        sepalLengthTextField.resignFirstResponder()
        sepalWidthTextField.resignFirstResponder()
        petalLengthTextField.resignFirstResponder()
        petalWidthTextField.resignFirstResponder()
    }
}

extension UIViewController : UITextFieldDelegate {
    public func textFieldDidEndEditing(_ textField: UITextField, reason:
      UITextField.DidEndEditingReason) {
        textField.resignFirstResponder()
    }
}
```

Testing the App

Save your project and run the app on the iOS Simulator. Specify values for the four feature variables and then tap on the background area of the screen to dismiss the keyboard. Tap the Get Iris Flower Species button and observe the results. Figure 8.17 depicts the results of running the app on the simulator.

NOTE You can download the code files for this chapter from wrox.com or from GitHub using the following URL:

https://github.com/asmtechnology/iosmlbook-chapter8.git

FIGURE 8.17
Results of running the
app on the iOS simulator

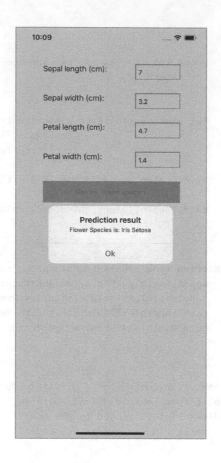

Summary

- In this chapter, a decision tree classification model was trained to classify the species of an Iris flower based on the measurements of its petals and sepals.

- The dataset was the popular Iris flowers dataset, consisting of 150 rows, each with four numeric features and one categorical target variable.

- A baseline model was created without any feature engineering or hyperparameter optimization.

- The decision tree generated by the model was visualized using graphviz.

- The decision tree model was also able to provide information about the relative importance of the training features.

- Core ML tools is a Python library that can be used to export Scikit-learn models into the Core ML format.

Chapter 9

Creating a Logistic Regression Model Using Scikit-learn and Core ML

WHAT'S IN THIS CHAPTER

- ◆ Training a logistic regression classifier with Scikit-learn
- ◆ Using Core ML Tools to convert a Scikit-learn model into the Core ML format
- ◆ Using the logistic regression model in an iOS application

In this chapter, you will use logistic regression to build a machine learning model that can be used to predict the onset of diabetes. The model will be trained on the Pima Indians diabetes dataset, a copy of which is included in the downloads that accompany this lesson. After the model is trained, you will use Core ML Tools to export the model into the Core ML file format and finally use the model in an iOS app that allows users to enter their information and determine whether they are likely to have type 2 diabetes.

NOTE You can download the code files for this chapter from wrox.com or from GitHub using the following URL:

https://github.com/asmtechnology/iosmlbook-chapter9.git

Examining the Dataset

This chapter uses the Pima Indians diabetes dataset, which was originally created by the National Institute of Diabetes and Digestive and Kidney Diseases. The dataset itself is a sample of a much larger dataset and consists of data for women from the Pima Indian heritage. The dataset was originally hosted at the UCI ML repository at http://www.ics.uci.edu/~mlearn/MLRepository.html. The dataset has been used in several studies and research papers. A copy of the dataset is also available at Kaggle.com and can be accessed via https://www.kaggle.com/uciml/pima-indians-diabetes-database.

The dataset contains the following attributes:

- ◆ **Pregnancies:** Number of pregnancies
- ◆ **Glucose:** Plasma glucose concentration after two hours in an oral glucose tolerance test
- ◆ **BloodPressure:** Diastolic blood pressure (mm HG)

- ◆ **SkinThickness:** Thickness of the triceps skin fold (mm)

- ◆ **Insulin:** Two-hour serum insulin level (mu U/ml)

- ◆ **BMI:** Body mass index (kg/m2)

- ◆ **Age:** The age of the subject

- ◆ **DiabetesPedigreeFunction:** A function that determines the risk of diabetes based on family history

- ◆ **Outcome:** 1 if the person was diagnosed with type 2 diabetes, 0 if not

Before we create the logistic regression model, let's spend some time analyzing the dataset. Download the code resources that accompany this chapter and create a new folder on your computer. Navigate to this folder using the macOS Terminal application and type the following command to start up a new Jupyter Notebook instance:

```
$ cd <your directory>
$ jupyter notebook
```

When Jupyter Notebook has finished loading in your web browser, create a new notebook file using the IOS_ML_BOOK kernel (see Figure 9.1) and name the file LogisticRegressionModel.ipnyb.

FIGURE 9.1
Creating a new
notebook file

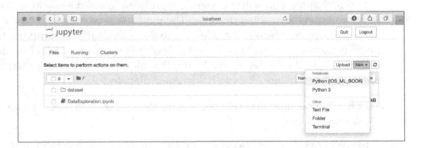

Type the following code in a notebook cell to load the dataset into a Pandas dataframe called df_diabetes. Do not forget to replace the path to the dataset CSV file with the appropriate value for your computer.

```
import numpy as np
import pandas as pd

# load the contents of a file into a pandas Dataframe
input_file = './dataset/diabetes_dataset/diabetes.csv'
df_diabetes = pd.read_csv(input_file)
```

The diabetes dataset consists of 768 rows, and each row has nine attributes (columns), one of which is the target attribute. You can verify the shape of the dataset using the following snippet:

```
# examine the shape of the dataset.
print ('df_diabetes has ' +
```

```
            str(df_diabetes.shape[0]) + ' rows and ' +
            str(df_diabetes.shape[1]) + ' columns')


>> df_diabetes has 768 rows and 9 columns
```

Figure 9.2 depicts the results of using the dataframe's head() method to inspect the first few rows of the dataframe.

FIGURE 9.2

Inspecting the first five rows of the diabetes dataset

```
In [2]: # view the first 5 rows of the dataframe
        pd.set_option('display.max_columns', None)
        df_diabetes.head()
Out[2]:
```

	Pregnancies	Glucose	BloodPressure	SkinThickness	Insulin	BMI	DiabetesPedigreeFunction	Age	Outcome
0	6	148	72	35	0	33.6	0.627	50	1
1	1	85	66	29	0	26.6	0.351	31	0
2	8	183	64	0	0	23.3	0.672	32	1
3	1	89	66	23	94	28.1	0.167	21	0
4	0	137	40	35	168	43.1	2.288	33	1

Use the following snippet to determine whether any of the columns of the dataset have missing values.

```
# how many missing values?
df_diabetes.isnull().sum()


Pregnancies                 0
Glucose                     0
BloodPressure               0
SkinThickness               0
Insulin                     0
BMI                         0
DiabetesPedigreeFunction    0
Age                         0
Outcome                     0
```

As you can see, none of the 768 rows contains missing data. Let's now examine the statistical characteristics of the nine columns using the Pandas describe() function. The results are depicted in Figure 9.3.

FIGURE 9.3

Inspecting the statistical characteristics of the diabetes dataset

```
In [4]: # examine the statistical characteristics of the dataframe.
        df_diabetes.describe()
Out[4]:
```

	Pregnancies	Glucose	BloodPressure	SkinThickness	Insulin	BMI	DiabetesPedigreeFunction	Age	Outcome
count	768.000000	768.000000	768.000000	768.000000	768.000000	768.000000	768.000000	768.000000	768.000000
mean	3.845052	120.894531	69.105469	20.536458	79.799479	31.992578	0.471876	33.240885	0.348958
std	3.369578	31.972618	19.355807	15.952218	115.244002	7.884160	0.331329	11.760232	0.476951
min	0.000000	0.000000	0.000000	0.000000	0.000000	0.000000	0.078000	21.000000	0.000000
25%	1.000000	99.000000	62.000000	0.000000	0.000000	27.300000	0.243750	24.000000	0.000000
50%	3.000000	117.000000	72.000000	23.000000	30.500000	32.000000	0.372500	29.000000	0.000000
75%	6.000000	140.250000	80.000000	32.000000	127.250000	36.600000	0.626250	41.000000	1.000000
max	17.000000	199.000000	122.000000	99.000000	846.000000	67.100000	2.420000	81.000000	1.000000

As you can see, the eight-feature columns have values in different ranges. For example, the Pregnancies column has a range of (0, 17), and the Insulin column has a range of (0, 846). Let's also create histograms of the columns of the dataframe to get an idea of the distribution of values. Type the following code in an empty notebook cell to generate histograms of the columns (see Figure 9.4):

```
# histogram of columns
import matplotlib
df_diabetes.hist(figsize=(12,12))
```

FIGURE 9.4
Histograms of the data in each column of the dataset

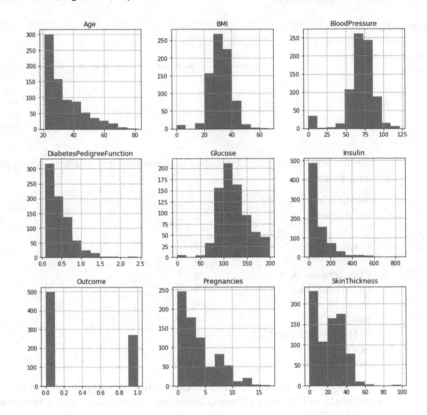

A couple of inferences can be made from the histograms:

◆ Three of the features appear to have outliers (BMI, Glucose, and BloodPressure).

◆ The binary target variable Outcome contains more samples with the value 0 (do not have diabetes) than 1. This is quite common in datasets that predict the occurrence of a negative condition (such as an illness), because most people do not have the condition.

Figure 9.5 depicts the histograms of the BMI, Glucose, and BloodPressure features. It is quite evident from these histograms that there are outliers in the range (0, 10) in the BMI feature, in the range (0, 25) in the Glucose feature, and in the range (0, 20) in the BloodPressure feature.

You could, at this point, choose to perform some feature engineering on the dataset, perhaps replace all the outliers with the median value of the corresponding feature, and then scale all the values to lie in the range (0, 1). However, without a baseline model, it is not possible to know whether making these changes will result in a better model.

FIGURE 9.5

Histograms of the
BMI, Glucose,
and BloodPressure
features

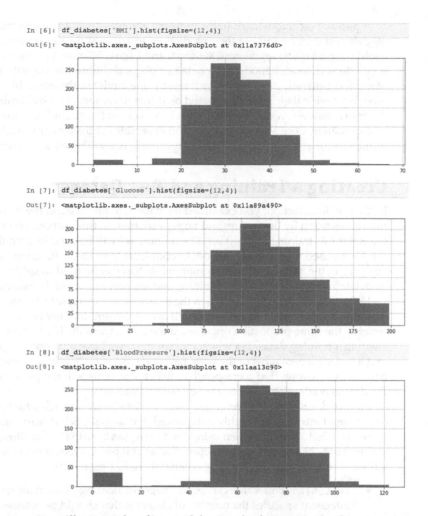

```
In [6]:  df_diabetes['BMI'].hist(figsize=(12,4))
```
```
Out[6]:  <matplotlib.axes._subplots.AxesSubplot at 0x11a7376d0>
```

```
In [7]:  df_diabetes['Glucose'].hist(figsize=(12,4))
```
```
Out[7]:  <matplotlib.axes._subplots.AxesSubplot at 0x11a89a490>
```

```
In [8]:  df_diabetes['BloodPressure'].hist(figsize=(12,4))
```
```
Out[8]:  <matplotlib.axes._subplots.AxesSubplot at 0x11aa13c90>
```

In this chapter, you will create a baseline model using the features in the dataset as-is. However, keep in mind that in a real-world situation, you will not stop at a baseline model. Instead, you will try to iteratively arrive at better models by one of the following means:

◆ Modify the dataset (remove outliers, scale feature values).

◆ Create new features (perhaps the square of the BMI has better predictive power than the BMI feature).

◆ Choose different sets of features (perhaps using fewer features may result in a better model).

◆ Try a different combination of hyperparameters.

◆ Try a different algorithm altogether (some advanced tree-based algorithms such as XGBoost, LightGBM, and CatBoost will almost always perform better at classification tasks).

A popular technique used in the industry involves creating an ensemble of different types of models and then combining their predictions to arrive at the final predictions. For instance, you could train a logistic regression, XGBoost, and LightGBM model on the same dataset; get three predictions from each model for a data sample; and choose the majority value. Ensembles made of models generally perform better than any one model in the ensemble, because the individual models provide their prediction based on different reasons, and by combining a collection of dissimilar models, your ensemble is likely to pick up the strengths of the individual models. Unfortunately, Core ML does not support ensembles of dissimilar models (when this chapter was written), so if you want to pursue this approach, you will need to use server-side inferencing.

Creating a Training and Test Dataset

In the previous section, you examined the dataset to understand the distribution and ranges of the values taken by the feature and target variables. In this section, you will split your 768-row dataset into a training and test set. The training set will be used to train the model, and the test set will be used to evaluate the model. Scikit-learn provides a function called `train_test_split()` in the `model_selection` submodule that can be used to split a Pandas dataframe into two dataframes, one for model building and the other for model evaluation.

However, since the two classes in the binary target variable `Outcome` are unbalanced (0 = no diabetes, 1 = diabetes detected), you will need to ensure that the test and train datasets have roughly the same proportion of values in the target variable. If you don't do this, then you risk creating a training dataset in which most of the rows have `Outcome` = 0 (implying no diabetes), and a test set where most of the rows have `Outcome` = 1. Clearly, a model built on a dataset that has a very few rows that correspond to diabetes patients will not perform well on a test set where the data is predominantly made up of diabetes patients.

Stratified sampling is a technique used by statisticians in such situations where the members of the target attribute are highly imbalanced. Fortunately, Scikit-learn makes it simple to implement stratified sampling when using the `train_test_split()` function.

The `test_train_split()` function has several parameters, most of which have default values. The following are the most commonly used parameters:

- `test_size`: This value can be an integer or floating-point number. When the value is an integer, it specifies the number of elements that should be retained for the test set. When the value is a floating-point number, it specifies the percentage of the original dataset to include in the test set.

- `random_state`: This is an integer value that is used to seed the random number generator used to shuffle the samples.

- `stratify`: The default value of this parameter is None, which implies stratified sampling must not be used. If you require the data to be split in a stratified manner, then this parameter must contain an array of class labels.

The output of the `train_test_split()` function is a list of four arrays in the following order:

- The first item of the list is an array that contains the training set features.

- The second item of the list is an array that contains the test set features.

◆ The third item of the list is an array that contains the training set labels (target variable).

◆ The fourth item of the list is an array that contains the test set labels.

You can find detailed information on the parameters of the `train_test_split()` function at `https://scikit-learn.org/stable/modules/generated/sklearn.model_selection.train_test_split.html`.

Type the following snippet into a empty notebook cell to split the nine-column dataframe `df_diabetes` into two dataframes—an eight-column dataframe called `df_diabetes_features` that contains all the feature attributes, and a one-column dataframe called `df_diabetes_target` that contains the target variable.

```
# split the df_diabetes dataframe into two,
# one with the features and the other with the target
df_diabetes_target = df_diabetes.loc[:,['Outcome']]
df_diabetes_features = df_diabetes.drop(['Outcome'], axis=1)
# You can inspect the number of items in each dataframe using the following
snippet:
print ('df_diabetes_target has ' +
        str(df_diabetes_target.shape[0]) + ' rows and ' +
        str(df_diabetes_target.shape[1]) + ' columns')

print ('df_diabetes_features has ' +
        str(df_diabetes_features.shape[0]) + ' rows and ' +
        str(df_diabetes_features.shape[1]) + ' columns')

df_diabetes_target has 768 rows and 1 columns
df_diabetes_features has 768 rows and 8 columns
```

After separating the `df_diabetes` dataframe into two dataframes, type the following code into an empty notebook cell to create the training and test datasets:

```
# create a training set and a test set.

from sklearn.model_selection import train_test_split
diabetes_split = train_test_split(df_diabetes_features, df_diabetes_target,
                                  test_size=0.25, random_state=17,
                                  stratify = df_diabetes_target['Outcome'])

df_diabetes_features_train = diabetes_split[0]
df_diabetes_features_test = diabetes_split[1]
df_diabetes_target_train = diabetes_split[2]
df_diabetes_target_test = diabetes_split[3]
```

NOTE Both the training and test datasets contain two dataframes each, one with the features and the other with the target attribute.

You can visualize the distribution of classes in the target variable both before and after creating the test-train split using the following snippet. The resulting plot is depicted in Figure 9.6. Note the distributions are roughly the same.

```
# visualize the distribution of target values in the
# original dataset and the test/train sets created by the train_test_split
function

import matplotlib.pyplot as plt

# use Pandas dataframe functions to plot a bar chart of the 'Embarked' attribute
fig, axes = plt.subplots(1, 3, figsize=(15,5))

axes[0].set_title('df_diabetes_target')
df_diabetes_target['Outcome'].value_counts(dropna=False).plot.bar(grid=True,
ax=axes[0])

axes[1].set_title('df_diabetes_target_train')
df_diabetes_target_train['Outcome'].value_counts(dropna=False).plot.bar(grid=True,
ax=axes[1])

axes[2].set_title('df_diabetes_target_test')
df_diabetes_target_test['Outcome'].value_counts(dropna=False).plot.bar(grid=True,
ax=axes[2])
```

FIGURE 9.6
Distribution of the classes in the target attribute of the original dataset, and the test/train split datasets

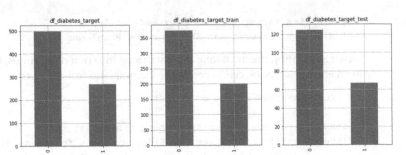

Creating the Logistic Regression Model with Scikit-learn

In the previous section, you prepared the stratified test/train datasets and learned that the target variable Outcome has two possible values, 1 and 0. Since the target variable is binary, the type of model you need to build is a binary classification model. In Chapter 1, you learned about different types of classification and regression models. In this chapter, you will train a binary classifier using the logistic regression algorithm. Logistic regression (also known as *logit regression*) is a simple algorithm that builds upon the output of linear regression and returns a probability that the data point is of one class or another. Recall that linear regression attempts to create a line (or hyperplane) that best fits all the data points, and the output of linear regression is a continuous unbounded value, whereas probabilities are continuous bounded values—bounded between 0.0 and 1.0.

To use a continuous value for binary classification, logistic regression converts it into a probability value between 0.0 and 1.0 by feeding the output of linear regression into the sigmoid function, which is defined as follows:

$$\text{Sigmoid}(x) = \frac{1}{1 + e^{-x}}$$

The graph of the sigmoid function is presented in Figure 9.7. The output of the sigmoid function will never go below 0.0 or above 1.0, regardless of the value of the input.

FIGURE 9.7

The Sigmoid function

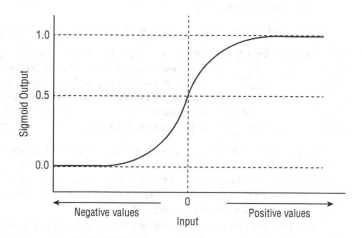

In the model that you will create in this chapter, a threshold value of 0.5 will be applied to the output of the sigmoid function. All values below 0.5 will be treated as class 0 (not diabetic), and all above 0.5 as class 1 (diabetic). See Figure 9.8.

FIGURE 9.8

Using the Sigmoid function for binary classification

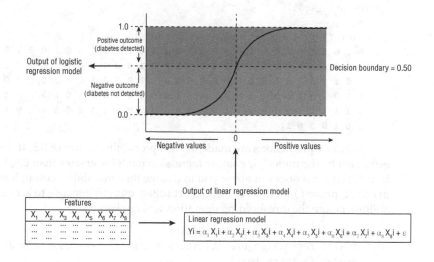

Scikit-learn provides the `LogisticRegression` class as part of the `linear_model` module. Type the following code snippet into an empty notebook cell to create a logistic regression classifier on the training set:

```
# train a logistic regression model on the diabetes dataset.
from sklearn.linear_model import LogisticRegression
logistic_regression_model = LogisticRegression(penalty='l2', fit_intercept=True,
solver='liblinear', multi_class='ovr')
logistic_regression_model.fit(df_diabetes_features_train, df_diabetes_target_
train.values.ravel())
```

Executing this code will return output similar to the following:

```
LogisticRegression(C=1.0, class_weight=None, dual=False, fit_intercept=True,
                   intercept_scaling=1, l1_ratio=None, max_iter=100,
                   multi_class='ovr', n_jobs=None, penalty='l2',
                   random_state=None, solver='liblinear', tol=0.0001,
                   verbose=0,
                   warm_start=False)
```

The constructor of the `LogisticRegression` class takes several parameters; since you have only provided valued for the penalty, `fit_intercept`, solver, and `multi_class` parameters, Scikit-learn uses default values for the remaining parameters. You can find out more about these parameters at `https://scikit-learn.org/stable/modules/generated/sklearn.linear_model.LogisticRegression.html`.

With the model created, you can use the model to make predictions on the test set using the `predict()` method provided by the `LogisticRegression` class. Type the following snippet into an empty notebook cell to make predictions and print the predicted values:

```
# get predictions (using default signoid threshold of 0.5)
logistic_regression_predictions = logistic_regression_model.predict(df_diabetes_
features_test)

print (logistic_regression_predictions)
[0 1 0 0 0 0 0 0 1 0 0 1 0 1 1 0 0 0 1 0 1 0 0 0 0 0 0 1 0 1 0 0 1 0 0 0
 1 0 0 1 0 1 0 1 1 0 0 0 1 0 0 1 0 0 1 0 0 0 0 0 0 0 1 0 0 1 1 0 0 0 1 0
 0 0 1 0 0 1 0 0 0 1 0 0 0 0 0 0 1 0 0 0 0 0 1 0 0 0 0 0 0 0 0 0 1 0 0 0
 1 1 0 0 0 1 1 0 0 0 0 0 0 0 1 0 0 0 0 0 0 1 0 0 0 0 0 0 1 1 1 0 0 0 1 1
 1 1 1 0 1 0 0 0 1 1 0 0 1 0 0 1 1 0 0 0 1 1 0 0 0 1 0 0 1 0 0 0 0 0 0 0
 1 0 1 0 0 0 1]
```

The binary predictions are made using a probability cutoff of 0.5. If the probability value estimated by the underlying linear regression model is greater than 0.5, then the output class will be 0. Scikit-learn does not allow you to change this probability cutoff; however, you can use the `predict_proba()` method of the `LogisticRegression` instance to access the prediction probabilities before the thresholding operation was applied.

```
# access class-wise probabilities
logistic_regression_probabilities = logistic_regression_model.predict_proba(df_
diabetes_features_test)
```

Since there are two output classes, the `predict_proba()` method will give you two probabilities per data point. The first column contains the probability that the point will be labeled 0, and the second column contains the probability that the point will be labeled 1.

```
print (logistic_regression_probabilities)

[[0.92906446 0.07093554]
 [0.3294155  0.6705845 ]
 [0.68119927 0.31880073]
 ...

 ...
 [0.74026741 0.25973259]
 [0.73397199 0.26602801]
 [0.11737272 0.88262728]]
```

Because these numbers represent probabilities, the sum of the prediction probabilities for any data point will be 1.0. Furthermore, since there are only two classes, you can use the information in any one column to work out the value of the other column by subtracting from 1.0. The following snippet uses the information in the first column (probability that the output class is 0) and implements custom thresholding logic at 0.8. Any probabilities greater than 0.8 will be labeled 0.

```
# implement custom thresholding logic
dfProbabilites = pd.DataFrame(logistic_regression_probabilities[:,0])
predictions_with_custom_threshold = dfProbabilites.applymap(lambda x: 0 if x >
0.8 else 1)
```

You can examine the predictions with this new threshold of 0.8 by printing the contents of predictions. Compare these predictions with the predictions made by the model with Scikit-learn's default cutoff threshold of 0.5.

```
print (predictions_with_custom_threshold.values.ravel())
[0 1 1 1 0 0 0 1 1 1 1 1 1 1 1 1 1 1 1 1 1 1 0 0 0 1 1 1 1 0 1 1 1 1
 1 1 1 1 1 0 1 1 1 1 1 0 1 1 0 1 1 0 1 1 1 0 1 0 0 1 0 1 1 1 0 1 1 1 1
 1 1 1 0 1 0 1 0 1 0 1 1 0 0 1 1 1 0 1 0 1 0 0 0 0 0 1 1 1 1 1 0 1 0
 1 1 1 1 1 1 0 1 0 0 0 1 0 1 1 1 0 1 0 0 1 1 0 1 0 0 1 1 1 1 1 1 1 1
 1 1 1 1 1 1 1 1 1 0 0 1 0 1 1 1 1 0 1 1 1 1 1 1 0 1 1 0 0 0 1 1 0
 1 1 1 0 1 1 1]
```

We will continue the rest of this chapter with the default cutoff threshold of 0.5. Let's now compute the value of a performance metric that we can use to evaluate the classifier. The metric being used in this chapter is accuracy and can be computed from the confusion matrix for the binary classifier. The following snippet computes the confusion matrix and the accuracy:

```
# compute confusion matrix and accuracy
#
# Note: the confusion matrix consists of 4 elements:
#            predicted no    predicted yes
# actual no      TN              FP
```

```
# actual yes       FN              TP
from sklearn.metrics import confusion_matrix
cm = confusion_matrix(df_diabetes_target_test, logistic_regression_predictions)
accuracy = (cm[0][0] + cm[1][1]) / df_diabetes_target_test.shape[0]

print ('accuracy: ' + str(accuracy))
accuracy: 0.796875
```

As you can see, the accuracy of this classifier is 79.68 percent on the predictions made on the test set. Recall that the test set consists of 25 percent of the 768 rows of the original dataset. The 25 percent of the samples that make up the test set were picked in a stratified manner based on the value of the target attribute Outcome. The main drawback with the idea of splitting the training dataset into a training and validation set is that it's possible for the samples in the training set to exhibit characteristics that may not be found in any of the samples in the test set. While shuffling the data can help mitigate this, the extent of the mitigation depends on various factors such as the size of the original dataset and the proportion of samples that exhibit a particular characteristic. The solution to avoid creating a model that is susceptible to character-istics only found in the training set is embodied in a technique called *k-fold cross-validation*. At a very high level, the k-fold cross-validation technique works as follows:

1. Choose a value of k.

2. Shuffle the data.

3. Split the data into k equal subsets.

4. For each value of k:

   ◆ Train a model that uses the kth subset as the test set and the samples of the k-1 subsets as the training set.

   ◆ Record the performance of the model when making predictions on the kth subset.

5. Compute the mean performance of the individual models to work out the overall performance.

If k=1, then the k-fold cross-validation approach becomes similar to the train/test split method discussed earlier in this chapter. If k = n, the number of samples in the training set, then in effect the test set contains only one sample, and each sample will get to be part of the test set during one of the iterations. This technique is also known as *leave-one-out cross-validation*. Many academic research papers use k = 5 or k=10; however, there is no hard and fast rule governing the value of k.

Scikit-learn provides two classes as part of the model_selection package that can be used to create the folds and enumerate through the folds. The classes are called KFold and StratifiedKFold, with the latter performing stratified sampling while preparing the k-folds. The constructor for the StratifiedKFold class is identical to the constructor of the KFold class and takes three parameters.

   ◆ n_splits: An integer that represents the number of folds required

   ◆ shuffle: An optional Boolean value that indicates whether the data should be shuffled before the folds are created

◆ random_state: An optional integer that is used to seed the random number generator used to shuffle the data

Both the StratifiedKFold and KFold classes provide two methods.

◆ get_n_splits(): Returns the number of folds

◆ split(): Gets the indices of the training and test set members for each fold

We will use the StratifiedKFold class in this chapter; you can find more information on the StratifiedKFold class at https://scikit-learn.org/stable/modules/generated/sklearn.model_selection.StratifiedKFold.html.

Type the following snippet into an empty notebook cell to use the StratifiedKFold class to split the contents of the diabetes dataset into 10 folds, train 10 logistic regression models, and compute the average across the 10 models.

```
# perform 10-fold cross-validation and
# compute the average accuracy across the 10 folds.

from sklearn.model_selection import StratifiedKFold
kf = StratifiedKFold(n_splits=10, shuffle=True)

fold_number = 1
fold_accuracy = []

for train_indices, test_indices in kf.split(df_diabetes_features,
y = df_diabetes_target['Outcome']):

    df_diabetes_features_train = df_diabetes_features.iloc[train_indices]
    df_diabetes_target_train = df_diabetes_target.iloc[train_indices]

    df_diabetes_features_test = df_diabetes_features.iloc[test_indices]
    df_diabetes_target_test = df_diabetes_target.iloc[test_indices]

    # train a logistic regression model
    model = LogisticRegression(penalty='l2',
                               fit_intercept=True,
                               solver='liblinear',
                               multi_class = 'ovr')

    model.fit(df_diabetes_features_train,
              df_diabetes_target_train.values.ravel())

    # get predictions (using default signoid threshold of 0.5)
    predictions = model.predict(df_diabetes_features_test)

    # compute fold accuracy, and append the value into the fold_accuracy array.
    cm = confusion_matrix(df_diabetes_target_test, predictions)
    accuracy = (cm[0][0] + cm[1][1]) / df_diabetes_target_test.shape[0]
    fold_accuracy.append(accuracy)
```

```
        print("Fold number:", fold_number)
        print ('Fold accuracy: ' + str(accuracy))

        fold_number = fold_number + 1

# compute average accuracy of the model across the folds.
print ('Average 10-fold accuracy: ' + str(np.mean(fold_accuracy)))
```

The results of executing the code should resemble the following, with the average 10-fold accuracy being close to 77.08 percent.

```
Fold number: 1
Fold accuracy: 0.7402597402597403
Fold number: 2
Fold accuracy: 0.8441558441558441
Fold number: 3
Fold accuracy: 0.7532467532467533
Fold number: 4
Fold accuracy: 0.7792207792207793
Fold number: 5
Fold accuracy: 0.7532467532467533
Fold number: 6
Fold accuracy: 0.7532467532467533
Fold number: 7
Fold accuracy: 0.7662337662337663
Fold number: 8
Fold accuracy: 0.7922077922077922
Fold number: 9
Fold accuracy: 0.7894736842105263
Fold number: 10
Fold accuracy: 0.7368421052631579
Average 10-fold accuracy: 0.7708133971291866
```

An average accuracy of 77.08 percent on the training dataset is not bad for a baseline model. In a real-world scenario you would now attempt to improve the accuracy of the model by trying different combinations of hyperparameters and features. Keep in mind that the dataset is very small, with just 768 rows. There isn't enough data to create a highly accurate model and, therefore, subsequent refinements to the model are not likely to improve the prediction accuracy significantly.

Using Core ML Tools to Convert the Scikit-learn Model to the Core ML Format

Core ML tools is an open source Python package provided by Apple that can be used to convert models made using libraries like Scikit-learn into the Core ML format. You can learn more about Core ML tools (at https://github.com/apple/coremltools).

Installing Core ML tools is a straightforward process. If you haven't already done so, launch a Terminal window on your Mac and execute the following statements:

```
$ conda activate IOS_ML_BOOK
$ pip install coremltools
```

With Core ML tools installed, type the following code into an empty notebook cell to export the model called `logistic_regression_model` that was trained earlier in this chapter, into the Core ML format.

```
# export the model to the Core ML format.
import coremltools

coreml_model = coremltools.converters.sklearn.convert(logistic_regression_model,
                                            ['Pregnancies', 'Glucose',
'BloodPressure', 'SkinThickness', 'Insulin', 'BMI',
'DiabetesPedigreeFunction', 'Age'],
                                                    'Outcome')
coreml_model.author = 'Abhishek Mishra'
coreml_model.short_description = 'Logistic regression model trained on the
Kaggle.com version of the PIMA Indians diabetes dataset. https://www.kaggle.com/
uciml/pima-indians-diabetes-database'

# feature descriptions
coreml_model.input_description['Pregnancies'] = 'Number of pregnancies.'
coreml_model.input_description['Glucose'] = 'Plasma glucose concentration after
2 hours in an oral glucose tolerance test.'
coreml_model.input_description['BloodPressure'] = 'Diastolic blood pressure.'
coreml_model.input_description['SkinThickness'] = 'Thickness of the triceps
skin folds.'
coreml_model.input_description['Insulin'] = '2-Hour serum insulin level.'
coreml_model.input_description['BMI'] = 'Body mass index.'
coreml_model.input_description['DiabetesPedigreeFunction'] = 'A function that
determines the risk of diabetes based on family history.'
coreml_model.input_description['Age'] = 'The age of the subject.'

# description of target variable
coreml_model.output_description['Outcome'] = 'A binary value, 1 indicates the
patient has type-2 diabetes.'
coreml_model.save('diabetes_logreg.mlmodel')
```

The `coremltools.converters` package provides a converter class called `sklearn` that can be used to convert Scikit-learn models into the Core ML format. The `sklearn` class exposes a method named `convert()` that performs the bulk of the work. The `convert()` method requires three arguments—the model to convert, an array of feature names, and the name of the target variable. The `convert()` method returns a Core ML–compatible Python object that can be saved to the Core ML file format using the `save()` method.

Prior to saving the model to a disk file, it is a good idea to set up some metadata about the model. This data will be visible in Xcode when you import the `.mlmodel` file. You can use the author and `short_description` attributes of the Core ML Python object to specify the name of the author and a general description of the type of model. You can also use the `input_descrip-tion` and `output_description` dictionaries to specify descriptions for each of the features and the target attribute, respectively. After executing the previous snippet, you should find a model file called `diabetes_logreg.mlmodel` in the same folder as the Jupyter Notebook file.

Creating the iOS Project

After exporting the Scikit-learn model to the Core ML format, launch Xcode on your Mac and create a new project using the Single View App template (see Figure 9.9).

FIGURE 9.9

Creating a new iOS project using the Single View App template

When prompted, use the following project options:

◆ **Product Name:** `DiabetesPredictor`

◆ **Organization Name:** *Provide a suitable value*

◆ **Organization Identifier:** *Provide a suitable value*

◆ **Language:** Swift

◆ **User Interface:** Storyboard

◆ **Use Core Data:** Unchecked

◆ **Include Unit Tests:** Unchecked

◆ **Include UI Tests:** Unchecked

Creating the User Interface

With the project created, set up the user interface of the project using these steps:

1. Open the `Main.storyboard` file and use the View ➤ Show Library menu item to access the object library window. Drag and drop eight label instances from the object library onto the default view controller scene.

2. Place these labels one below the other and use the Attributes Inspector to change the captions of these labels according to the list. You can access the Attributes Inspector using the View ➤ Inspectors ➤ Show Attributes Inspector menu item.

    ◆ Number of pregnancies:

    ◆ Glucose level:

    ◆ Blood pressure:

    ◆ Skin thickness:

    ◆ Insulin level:

    ◆ BMI:

    ◆ Diabetes pedigree function:

    ◆ Age:

3. Drag and drop eight text field instances from the object library onto the default view controller scene and arrange them one below the other, to the right of the labels you have created in the previous step. To make the text fields easily visible, use the Attributes Inspector to make the border style of each of the text fields to Line (see Figure 9.10).

FIGURE 9.10

Using the Attributes Inspector to change the border style of the text fields

4. Drag and drop a button from the object library onto the default view controller scene. Place the button at the bottom of the scene, below all the text fields and labels. Use the Attributes Inspector to change the caption of the button to *Check for Type 2 Diabetes*. Change the background color of the buttons to a shade of gray to make it easier to see on the storyboard scene.

5. Drag and drop a tap gesture recognizer object from the object library onto the default view controller.

6. Organize the elements on the default view controller scene to resemble Figure 9.11 and set up the appropriate storyboard constraints.

FIGURE 9.11
Application storyboard
with default view
controller scene

7. Use the Editor ➢ Assistant menu item to access the assistant editor and ensure the `ViewController.swift` file is open in the assistant editor. Create eight outlets in the view controller class per the following list:

   ◆ `pregnanciesTextField`

   ◆ `glucoseLevelTextField`

   ◆ `bloodPressureTextField`

   ◆ `skinThicknessTextField`

   ◆ `insulinLevelTextField`

   ◆ `bmiTextField`

   ◆ `pedigreeFunctionTextField`

   ◆ `ageTextField`

Associate these outlets with the corresponding text fields of the storyboard scene (see Figure 9.12).

8. Set up the view controller class to act as the delegate for each of the text fields in the storyboard scene. There are many ways to do this. One way is to Ctrl-click on a text field in the storyboard and connect the delegate outlet to the View Controller object (see Figure 9.13).

9. Create an action method in the `ViewController.swift` file called `onCheckForType2Diabetes(_ sender: Any)` and associate this method with the `Touch Up Inside` event of the button.

FIGURE 9.12
Using the Assistant
Editor to create outlets

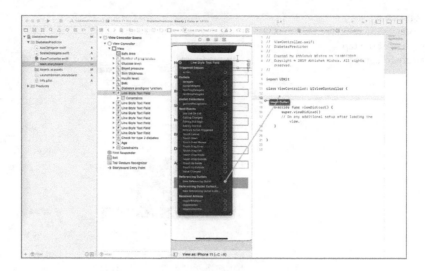

FIGURE 9.13
Setting up the text
field delegate

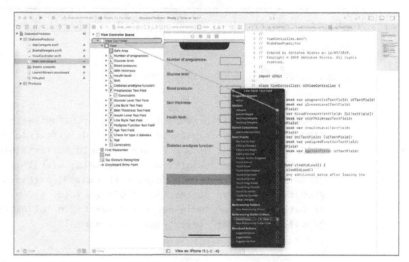

10. Create an action method in the `ViewController.swift` file called `onBackground-Tapped(_ sender: Any)` and associate this method with the `selector` property of the tap gesture recognizer (see Figure 9.14).

The code in your `ViewController.swift` file should now resemble Listing 9.1.

FIGURE 9.14
Setting up the selector property of the tap gesture recognizer

LISTING 9.1:   ViewController.swift File with Outlets and Actions

```swift
import UIKit

class ViewController: UIViewController {


    @IBOutlet weak var pregnanciesTextField: UITextField!
    @IBOutlet weak var glucoseLevelTextField: UITextField!
    @IBOutlet weak var bloodPressureTextField: UITextField!
    @IBOutlet weak var skinThicknessTextField: UITextField!
    @IBOutlet weak var insulinLevelTextField: UITextField!
    @IBOutlet weak var bmiTextField: UITextField!
    @IBOutlet weak var pedigreeFunctionTextField: UITextField!
    @IBOutlet weak var ageTextField: UITextField!


    override func viewDidLoad() {
        super.viewDidLoad()
        // Do any additional setup after loading the view.
    }

    @IBAction func onCheckForType2Diabetes(_ sender: Any) {
    }

    @IBAction func onBackgroundTapped(_ sender: Any) {
    }

}
```

11. Update the `viewDidLoad()` method in your `ViewController.swift` file to resemble the following snippet. This code ensures that the number pad is displayed as the default keyboard when the text field becomes the first responder.

```
override func viewDidLoad() {
    super.viewDidLoad()

    pregnanciesTextField.keyboardType = .decimalPad
    glucoseLevelTextField.keyboardType = .decimalPad
    bloodPressureTextField.keyboardType = .decimalPad
    skinThicknessTextField.keyboardType = .decimalPad
    insulinLevelTextField.keyboardType = .decimalPad
    bmiTextField.keyboardType = .decimalPad
    pedigreeFunctionTextField.keyboardType = .decimalPad
    ageTextField.keyboardType = .decimalPad
}
```

12. Update the implementation of the `onBackgroundTapped(_ sender: Any)` method to the following:

```
@IBAction func onBackgroundTapped(_ sender: Any) {
    pregnanciesTextField.resignFirstResponder()
    glucoseLevelTextField.resignFirstResponder()
    bloodPressureTextField.resignFirstResponder()
    skinThicknessTextField.resignFirstResponder()
    insulinLevelTextField.resignFirstResponder()
    bmiTextField.resignFirstResponder()
    pedigreeFunctionTextField.resignFirstResponder()
    ageTextField.resignFirstResponder()
}
```

This code uses dismisses the keyboard when a tap is detected in the background areas of the screen.

13. Implement the `UITextFieldDelegate` method `textFieldDidEndEditing(_, reason)` in a class extension as follows:

```
extension UIViewController : UITextFieldDelegate {
    public func textFieldDidEndEditing(_ textField: UITextField, reason:
UITextField.DidEndEditingReason) {
        textField.resignFirstResponder()
    }
}
```

The code in `ViewController.swift` should resemble Listing 9.2.

LISTING 9.2:   ViewController.swift File with Code to Dismiss the Keypad

```swift
import UIKit

class ViewController: UIViewController {

    @IBOutlet weak var pregnanciesTextField: UITextField!
    @IBOutlet weak var glucoseLevelTextField: UITextField!
    @IBOutlet weak var bloodPressureTextField: UITextField!
    @IBOutlet weak var skinThicknessTextField: UITextField!
    @IBOutlet weak var insulinLevelTextField: UITextField!
    @IBOutlet weak var bmiTextField: UITextField!
    @IBOutlet weak var pedigreeFunctionTextField: UITextField!
    @IBOutlet weak var ageTextField: UITextField!

    override func viewDidLoad() {
        super.viewDidLoad()

        pregnanciesTextField.keyboardType = .decimalPad
        glucoseLevelTextField.keyboardType = .decimalPad
        bloodPressureTextField.keyboardType = .decimalPad
        skinThicknessTextField.keyboardType = .decimalPad
        insulinLevelTextField.keyboardType = .decimalPad
        bmiTextField.keyboardType = .decimalPad
        pedigreeFunctionTextField.keyboardType = .decimalPad
        ageTextField.keyboardType = .decimalPad
    }

    @IBAction func onCheckForType2Diabetes(_ sender: Any) {


    }

    @IBAction func onBackgroundTapped(_ sender: Any) {
        pregnanciesTextField.resignFirstResponder()
        glucoseLevelTextField.resignFirstResponder()
        bloodPressureTextField.resignFirstResponder()
        skinThicknessTextField.resignFirstResponder()
        insulinLevelTextField.resignFirstResponder()
        bmiTextField.resignFirstResponder()
        pedigreeFunctionTextField.resignFirstResponder()
        ageTextField.resignFirstResponder()
    }

}
```

```
extension UIViewController : UITextFieldDelegate {
    public func textFieldDidEndEditing(_ textField: UITextField, reason:
      UITextField.DidEndEditingReason) {
        textField.resignFirstResponder()
    }
}
```

Using the Scikit-learn Model in the iOS Project

Now that we have built the app's user interface, it is time to use the logistic regression model that was created in an earlier section to predict the onset of diabetes. Perform the following steps:

1. Control-click the DiabetesPredictor folder group in the Project navigator window and select the Add Files to DiabetesPredictor menu item. Navigate to the diabetes_logreg.mlmodel file in your Jupyter Notebook folder and ensure that the Copy Items If Needed option is checked and the DiabetesPredictor target is selected in the dialog box (see Figure 9.15).

FIGURE 9.15
Import settings for the diabetes_logreg .mlmodel file

2. Select the diabetes_logreg.mlmodel file in the Project navigator to get an overview of the model (see Figure 9.16).

As you can see from the model overview screen, the size of the model is just 1KB, and the inputs to the model are eight double-precision numbers, with the same names that you have specified while exporting the model using Core ML tools.

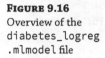

FIGURE 9.16
Overview of the
diabetes_logreg
.mlmodel file

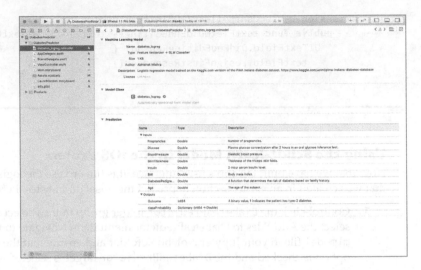

3. Access the autogenerated Swift class from the Model Class section of the model overview page (see Figure 9.17).

FIGURE 9.17
Accessing the Swift
interface to the Core ML
model file

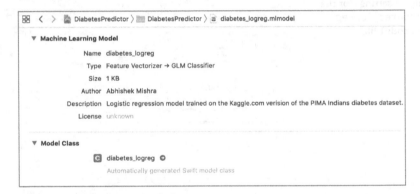

Locate the definition of a class call `diabetes_logregInput` in the autogenerated `diabetes_logreg.swift` file. This class represents the input for the Core ML model. The initializer for this class is listed next. Your eight individual input variables (which you will collect from the text fields) will need to be wrapped into a `diabetes_logregInput` instance before being passed along as the input to the Core ML model.

```
init(Pregnancies: Double, Glucose: Double, BloodPressure: Double,
SkinThickness: Double, Insulin: Double, BMI: Double, DiabetesPedigreeFunction:
Double, Age: Double) {
        self.Pregnancies = Pregnancies
        self.Glucose = Glucose
        self.BloodPressure = BloodPressure
        self.SkinThickness = SkinThickness
```

```
        self.Insulin = Insulin
        self.BMI = BMI
        self.DiabetesPedigreeFunction = DiabetesPedigreeFunction
        self.Age = Age
    }
```

4. Select the `ViewController.swift` file in the Project navigator and add the following `import` statement to the top of the file to import the Core ML framework.

```
import CoreML
```

5. Modify the onCheckForType2Diabetes(_ sender:Any) method in the `ViewController.swift` file to resemble the following:

```
@IBAction func onCheckForType2Diabetes(_ sender: Any) {
    // read data from text fields

    guard let pregnancyCount = Double(pregnanciesTextField.text ?? "0.0"),
        let glucoseLevel = Double(glucoseLevelTextField.text ?? "0.0"),
        let bloodPressure = Double(bloodPressureTextField.text ?? "0.0"),
        let skinThickness = Double(skinThicknessTextField.text ?? "0.0"),
        let insulinLevel = Double(insulinLevelTextField.text ?? "0.0"),
        let bmi = Double(bmiTextField.text ?? "0.0"),
        let pedigreeFunction = Double(pedigreeFunctionTextField.text ?? "0.0"),
        let age = Double(ageTextField.text ?? "0.0") else {

            let alertController = UIAlertController(title: "Error",
                message: "One or more fields contain non-numeric data.",
                preferredStyle: .alert)

            alertController.addAction(UIAlertAction(title: "Ok",
                                        style: .cancel, handler: nil))
            self.present(alertController, animated: true, completion: nil)
            return

    }

    let input = diabetes_logregInput(Pregnancies: pregnancyCount,
                                    Glucose: glucoseLevel,
                                    BloodPressure: bloodPressure,
                                    SkinThickness: skinThickness,
                                    Insulin: insulinLevel,
                                    BMI: bmi,
                           DiabetesPedigreeFunction: pedigreeFunction,
                                    Age: age)

    let model = diabetes_logreg()
```

```swift
        guard let result = try? model.prediction(input: input) else {

            let alertController = UIAlertController(title: "Core ML Error",
                                    message: "An unexpected error occurred.",
                                    preferredStyle: .alert)

            alertController.addAction(UIAlertAction(title: "Ok",
                                                style: .cancel, handler: nil))
            self.present(alertController, animated: true, completion: nil)
            return
        }

        if result.Outcome == 1 {
            let alertController = UIAlertController(title: "Prediction result",
                                    message: "Type 2 diabetes detected.",
                                    preferredStyle: .alert)

            alertController.addAction(UIAlertAction(title: "Ok",
                                                style: .cancel, handler: nil))
            self.present(alertController, animated: true, completion: nil)
        } else {
            let alertController = UIAlertController(title: "Prediction result",
                                    message: "Type 2 diabetes not detected.",
                                    preferredStyle: .alert)

            alertController.addAction(UIAlertAction(title: "Ok",
                                                style: .cancel, handler: nil))
            self.present(alertController, animated: true, completion: nil)
        }
    }
```

This method is called when the Check For Diabetes button is tapped. It reads all the values from the text fields and attempts to convert the values to double-precision numbers. If the conversion fails, then an error message is displayed to the user.

```swift
        guard let pregnancyCount = Double(pregnanciesTextField.text ?? "0.0"),
            let glucoseLevel = Double(glucoseLevelTextField.text ?? "0.0"),
            let bloodPressure = Double(bloodPressureTextField.text ?? "0.0"),
            let skinThickness = Double(skinThicknessTextField.text ?? "0.0"),
            let insulinLevel = Double(insulinLevelTextField.text ?? "0.0"),
            let bmi = Double(bmiTextField.text ?? "0.0"),
            let pedigreeFunction = Double(pedigreeFunctionTextField.text ?? "0.0"),
            let age = Double(ageTextField.text ?? "0.0") else {

            let alertController = UIAlertController(title: "Error",
```

```
            message: "One or more fields contain non-numeric data.",
            preferredStyle: .alert)

    alertController.addAction(UIAlertAction(title: "Ok",
                                style: .cancel, handler: nil))
    self.present(alertController, animated: true, completion: nil)
    return

}
```

If the conversion is successful, the code creates an instance of a `diabetes_logregInput` from the values typed by the user.

```
let input = diabetes_logregInput(Pregnancies: pregnancyCount,
                            Glucose: glucoseLevel,
                            BloodPressure: bloodPressure,
                            SkinThickness: skinThickness,
                            Insulin: insulinLevel,
                            BMI: bmi,
                DiabetesPedigreeFunction: pedigreeFunction,
                            Age: age)
```

An instance of the Core ML model wrapper class `diabetes_logreg` is created next, and the `prediction()` method is called on the instance. The `prediction` method can throw an exception. The code that is presented in this chapter displays a generic error to the user if an exception is detected.

```
let model = diabetes_logreg()

guard let result = try? model.prediction(input: input) else {

    let alertController = UIAlertController(title: "Core ML Error",
                        message: "An unexpected error occurred.",
                        preferredStyle: .alert)

    alertController.addAction(UIAlertAction(title: "Ok",
                                        style: .cancel, handler: nil))
    self.present(alertController, animated: true, completion: nil)
    return
}
```

If no exceptions occurred, the result of the prediction is an object of type `diabetes_logregOutput`, which is also declared in the autogenerated Core ML wrapper class. The `diabetes_logregOutput` class contains a member variable called `Outcome`, which corresponds to the target variable of the machine learning model.

The complete code in the `ViewController.swift` file is presented in Listing 9.3.

LISTING 9.3:   Completed ViewController.swift File

```swift
import UIKit
import CoreML

class ViewController: UIViewController {

    @IBOutlet weak var pregnanciesTextField: UITextField!
    @IBOutlet weak var glucoseLevelTextField: UITextField!
    @IBOutlet weak var bloodPressureTextField: UITextField!
    @IBOutlet weak var skinThicknessTextField: UITextField!
    @IBOutlet weak var insulinLevelTextField: UITextField!
    @IBOutlet weak var bmiTextField: UITextField!
    @IBOutlet weak var pedigreeFunctionTextField: UITextField!
    @IBOutlet weak var ageTextField: UITextField!

    override func viewDidLoad() {
        super.viewDidLoad()

        pregnanciesTextField.keyboardType = .decimalPad
        glucoseLevelTextField.keyboardType = .decimalPad
        bloodPressureTextField.keyboardType = .decimalPad
        skinThicknessTextField.keyboardType = .decimalPad
        insulinLevelTextField.keyboardType = .decimalPad
        bmiTextField.keyboardType = .decimalPad
        pedigreeFunctionTextField.keyboardType = .decimalPad
        ageTextField.keyboardType = .decimalPad
    }

    @IBAction func onCheckForType2Diabetes(_ sender: Any) {
        // read data from text fields

        guard let pregnancyCount = Double(pregnanciesTextField.text ?? "0.0"),
            let glucoseLevel = Double(glucoseLevelTextField.text ?? "0.0"),
            let bloodPressure = Double(bloodPressureTextField.text ?? "0.0"),
            let skinThickness = Double(skinThicknessTextField.text ?? "0.0"),
            let insulinLevel = Double(insulinLevelTextField.text ?? "0.0"),
            let bmi = Double(bmiTextField.text ?? "0.0"),
            let pedigreeFunction = Double(pedigreeFunctionTextField.text ??
    "0.0"),
            let age = Double(ageTextField.text ?? "0.0") else {
```

```swift
            let alertController = UIAlertController(title: "Error",
                                      message: "One or more fields contain
non-numeric data.",
                                      preferredStyle: .alert)

            alertController.addAction(UIAlertAction(title: "Ok", style:
.cancel, handler: nil))
            self.present(alertController, animated: true, completion: nil)
            return

        }

    let input = diabetes_logregInput(Pregnancies: pregnancyCount,
                                 Glucose: glucoseLevel,
                                 BloodPressure: bloodPressure,
                                 SkinThickness: skinThickness,
                                 Insulin: insulinLevel,
                                 BMI: bmi,
                                 DiabetesPedigreeFunction:
pedigreeFunction,
                                 Age: age)

    let model = diabetes_logreg()

    guard let result = try? model.prediction(input: input) else {

        let alertController = UIAlertController(title: "Core ML Error",
                                 message: "An unexpected error occurred.",
                                 preferredStyle: .alert)

        alertController.addAction(UIAlertAction(title: "Ok", style:
.cancel, handler: nil))
        self.present(alertController, animated: true, completion: nil)
        return
    }

    if result.Outcome == 1 {
        let alertController = UIAlertController(title: "Prediction result",
                                 message: "Type 2 diabetes detected.",
                                 preferredStyle: .alert)

        alertController.addAction(UIAlertAction(title: "Ok", style:
.cancel, handler: nil))
```

```
                self.present(alertController, animated: true, completion: nil)
            } else {
                let alertController = UIAlertController(title: "Prediction result",
                                    message: "Type 2 diabetes not detected.",
                                    preferredStyle: .alert)

                alertController.addAction(UIAlertAction(title: "Ok", style:
        .cancel, handler: nil))
                self.present(alertController, animated: true, completion: nil)
            }
        }

        @IBAction func onBackgroundTapped(_ sender: Any) {
            pregnanciesTextField.resignFirstResponder()
            glucoseLevelTextField.resignFirstResponder()
            bloodPressureTextField.resignFirstResponder()
            skinThicknessTextField.resignFirstResponder()
            insulinLevelTextField.resignFirstResponder()
            bmiTextField.resignFirstResponder()
            pedigreeFunctionTextField.resignFirstResponder()
            ageTextField.resignFirstResponder()
        }

    }

    extension UIViewController : UITextFieldDelegate {
        public func textFieldDidEndEditing(_ textField: UITextField, reason:
          UITextField.DidEndEditingReason) {
            textField.resignFirstResponder()
        }
    }
```

Testing the App

Save your project and run the app on the iOS simulator. Specify values for the eight feature variables and then tap on the background area of the screen to dismiss the keyboard. Tap the Check for Type 2 Diabetes button and observe the results. Figure 9.18 depicts the results of running the app on the simulator.

NOTE   You can download the code files for this chapter from wrox.com or from GitHub using the following URL:

https://github.com/asmtechnology/iosmlbook-chapter9.git

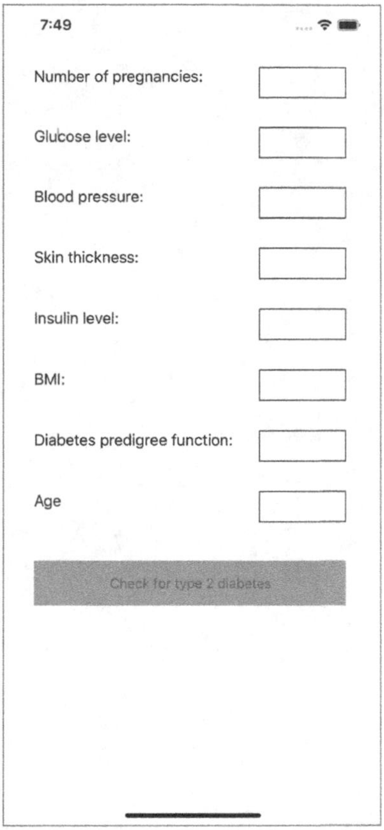

FIGURE 9.18
Results of running the
app on the iOS simulator

Summary

- In this chapter, a logistic regression model to predict the onset of diabetes was trained using the Pima Indian diabetes dataset.

- The dataset has eight numeric features and one binary target variable.

- Some of the features appeared to have outliers.

- A baseline model was created without any feature engineering or hyperparameter optimization.

- Because of the class-wise imbalance in the target variable, we used stratified sampling to split the dataset into separate training and test sets.

- You used k-fold cross-validation to compute the average accuracy of the model across the entire dataset.

- Core ML Tools is a Python library that can be used to export Scikit-learn models into the Core ML format.

Chapter 10

Building a Deep Convolutional Neural Network with Keras

WHAT'S IN THIS CHAPTER

◆ Introducing the Inception family of networks

◆ Introducing Keras

◆ Creating an Inception-v4 network with the Keras functional API

◆ Training an Inception-v4 network

◆ Loading pre-trained weights

◆ Using the Inceptionv4 network in an iOS app

In Chapter 5, you learned about the basics of convolutional neural networks (CNNs) and downloaded a pre-trained convolutional neural network model from Apple. In this chapter, you will create a deep convolutional neural network from scratch using the Keras functional API, train this network on a small publicly available dataset, and then use the trained model in an iOS app.

The dataset used to train this model is the Dogs vs. Cats dataset, available on Kaggle.com at https://www.kaggle.com/c/dogs-vs-cats/data. The dataset is provided by Kaggle as part of a competition to create a model that can detect dogs and cats in images. The dataset consists of two folders.

◆ Train: Contains 12,500 images; 6,250 are images of dogs, and the rest are images of cats. The filenames make it clear whether the image contains a dog or a cat.

◆ Test: Contains an additional 12,500 unlabeled images, the objective of the completion is to accurately classify the images as containing either dogs or cats. The dataset creators have ensured that there are no images that contain both dogs and cats.

Since the aim of this chapter is to teach you how to build a deep learning model from scratch with Keras, and not take part in the competition, you will use only the labeled images in the train folder. A copy of this folder has been provided with the downloads that accompany this lesson.

This dataset was chosen because of its relatively small size (less than 1 GB). You can, if you want, attempt to train the model that is built in this chapter on larger datasets such as the ImageNet datasets.

NOTE You can download the code files for this chapter from `wrox.com` or from GitHub using the following URL:

`https://github.com/asmtechnology/iosmlbook-chapter10.git`

The resources for this chapter also include the model weights and the trained model file. These files are too large to be hosted on GitHub, and you can download them from `wrox.com`.

Introduction to the Inception Family of Deep Convolutional Neural Networks

There are a number of popular architectures for convolutional neural networks that have been proposed by researchers after AlexNet's success in the 2012 ImageNet Large Scale Visual Recognition Challenge (ILSVRC). This chapter focuses on the Inception family of networks and implements Inception-v4 from scratch using Keras. The first version of the Inception deep learning network was proposed in 2014 by Christian Szegedy et al. in the paper titled "Going Deeper with Convolutions." You can read the original paper at `https://arxiv.org/pdf/1409.4842v1.pdf`.

The development of the Inception network represented an important milestone in deep learning. Prior to this network, deep networks were primarily focused on stacking more and more convolutional layers on top of each other. The Inception network, on the other hand, used a number of techniques to optimize the computation cost as well as increase the overall performance of convolutional neural networks. The Inception family of networks includes the original Inception network as well as four additional variants.

- Inception-v1
- Inception-v2 and Inception-v3
- Inception-v4 and Inception-ResNet

GoogLeNet (aka Inception-v1)

The central premise of the first version of the Inception network architecture was that the same object can appear at vastly different scales in different images and, therefore, no single filter size will perform well across all images. Figure 10.1 shows a 3×3 convolution operation.

A convolution operation, by design, processes a small region of the image, and while tiling this operation horizontally and vertically can result in useful features, some large-scale features will be missed. This is because, fundamentally, the size of a convolution filter (3×3, 5×5, or 7×7) places an upper limit on the area of the image the filter can process. The solution proposed by the authors of the Inception-v1 network was to include filters of different sizes at the same level of the network and concatenate their results. The authors were also conscious of the computational cost of stacked convolutional operations and the fact that deeper networks were prone to overfitting. To remediate these concerns, they chose to design their networks wider instead of deeper (see Figure 10.2).

FIGURE 10.1

A 3×3 convolution operation tiled across a larger image

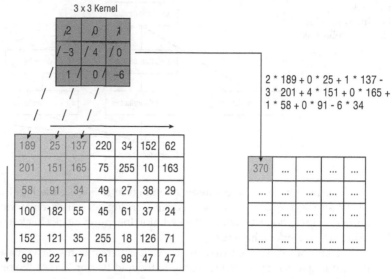

FIGURE 10.2

An Inception block

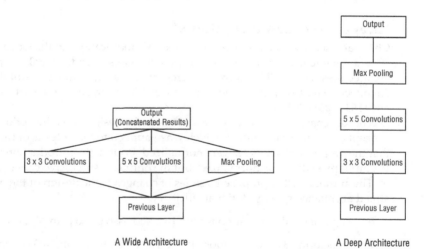

The authors also decided to use 1×1 convolution operations to reduce the number of inputs before the parallel convolutional operations. A 1×1 convolution operation is a convolution operation that uses a single-element kernel. 1×1 convolution operations were introduced by Min Lin et al. in a paper titled "Network in Network" and have several uses in deep learning, including the ability to manage the computational complexity of deep learning networks. A copy of the paper can be found at https://arxiv.org/pdf/1312.4400.pdf. Figure 10.3 shows the result of incorporating 1×1 convolutions with a wider network design.

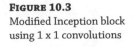

FIGURE 10.3
Modified Inception block
using 1 x 1 convolutions

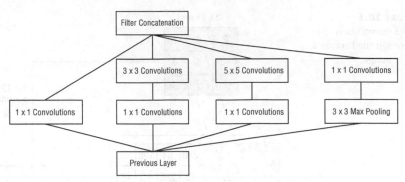

The arrangement of layers depicted in Figure 10.3 was called an Inception block, and Christian Szegedy et al. proposed a deep learning network architecture called *GoogLeNet* (also known as Inception-v1), which stacked nine Inception blocks back to back. Figure 10.4 shows the resulting network architecture.

The authors also added two auxiliary classifiers into the network architecture to ensure that the training loss propagated correctly to the middle portions of the network. During training, the objective was to minimize a loss function that consisted of the primary and auxiliary outputs. The auxiliary outputs were not used when the model was used to make predictions.

Inception-v2 and Inception-v3

Christian Szegedy et al. proposed a number of modifications to the GoogLeNet architecture in 2015, aiming to make it computationally efficient to stack additional Inception blocks in deeper architectures. The modifications were presented in a paper titled "Rethinking the Inception Architecture for Computer Vision," a copy of which can be found at https://arxiv.org/pdf/1512.00567v3.pdf.

The key change proposed by the authors in the design of the Inception-v2 network was the concept of batch normalization, which when applied to the outputs of Inception blocks ensured that the outputs of the blocks were normalized. Prior to the introduction of batch normalization, the input pixel data was normalized, but the output of successive convolution layers was not.

The authors further proposed a series of changes to the design of the original Inception block, aimed at enhancing computational efficiency.

◆ Replacing 5×5 convolutions with two successive 3×3 convolutions.

◆ Refactoring 3×3 convolutions into a 1×3 convolution and a 3×1 convolution.

◆ The refactored convolutional operations were designed to be wider instead of deeper.

These changes resulted in the creation of three distinct Inception blocks, which are depicted in Figure 10.5.

A new deep learning network architecture was proposed using the suggested modifications and was called Inception-v3. This new architecture also used only one auxiliary classifier instead of two.

FIGURE 10.4
GoogLeNet
(Inception-v1)
architecture

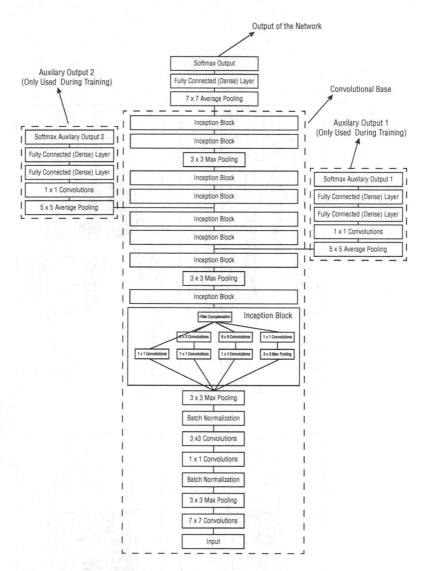

Inception-v4 and Inception-ResNet

In 2016, the authors of the Inception network (Christian Szegedy et al.) proposed a new variant of their network architecture in a paper titled "Inception-v4, Inception-ResNet, and the Impact of Residual Connections on Learning." A copy of the paper is located at https://arxiv.org/pdf/1602.07261.pdf.

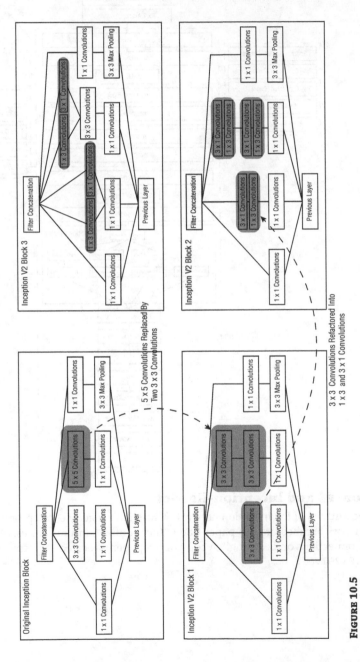

FIGURE 10.5
Inception-v3 blocks

The Inception V4 network architecture they proposed had both a more simplified architecture and more Inception blocks than its predecessor. In addition, the recent work by scientists at Microsoft had proven that the use of residual connections in CNNs significantly improved the performance of older network architectures. It stood to reason, therefore, that the use of similar residual connections in an Inception network could lead to a combination of reduced training time and better classification accuracy. To that end, the authors proposed two additional versions of their Inception architecture in the same paper. These residual variants were called Inception-ResNet and Inception-ResNet-v2 and used residual connections in the filter concatenation stage.

The Inception-v4 and Inception-ResNet architectures are popular deep learning architectures today and are usually part of an ensemble of networks that include different architectures. Figure 10.6 shows the architecture of the Inception-v4 network.

FIGURE 10.6
Inception-v4 network architecture

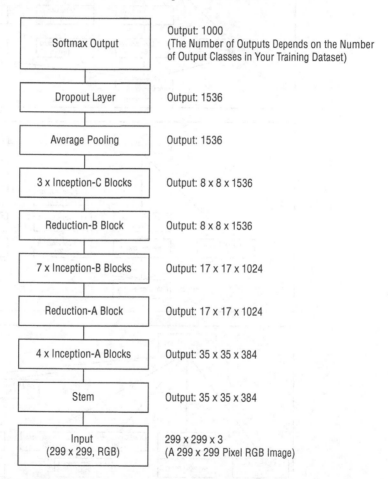

The network architecture proposed by Christian Szegedy et al. in their paper required input images to be 299×299 pixel, RGB. The output of the network was the class-wise classification probabilities of 1,000 object classes. The reason for the 1,000-class output is that the network was designed for the ImageNet ILSVRC competition, where the training data consists of images from 1,000 classes. It is important to note that you are free to choose a different input size and number of output classes, depending on the problem you are trying to apply the network to. Later in this chapter, we will create an Inception-v4 network from scratch, with just two output classes.

Figure 10.7 shows the structure of the three Inception blocks.

FIGURE 10.7
Inception-A,
Inception-B,
Inception-C blocks

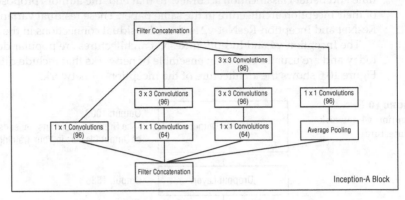

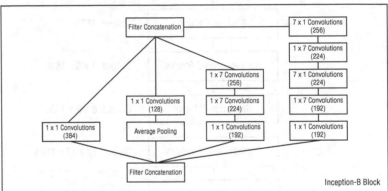

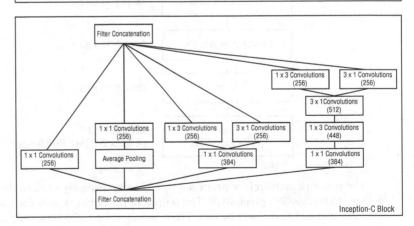

Figure 10.8 shows the structure of the stem. The stem of the network is the portion of the network before the first Inception block.

FIGURE 10.8
Structure of the stem of the Inception-v4 network

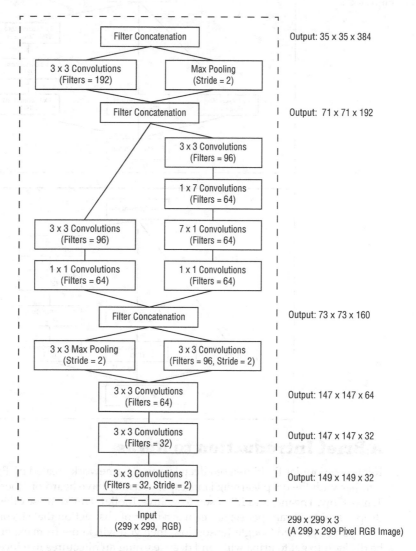

The Inception-v4 architecture also introduces the concept of reduction blocks. The purpose of these blocks is to reduce the computational complexity of the network. There are two reduction blocks in the network, labeled Reduction-A and Reduction-B, respectively. Figure 10.9 shows the architecture of these reduction blocks.

This concludes the architecture of the Inception-v4 network. In the next section, you will learn about the Keras functional API and implement the Inception-v4 network from scratch.

FIGURE 10.9
Reduction-A and
Reduction-B blocks

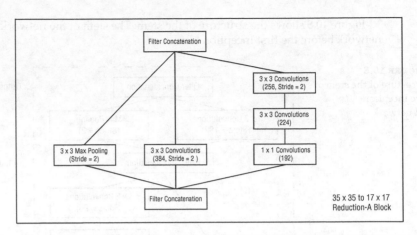

35 x 35 to 17 x 17
Reduction-A Block

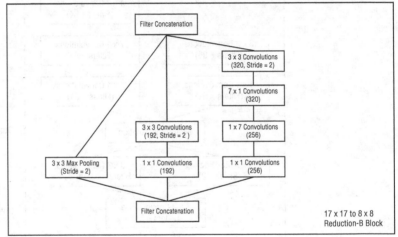

17 x 17 to 8 x 8
Reduction-B Block

A Brief Introduction to Keras

Keras is a popular Python-based deep learning framework created by François Chollet. If you are familiar with the deep learning landscape, you may have heard of other libraries like Google TensorFlow, Theano, and Microsoft Cognitive Toolkit. Unlike these other libraries, Keras is not a deep-learning library per se; rather, it is a layer of abstraction that sits on top of these libraries.

If you have used Google TensorFlow, then you will know from experience that its syntax can be difficult to get to grips with, and deep learning architectures like Inception-v4 can be quite difficult to represent in the Google TensorFlow syntax. Keras was created to provide a simplified user-friendly API to Google TensorFlow and today provides a number of advantages such as the following:

◆ Support for alternate deep learning backend frameworks like Google TensorFlow, Microsoft Cognitive Toolkit (CNTK), and Theano

◆ The ability to use the same code on a CPU- or a GPU-based machine

◆ Implementations of popular convolutional neural network layers

◆ A model zoo with implementations of ready-to-use deep learning models

◆ The ability to define any kind of neural network architecture

It is important to note that Keras is used in conjunction with a lower-level tensor processing library, and hence you need to install both Keras and the lower-level library. Out of the box, Keras uses Google TensorFlow; however, it can be configured to use other backend libraries (see Figure 10.10).

FIGURE 10.10
Keras' modular architecture

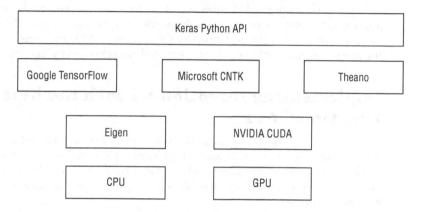

If you are interested in learning more about the back-end libraries, use the following links:

◆ Google TensorFlow: `https://www.tensorflow.org`

◆ Microsoft Cognitive Toolkit: `https://github.com/microsoft/CNTK`

◆ Theano: `http://deeplearning.net/software/theano/`

The backend tensor libraries listed here in turn use lower-level libraries to interact with the CPU/GPU. Eigen is a popular library that is used by Google TensorFlow to perform matrix/tensor operations on the CPU. NVIDIA's CUDA and CUDA Deep Neural Network Library (cuDNN) are commonly used to perform matrix/tensor operations on NVIDIA GPUs. You do not need to know anything about these lower-level libraries in order to use Keras.

When building models with Keras, the general workflow involves the following steps:

1. Prepare your training, test, and validation datasets.

2. Write Python code to define a deep learning model architecture. This can be achieved by either writing code to define the model from scratch or using one of the pre-built models that come with Keras.

3. Compile the model.

4. Train the model.

Keras provides two model-building APIs, the sequential API and the functional API. The sequential API is somewhat easier to understand but is only capable of creating models whose architectures consist of a linear stack of layers. If the model architecture consists of branches, then you need to use the functional API.

The data a neural network operates on is an n-dimensional matrix called a *tensor*. For example, a 2D color image can be represented by a 3D tensor (height, width, and number of channels). The input image tensor is transformed by each layer as it flows through the network until it reaches the final (output) layer of the network. These transformations can be to both the content and the shape of the tensor.

The Keras functional API allows you to represent each layer of the network as a function and apply this function to the output of the previous layer. The functional API is capable of creating any architecture that can be defined by the sequential API, and more. You can learn more about the Keras functional API at https://keras.io/getting-started/functional-api-guide/.

Implementing Inception-v4 with the Keras Functional API

In the previous sections of this chapter, you learned about the architecture of the Inception-v4 network and the basics of the Keras deep-learning library. In this section, you will implement the Inception-v4 network in Python with the Keras functional API. To get started, launch the macOS Terminal application and type the following command to start up a new Jupyter Notebook instance.

```
$ cd <your directory>
$ jupyter notebookf
```

When Jupyter Notebook has finished loading in your web browser, create a new notebook file using the IOS_ML_BOOK kernel (see Figure 10.11) and name the file Inceptionv4.ipnyb.

FIGURE 10.11
Creating a new notebook file

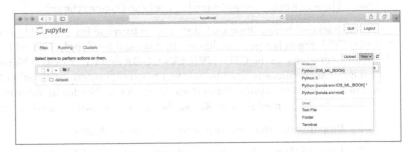

Execute the following code in an empty notebook cell to load all the Keras modules:

```
from keras.layers.convolutional import MaxPooling2D, Conv2D, AveragePooling2D
from keras.layers import Input, Dropout, Dense, Flatten, Activation
from keras.layers.normalization import BatchNormalization
from keras.layers.merge import concatenate
from keras import regularizers
from keras import initializers
```

```
from keras.models import Model
from keras.optimizers import Adam
from keras import backend as K
```

Execute the following code in an empty notebook cell to determine the current image data format:

```
# Check the data ordering format. If you are using Tensorflow as
# the backend, this should be channels_last.
print (K.image_data_format())
```

channels_last

The image data format determines the structure of the input image data tensors into the network. There are two possible values.

◆ channels_last: This means the input data is to be supplied as a tuple of three values (number of rows, number of columns, and number of channels). In the case of a 300×300 RGB image, this would be (300, 300, 3). This is the format used by the TensorFlow and CNTK backends and is what Keras is configured to use out of the box.

◆ channels_first: This means that the input data is to be supplied as a tuple of three values (number of channels, number of rows, and number of columns). In the case of a 300×300 RGB image, this would be (3, 300, 300). This is the format used by Theano, which is another popular deep learning library that can be used as the backend with Keras.

The code in this section assumes that you are using the channels_last ordering format. If the image data format is reported as channels_first, then you can use the following snippet to force the channel ordering format:

```
# if the data ordering format is not channels_last, you
# can use this snippet to force the ordering format
K.set_image_data_format('channels_last')
print (K.image_data_format())
```

Type the following code in an empty notebook cell to create a helper function called conv2d_batchnorm_relu. This function is used to create a 2D convolutional layer, apply batch normalization to the output of the convolutional layer, and then apply a rectified linear unit (RELU) activation function to the normalized output.

```
# create a 2d convolutional layer with 'num_kernels' convolutional kernels,
# each  with dimensions (height = kernel_rows x width = kernel_cols)
#
# add a batch normalization layer to the output of the 2d convolutional layer.
#
# add a Relu activation later to the output of the batch normalization layer.
#
# based on IncpetionV3 keras implementation by François Chollet at
# https://github.com/keras-team/keras-applications
def conv2d_batchnorm_relu(input,
                num_kernels,
```

```
                           kernel_rows, kernel_cols,
                           padding='same',
                           strides=(1, 1)):

    x = Conv2D(num_kernels,
               (kernel_rows, kernel_cols),
               strides=strides,
               padding=padding,
               use_bias=False,
               kernel_regularizer =
               regularizers.l2(L2_REGULARIZATION_AMOUNT),
               kernel_initializer =
               initializers.glorot_normal(seed=42))(input)

    x = BatchNormalization()(x)

    output = Activation('relu')(x)

    return output
```

The input parameter represents the previous layer of the network (or the input image tensor). The num_kernels parameter represents the number of convolutional kernels that should be used. Convolutional kernels are sometimes also referred to as *filters*. It is important to note that most convolutional neural networks use several kernels at each convolutional layer, and the objective of training the network is to determine the numbers in these kernels that will yield the best overall result.

The kernel_rows and kernel_cols parameters control the height and width of the kernels (such as 3×3, 1×3, 1×7, etc.). The padding parameter determines whether any padding should be applied to the input data before performing the convolutional operation. The default value implies that the input data will be padded with rows and columns that contain zeros to ensure that the height and width of the results of the convolution operation are the same as the input dimensions (see Figure 10.12).

The conv2d_batchnorm_relu function first calls the Conv2D() Keras function to create the convolutional layer, passing in the num_kernels, kernel_rows, kernel_cols, padding, and strides arguments without modifications. In addition to these arguments, an l2 regularizer object is used to apply L2 regularization, and the glorot_normal initializer is used. A regularizer ensures that the weights of the convolutional filters do not get too large during training, and thus it prevents overfitting. An initializer object is used to provide the initial default values of the convolutional kernels before training. You can learn more about the Conv2D() function at https://keras.io/layers/convolutional/. You can learn more about regularizers at https://keras.io/regularizers/ and more about initializers at https://keras.io/initializers/.

The output of the 2D convolutional layer is passed into the Keras BatchNormalization() function that adds a batch normalization layer on top of the convolutional layer. The batch normalization layer ensures that the outputs of the convolutional operations are normalized at the end of each training batch to have a mean close to 0 and a standard deviation close to 1. The Keras BatchNormalization() function accepts several arguments, all of which have default values. You can learn more about the BatchNormialization() function at https://keras.io/layers/normalization/.

FIGURE 10.12
Padding options for
convolutional layers

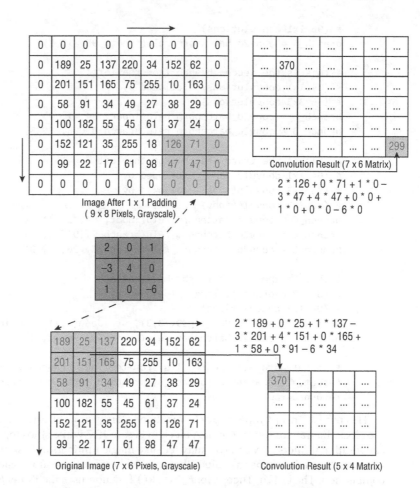

Image After 1 x 1 Padding
(9 x 8 Pixels, Grayscale)

Convolution Result (7 x 6 Matrix)

$2 * 126 + 0 * 71 + 1 * 0 -$
$3 * 47 + 4 * 47 + 0 * 0 +$
$1 * 0 + 0 * 0 - 6 * 0$

$2 * 189 + 0 * 25 + 1 * 137 -$
$3 * 201 + 4 * 151 + 0 * 165 +$
$1 * 58 + 0 * 91 - 6 * 34$

Original Image (7 x 6 Pixels, Grayscale)

Convolution Result (5 x 4 Matrix)

The output of the batch normalization layer is passed into a Keras `Activation()` function, which adds an activation layer on top of the batch normalization layer. The input to the `Activation()` function is the string `relu`, which ensures that Keras will use the rectified linear unit activation function. You can learn more about Keras' activation layers at `https://keras.io/activations/`.

Now that you have a function that can create a 2D convolutional layer with batch normalization and an activation function, you can implement the three Inception-v4 blocks. These blocks are called InceptionA, InceptionB, and InceptionC blocks in the paper by Szegedy et al. Type the following code in an empty notebook cell to define a function called `build_InceptionA_block()` that uses the `conv2d_batchnorm_relu` function defined earlier to implement the InceptionA block:

```
def build_InceptionA_block(input):

    # refer to Figure 10.7 for a visual representation of this block.

    # this is the first branch from the left
```

```
# (96 1x1 convolutions)
branch_A = conv2d_batchnorm_relu(input, 96, 1, 1)

# this is the second branch from the left
# (64 1x1 convolutions), followed by
# (96 3x3 convolutions)
branch_B = conv2d_batchnorm_relu(input, 64, 1, 1)
branch_B = conv2d_batchnorm_relu(branch_B, 96, 3, 3)

# this is the third branch from the left
# (64 1x1 convolutions), followed by
# (96 3x3 convolutions), followed by
# (96 3x3 convolutions)
branch_C = conv2d_batchnorm_relu(input, 64, 1, 1)
branch_C = conv2d_batchnorm_relu(branch_C, 96, 3, 3)
branch_C = conv2d_batchnorm_relu(branch_C, 96, 3, 3)

# this is the fourth (right-most) branch
# (3 x 3 average pooling), followed by
# (96 1x1 convolutions)
branch_D = AveragePooling2D((3,3), strides=(1,1), padding='same')(input)
branch_D = conv2d_batchnorm_relu(branch_D, 96, 1, 1)

# concatenate all the results from the four branches.
output = concatenate([branch_A, branch_B, branch_C, branch_D], axis=-1)
return output
```

This `build_InceptionA_block()` function is fairly straightforward. It may help if you look at the block diagram of the InceptionA block in Figure 10.7 while studying this code. The number of convolutional filters at each layer may feel like magic numbers at first, but they were proposed in Christian Szegedy's paper as values that worked best for their submission to the ILSVRC competition. The `build_InceptionA_block()` function uses the Keras `AveragePooling2D()` function to add a layer that implements 3x3 average pooling on its inputs, and the Keras `concatenate()` function to add a layer that concatenates the outputs of the four input branches. You can learn more about the `AveragePooling2D()` function at https://keras.io/layers/pooling/. You can learn more about the `concatenate()` function at https://keras.io/layers/merge/.

Type the following code in a new notebook cell to define a function called `build_InceptionB_block()` that will create an InceptionB block:

```
def build_InceptionB_block(input):

    # refer to Figure 10.7 for a visual representation of this block.

    # this is the first branch from the left
    # (384 1x1 convolutions)
    branch_A = conv2d_batchnorm_relu(input, 384, 1, 1)
```

```
# this is the second branch from the left
# (3 x 3 average pooling), followed by
# (128 1x1 convolutions)
branch_B = AveragePooling2D((3,3), strides=(1,1), padding='same')(input)
branch_B = conv2d_batchnorm_relu(branch_B, 128, 1, 1)

# this is the third branch from the left
# (192 1x1 convolutions), followed by
# (224 1x7 convolutions), followed by
# (256 7x1 convolutions)
branch_C = conv2d_batchnorm_relu(input, 192, 1, 1)
branch_C = conv2d_batchnorm_relu(branch_C, 224, 1, 7)
branch_C = conv2d_batchnorm_relu(branch_C, 256, 7, 1)

# this is the fourth (right-most) branch
# (192 1x1 convolutions), followed by
# (192 1x7 convolutions), followed by
# (224 7x1 convolutions), followed by
# (224 1x7 convolutions), followed by
# (256 7x1 convolutions)
branch_D = conv2d_batchnorm_relu(input, 192, 1, 1)
branch_D = conv2d_batchnorm_relu(branch_D, 192, 1, 7)
branch_D = conv2d_batchnorm_relu(branch_D, 224, 7, 1)
branch_D = conv2d_batchnorm_relu(branch_D, 224, 1, 7)
branch_D = conv2d_batchnorm_relu(branch_D, 256, 7, 1)

# concatenate all the results from the four branches.
output = concatenate([branch_A, branch_B, branch_C, branch_D], axis=-1)
return output
```

The code in the build_InceptionB_block() function is similar to the code in the build_InceptionA_block() function. The block diagram for the InceptionB block was presented in Figure 10.7. Type the following code in a new notebook cell to define a function called build_InceptionC_block() that will create an InceptionC block:

```
def build_InceptionC_block(input):

    # refer to Figure 10.7 for a visual representation of this block.

    # this is the first branch from the left
    # (256 1x1 convolutions)
    branch_A = conv2d_batchnorm_relu(input, 256, 1, 1)

    # this is the second branch from the left
    # (3 x 3 average pooling), followed by
    # (256 1x1 convolutions)
    branch_B = AveragePooling2D((3, 3), strides=(1, 1), padding='same')(input)
    branch_B = conv2d_batchnorm_relu(branch_B, 256, 1, 1)
```

```
    # this is the third branch from the left
    # (384 1x1 convolutions), followed by
    # (256 1x3 and 3x1 convolutions in parallel)
    branch_C = conv2d_batchnorm_relu(input, 384, 1, 1)
    branch_C_left = conv2d_batchnorm_relu(branch_C, 256, 1, 3)
    branch_C_right = conv2d_batchnorm_relu(branch_C, 256, 3, 1)

    # this is the fourth (right-most) branch
    # (384 1x1 convolutions), followed by
    # (448 1x3 convolutions), followed by
    # (512 3x1 convolutions), followed by
    # (256 1x3 and 3x1 convolutions in parallel)
    branch_D = conv2d_batchnorm_relu(input, 384, 1, 1)
    branch_D = conv2d_batchnorm_relu(branch_D, 448, 1, 3)
    branch_D = conv2d_batchnorm_relu(branch_D, 512, 3, 1)
    branch_D_left = conv2d_batchnorm_relu(branch_D, 256, 1, 3)
    branch_D_right = conv2d_batchnorm_relu(branch_D, 256, 3, 1)

    output = concatenate([branch_A,
                    branch_B ,
                    branch_C_left, branch_C_right,
                    branch_D_left, branch_D_right],
                    axis=-1)
    return output
```

The code in the `build_InceptionC_block()` function is similar to the code that builds the InceptionA and InceptionB blocks and follows the architecture depicted in Figure 10.7.

Having written the code to create the three Inception-v4 blocks, you can now create the two reduction blocks. Type the following code in an empty notebook cell to create a function called `build_ReductionA_block()`:

```
def build_ReductionA_block(input):

    # refer to Figure 10.9 for a visual representation of this block.
    #
    # The purpose of this block is to reduce a 35 x 35 input into a 17 x 17
input.

    # this is the first branch from the left
    # (3 x 3 Max pooling)  - stride is 2 x 2 , no padding is used.
    branch_left = MaxPooling2D((3,3), strides=(2,2), padding='valid')(input)

    # this is the middle branch
    # (384 3x3 convolutions) - stride = 2 x 2, no padding is used.
    branch_middle = conv2d_batchnorm_relu(input, 384, 3, 3, strides=(2,2),
padding='valid')

    # this is the right branch.
    # (192 1x1 convolutions), followed by
```

```
    # (224 3x3 convolutions), followed by
    # (256 3x3 convolutions) - stride = 2 x 2, no padding is used.
    branch_right = conv2d_batchnorm_relu(input, 192, 1, 1)
    branch_right = conv2d_batchnorm_relu(branch_right, 224, 3, 3)
    branch_right = conv2d_batchnorm_relu(branch_right, 256, 3, 3, strides=(2,2),
padding='valid')

    output = concatenate([branch_left, branch_middle, branch_right], axis=-1)
    return output
```

The purpose of the ReductionA block is to transform a 35×35 input into a 17×17 input in an efficient manner. The architecture of the block was presented in Figure 10.9. The key points to note in the implementation of the reduction block is the use of the `strides=(2 x 2)` and the use of the `padding=valid` argument in some layers, which implies no input padding will be performed. When input padding is not used, the dimensions of the output of a convolution operation are always smaller than the dimensions of the input. The use of a horizontal and vertical stride greater than 1 implies that every alternate position will be skipped in the original image, thereby providing a further reduction in the dimensions of the output. The concept of a strided convolution is best illustrated with a simple one-dimensional example (see Figure 10.13). The convolutional filter is a single number (or a 1×1 kernel), and every alternate input value is ignored.

FIGURE 10.13
A one-dimensional
strided convolu-
tion operation

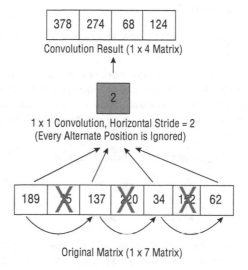

Type the following code in an empty notebook cell to create a function called `build_ReductionB_block()`:

```
def build_ReductionB_block(input):

    # refer to Figure 10.9 for a visual representation of this block.
    #
```

```
# The purpose of this block is to reduce a 17 x 7 input into a 8 x 8 input.

# this is the first branch from the left
# (3 x 3 Max pooling)  - stride is 2 x 2 , no padding is used.
branch_left = MaxPooling2D((3,3), strides=(2,2), padding='valid')(input)

# this is the middle branch
# (192 1x1 convolutions), followed by
# (192 3x3 convolutions) - stride = 2 x 2, no padding is used.
branch_middle = conv2d_batchnorm_relu(input, 192, 1, 1)
branch_middle = conv2d_batchnorm_relu(branch_middle, 192, 3, 3, strides=(2,
2), padding='valid')

# this is the right branch.
# (256 1x1 convolutions), followed by
# (256 1x7 convolutions), followed by
# (320 7x1 convolutions), followed by
# (320 3x3 convolutions) - stride = 2 x 2, no padding is used.
branch_right = conv2d_batchnorm_relu(input, 256, 1, 1)
branch_right = conv2d_batchnorm_relu(branch_right, 256, 1, 7)
branch_right = conv2d_batchnorm_relu(branch_right, 320, 7, 1)
branch_right = conv2d_batchnorm_relu(branch_right, 320, 3, 3, strides=(2,2),
padding='valid')

output = concatenate([branch_left, branch_middle, branch_right], axis=-1)
return output
```

The purpose of the second reduction block is to reduce the dimensions of the input data from 17×17 to 8×8 efficiently. The code to implement the ReductionB block is similar to the code for the ReductionA block. The architecture of the ReductionB block was depicted in Figure 10.9.

Type the following code in a new notebook cell to create the stem of the Inception-v4 network:

```
def build_InceptionV4_stem(input):

    # refer to Figure 10.8 for a visual representation of this block.

    # First stage of the stem:
    #
    # (32 3x3 convolutions) - stride = 2 x 2, no padding is used, followed by
    # (32 3x3 convolutions) - stride = 1 x 1, no padding is used, followed by
    # (64 3x3 convolutions).
    #
    # Assuming input image dimensions are (299 x 299 x 3),
    # the output from this stage will have dimensions (147 x 147 x 64)
    stem = conv2d_batchnorm_relu(input, 32, 3, 3, strides=(2,2), padding='valid')
    stem = conv2d_batchnorm_relu(stem, 32, 3, 3, padding='valid')
    stem = conv2d_batchnorm_relu(stem, 64, 3, 3)
```

```
    # Second stage of the stem:
    #
    # left branch: (3 x 3 Max pooling)  - stride is 2 x 2 , no padding.
    # right branch: (96 3x3 convolutions) - stride = 2 x 2, no padding.
    #
    # the output from this stage will have dimensions (73 x 73 x 160)
    left_1 = MaxPooling2D((3,3), strides=(2,2), padding='valid')(stem)
    right_1 = conv2d_batchnorm_relu(stem, 96, 3, 3, strides=(2,2),
padding='valid')
    stem = concatenate([left_1, right_1], axis=-1)


    # Third stage of the stem:
    #
    # left branch:
    # (64 1x1 convolutions), followed by
    # (96 3x3 convolutions) - stride = 1 x 1, no padding.
    #
    # right branch:
    # (64 1x1 convolutions), followed by
    # (64 1x7 convolutions), followed by
    # (64 7x1 convolutions), followed by
    # (96 3x3 convolutions) - stride = 2 x 2, no padding.
    #
    # the output from this stage will have dimensions (71 x 71 x 192)
    left_2 = conv2d_batchnorm_relu(stem, 64, 1, 1)
    left_2 = conv2d_batchnorm_relu(left_2, 96, 3, 3, padding='valid')

    right_2 = conv2d_batchnorm_relu(stem, 64, 1, 1)
    right_2 = conv2d_batchnorm_relu(right_2, 64, 1, 7)
    right_2 = conv2d_batchnorm_relu(right_2, 64, 7, 1)
    right_2 = conv2d_batchnorm_relu(right_2, 96, 3, 3, padding='valid')

    stem = concatenate([left_2, right_2], axis=-1)


    # Fourth stage of the stem:
    #
    # left branch: (192 3x3 convolutions) - stride = 2 x 2, no padding.
    # right branch: (3 x 3 Max pooling)  - stride is 2 x 2 , no padding.
    #
    # the output from this stage will have dimensions (35 x 35 x 384)
    left_3 = conv2d_batchnorm_relu(stem, 192, 3, 3, strides=(2,2),
padding='valid')
right_3 = MaxPooling2D((3,3), strides=(2,2), padding='valid')(stem)
    stem = concatenate([left_3, right_3], axis=-1)

    return stem
```

The stem of the network consists of a series of convolutional and pooling operations that prepare the image for the first InceptionA block. The architecture of the Inception-v4 stem was depicted in Figure 10.8.

Now you'll create a Python function that will use the functions that you have built so far in this section to create the convolutional base of the Inception-v4 network. Type the following code in a new notebook cell:

```
# builds the convolutional base portion of the InceptionV4 network.
def build_InceptionV4_convbase(input):

    # the stem
    convbase = build_InceptionV4_stem (input)

    # 4 InceptionA blocks
    # 1 ReductionA block
    # 7 InceptionB blocks
    # 1 ReductionB block
    # 3 InceptionC blocks


    convbase = build_InceptionA_block(convbase)
    convbase = build_InceptionA_block(convbase)
    convbase = build_InceptionA_block(convbase)
    convbase = build_InceptionA_block(convbase)

    convbase = build_ReductionA_block(convbase)

    convbase = build_InceptionB_block(convbase)
    convbase = build_InceptionB_block(convbase)
    convbase = build_InceptionB_block(convbase)
    convbase = build_InceptionB_block(convbase)
    convbase = build_InceptionB_block(convbase)
    convbase = build_InceptionB_block(convbase)
    convbase = build_InceptionB_block(convbase)

    convbase = build_ReductionB_block(convbase)

    convbase = build_InceptionC_block(convbase)
    convbase = build_InceptionC_block(convbase)
    convbase = build_InceptionC_block(convbase)

    return convbase
```

The build_Inceptionv4_convbase() function is rather straightforward. All it does is use the functions that have been defined earlier to build the stem, and stack four InceptionA blocks, one ReductionA block, seven InceptionB blocks, one ReductionB block, and three InceptionC blocks in sequence.

Now that you have created Python functions that can create the convolutional base of the Inception-v4 network, you can add a dense, fully connected classifier on top of the base to create a complete Inception-v4 network. Type the following code in an empty notebook cell:

```
# create an InceptionV4 network.
#
# The dimensions of input images expected by this network are
# (height = IMAGE_HEIGHT, width = IMAGE_WIDTH, channels = IMAGE_CHANNELS)
# In the original paper these are 299, 299, 3 respectively.
#
# The output of the network is an array of class-wise probabilities.

# set up IMAGE_HEIGHT, IMAGE_WIDTH, and IMAGE_CHANNELS to match your input images
IMAGE_HEIGHT = 299
IMAGE_WIDTH = 299
IMAGE_CHANNELS = 3

# hyperparameters you can adjust
DROPOUT_PROBABILITY = 0.1
INITIAL_LEARNING_RATE = 0.001

input_tensor = Input((IMAGE_HEIGHT, IMAGE_WIDTH, IMAGE_CHANNELS))

# convolutional base
conv_base = build_InceptionV4_convbase(input_tensor)

# this is the classifier on top of the inception-v4 convolutional base.
# it consists of an 8 x 8 Average pooling operation, a flattening operation,
# a Dropout layer and a Dense layer that serves as the output of the network.
pool_output = AveragePooling2D((8,8), padding='valid')(conv_base)
dropout_output = Dropout(DROPOUT_PROBABILITY)(pool_output)
flattened_output = Flatten()(dropout_output)
network_output = Dense(units=2, activation='softmax')(flattened_output)

# use a Adam optimizer and compile the model.
adam_optimizer = Adam(lr = INITIAL_LEARNING_RATE)
model = Model(input_tensor, network_output, name='InceptionV4')
model.compile(optimizer = adam_optimizer, loss = 'binary_crossentropy', metrics
= ["accuracy"])

# print a summary of the layers of the model.
model.summary()
```

In the original paper where the Inception-v4 network architecture was described, the authors chose an input image size of 299×299 pixels and three color channels. The dimensions of the input image are specified when the input layer is constructed using the Keras Input() function.

```
input_tensor = Input((IMAGE_HEIGHT, IMAGE_WIDTH, IMAGE_CHANNELS))
```

This code snippet uses the values specified in the constants `IMAGE_HEIGHT`, `IMAGE_WIDTH`, and `IMAGE_CHANNELS`, respectively. These are set to 299, 299, and 3, respectively, in the second notebook cell. You can learn more about the Keras `Input()` function at `https://keras.io/layers/core/`.

The following lines create the classifier network that is added on top of the convolutional base:

```
pool_output = AveragePooling2D((8,8), padding='valid')(conv_base)
dropout_output = Dropout(DROPOUT_PROBABILITY)(pool_output)
flattened_output = Flatten()(dropout_output)
network_output = Dense(units=2, activation='softmax')(flattened_output)
```

The `AveragePooling2D` layer is used to reduce the dimensions of the output of the convolutional base. The output of the convolutional base is an 8×8 x1536 tensor, which means there are 1536 8×8 matrices. The use of an 8×8 average pooling effectively takes one number from each of the 1,536 matrices, converting an 8×8×1536 input into a 1×1536 output.

A `Dropout` layer is applied to the 1×1536 tensor that is generated by the average pooling operation. A dropout layer prevents overfitting by randomly setting a fraction of the input values to zero. The fraction is specified by the constant `DROPOUT_PROBABILITY`, which is defined earlier in the notebook.

The concept of dropouts was first described by Nitish Srivastava et al. in a paper titled "Dropout: A Simple Way to Prevent Neural Networks from Overfitting." You can find a copy of this paper at `http://www.jmlr.org/papers/volume15/srivastava14a/srivastava14a.pdf`.

A `Flatten` layer is applied to the output of the `Dropout` layer. The purpose of this is to convert the 1× 1536 tensor into a one-dimensional array of numbers. The shape of the output of the `Flatten` layer is (`None, 1536`), implying that it is just an array of 1536 values.

Finally, a `Dense` (fully connected) layer is added on top of the output of the flattening operation. The number of neurons in this layer corresponds to the number of object classes in your training dataset. A value of 2 is specified because you will use this network to classify images of dogs and cats (which are two distinct classes). The original Inception-v4 network was built for the ILSVRC challenge, which has 1,000 object classes. The use of the `softmax` activation function ensures that the sum of the probabilities of the network outputs will total 1.0.

The final step in building a Keras model is to compile the model, which is achieved using the following statements:

```
adam_optimizer = keras.optimizers.Adam(learning_rate = INITIAL_LEARNING_RATE,
beta_1 = 0.9, beta_2 = 0.999, amsgrad=False)
model = Model(input_tensor, network_output, name='InceptionV4')
model.compile(optimizer = adam_optimizer, loss = 'binary_crossentropy', metrics
= ["accuracy"])
```

While you are compiling the model, you need to provide an optimizer, the loss function, and the error metric that you want to use. An optimizer, as its name suggests, is an optimization function that is used during the training process to update the weights of the neurons in the network in such a way to minimize the value of a loss function. The Adam optimizer is an efficient optimizer. Keras provides implementations of several optimizers, including the SGD (stochastic gradient descent) optimizer. The learning rate is a hyperparameter that is provided as an argument to the optimizer. Execute the code in all the notebook cells using the Cell ➤ Run All menu item. After a few minutes, you will see a summary of the structure of the compiled model. The final section of the summary should resemble the following:

```
Total params: 41,209,058
Trainable params: 41,145,890
Non-trainable params: 63,168
```

As you can see, there are more than 41 million weights in the model. At this point, they are assigned random values. In the next section, you will learn how to train this model on the Dogs vs. Cats dataset.

Training the Inception-v4 Model

Training an Inception-v4 model on a computer without a NVIDIA GPU is an extremely time-consuming process, and for that reason a set of pre-trained weights are included along with the downloads that accompany this chapter. If you do not have access to a computer with a high-end NVIDIA GPU, then you can execute the following code snippet in a notebook cell to load the pre-trained weights into the compiled model and skip the rest of this section.

```
weights_path = './inceptionv4_dogscats_weights.h5'
model.load_weights(weights_path, by_name=True)
```

If, however, you have access to a physical or cloud-based GPU instance or are just interested in learning how Keras models are trained, read on.

The code in this section was used to train the model on the Kaggle Dogs vs. Cats dataset, which consists of 25,000 images that contain dogs or cats (but not both). In some images the pets are seen with people and in others by themselves. A copy of the dataset is included with the downloads that accompany this section. The images themselves are named so as to clearly indicate whether they are dog images or cat images, with the word *dog* or *cat* appearing at the start of the filename. For example, the filename `cat.126.jpg` contains the image of a cat.

The following Python code snippet can be used to read the contents of the `datasets/dogs-vs-cats/train/` directory into a two-column Pandas dataframe. The first column is called `Filename` and, as you would expect, contains the filenames from the `train` directory. The second column is called `ObjectClass` and contains the string '0' or '1'. The string '0' is used to signify that the filename referenced in the corresponding position of the first contains a cat, and '1' signifies that it contains a dog.

```
import os
import pandas as pd

# load all filenames in the /datasets/dogs-vs-cats/train directory into a
dataframe.
imagedir = './datasets/dogs-vs-cats/train/'

# enumerate all files in source directory
# and prepare an array that only contains filenames that this
# code can support (.jpg, .png)
file_names_temp = next(os.walk(imagedir))[2]
```

```
file_names = []
object_classes = []

for filename in file_names_temp:
    name, extension = os.path.splitext(filename)
    if extension.lower() == '.jpg':
        file_names.append(filename)

        if name.startswith('cat') == True:
            object_classes.append('0')
        elif name.startswith('dog') == True:
            object_classes.append('1')


dfTrainingData = pd.DataFrame(list(zip(file_names, object_classes)),
                    columns =['Filename', 'ObjectClass'])
```

You can use the dataframe's head() method to preview the first few rows. Figure 10.14 depicts the results of the head() method.

FIGURE 10.14
Inspecting the first few rows of the dfTrainingData dataframe

```
In [3]:  dfTrainingData.head()

Out[3]:
                Filename   ObjectClass

        0    dog.8011.jpg        1
        1    cat.5077.jpg        0
        2    dog.7322.jpg        1
        3    cat.2718.jpg        0
        4   cat.10151.jpg        0
```

The next step in the training process is to split the labeled training data into separate training and test sets. Scikit-learn's train_test_split() function is used to create a 75/25 split.

```
# create train and test sets
from sklearn.model_selection import train_test_split
x_train, x_test, y_train, y_test = train_test_split(dfTrainingData['Filename'],
                                        dfTrainingData['ObjectClass'],
                                        test_size=0.25,
                                        random_state=42,
                                stratify=dfTrainingData['ObjectClass'])


num_train_samples = len(x_train)
num_test_samples = len(x_test)
```

```
dfTrain = pd.DataFrame(list(zip(x_train, y_train)),
            columns =['Filename', 'ObjectClass'])

dfTest = pd.DataFrame(list(zip(x_test, y_test)),
            columns =['Filename', 'ObjectClass'])

del x_train, x_test, y_train, y_test
```

Training a deep learning model involves presenting the labeled training data to the model, evaluating the classification error using a suitable metric, adjusting the weights of the network, and then repeating this process iteratively until the classification error stops reducing. To optimize the training process, the training data is split into a number of equal-sized batches, and each batch is presented to the network sequentially. When all the training images have been presented to the network, an epoch is said to have elapsed. A typical training process runs for several epochs.

To allow the training data to be fed in batches, Keras uses Python generators. A generator is a function that generates some data and in the context of the training process will generate a batch of samples. Generators provide a layer of abstraction between the actual training data and the model. You can modify the data as it flows through the generator and even generate data algorithmically.

You may be wondering why you can't simply extract rows from the Pandas dataframe dfTrain and feed them into the model. There are a number of reasons for this.

◆ The dfTrain dataframe does not contain the actual image data. It contains only the filename. You need to write some code that will read the filename from the dataframe and load the image data into memory.

◆ The Keras model's input layer is expecting a tensor of dimensions (299, 299, 3). Most of the input images are larger or smaller than that, and you need to write some code to resize the images on the fly.

◆ To make your model more robust to changes in image orientation, scale, and lighting conditions, you want to randomly perform image processing operations such as rotations, shearing, and brightness enhancements to the images on the fly.

◆ The model expects the input tensors to be normalized. Digital images contain pixel values in the range of 0–255. You will need to write some code that converts the pixel values from [0, 255] to [0.0, 1.0] on the fly.

All of these objectives can be met using Keras' built-in image-processing support and Python generators. The following code snippet creates a Keras ImageDataGenerator object that is used to perform pixel scaling and image processing operations on a batch of images and then uses the flow_from_dataframe method to return a Python generator that will be used as one of the inputs in the training process:

```
# create Keras generator for training data
from keras.preprocessing.image import ImageDataGenerator
```

```
# rescale all pixel values to the range 0.0 to 1.0
# apply in-memory augmentations to original data
train_datagen = ImageDataGenerator(
        rescale=1./255,
        shear_range=0.2,
        zoom_range=0.2,
        brightness_range = [0.75, 1.25],
        height_shift_range = 0.2,
        width_shift_range = 0.2,
        rotation_range=180.0,
        horizontal_flip=True)

train_generator = train_datagen.flow_from_dataframe(
        dataframe = dfTrain,
        directory = imagedir,
        x_col = "Filename",
        y_col = "ObjectClass",
        target_size = (IMAGE_WIDTH, IMAGE_HEIGHT),
        batch_size = BATCH_SIZE,
        class_mode = 'categorical')
```

You can learn more about the `ImageDataGenerator` class at `https://keras.io/preproc-essing/image/`. It is important to note that the `flow_from_dataframe()` method returns a Python generator, and you could have created such a function without using the Keras `ImageDataGenerator` class. You may want to create your own Python generator function if the preprocessing capabilities provided by the `ImageDataGenerator` class are not sufficient for your needs. For instance, the `ImageDataGenerator` class cannot perform contrast enhancements, Gaussian blurring, or color space conversions on the fly.

You will also need to create a Python generator for the data in the `dfTest` dataframe. This is needed because Keras needs the test data to evaluate the quality of the model as the training progresses through each epoch. The following snippet creates a generator object for the data in the `dfTest` dataframe:

```
# create Keras generator for test data

# rescale all pixel values to the range 0.0 to 1.0
test_datagen = ImageDataGenerator(rescale=1./255)

test_generator = test_datagen.flow_from_dataframe(
        dataframe = dfTest,
        directory = imagedir,
        x_col = "Filename",
        y_col = "ObjectClass",
        target_size = (IMAGE_WIDTH, IMAGE_HEIGHT),
        batch_size = BATCH_SIZE,
        class_mode = 'categorical')
```

The code to create the test data generator is similar to the code that created the training data generator. The key difference is that you do not need to perform on-the-fly image processing operations on the test data. The purpose of making subtle random enhancements to the brightness, scale, and rotation of the training images was to generate a more robust model. Those modifications are not needed on the test data. Once you have created both the training and test data generators, you can train the model with the following snippet:

```
# train the model for 30 epochs
import math
import datetime
from keras.callbacks import EarlyStopping, ModelCheckpoint, ReduceLROnPlateau

start_time = datetime.datetime.now()

callbacks = [
    EarlyStopping(patience=10, verbose=1),
    ReduceLROnPlateau(factor=0.1, patience=5, min_lr=0.00001, verbose=1),
    ModelCheckpoint('inceptionv4_checkpoint_weights.h5', verbose=1,
save_best_only=True, save_weights_only=True)
]

history = model.fit_generator(train_generator,
                        steps_per_epoch = math.ceil(num_train_samples /
BATCH_SIZE),
                        epochs = 30,
                        callbacks=callbacks,
                        validation_data = test_generator,
                        validation_steps = math.ceil(num_test_samples /
BATCH_SIZE))

model.save('./inceptionv4_dogscats_fullmodel.mod')
model.save_weights('inceptionv4_dogscats_weights.h5')

end_time = datetime.datetime.now()
print('training completed in:')
print(end_time - start_time)
```

The training is initiated by calling the `fit_generator()` method on a compiled Keras generator. The `fit_generator()` method requires several parameters that include the train and test generators, and the number of training epochs. You can learn more about the `fit_genera-tor()` method at https://keras.io/models/model/.

Since training a deep-learning model is a time-consuming process (sometimes several days long), it is useful to have the ability to control some aspects of the training process (such as the learning rate) while the training process is underway. This may seem counterintuitive at first but in fact is a common practice. The learning rate used when creating the optimizer is constant;

however, if the performance of the model has not improved for a number of epochs, you may want to reduce (or increase) the learning rate. Similarly, if the value of the loss function has not decreased for a number of epochs, you may want to stop training the model altogether. Another common control that you would want is the ability to save the best version of your model as each epoch elapses. It is not guaranteed that the best model is the one at the end of the final epoch.

Keras provides callback events that you can monitor during the training process. If one of those events is triggered, then a function that you specify at the start of the training process will be invoked. These callback functions can terminate the training process, modify the learning rate, and save snapshots of the best version of your model during the training process. A detailed discussion of Keras callbacks is beyond the scope of this book. If you want to learn more about Keras callbacks, you can access the documentation at `https://keras.io/callbacks/`.

The code to train the model uses three callback functions.

```
callbacks = [
    EarlyStopping(patience=10, verbose=1),
    ReduceLROnPlateau(factor=0.1, patience=5, min_lr=0.00001, verbose=1),
    ModelCheckpoint('inceptionv4_checkpoint_weights.h5', verbose=1,
save_best_only=True, save_weights_only=True)
]
```

The `EarlyStopping` callback function is part of the Keras library and will abort the training if the value of the loss function has not improved for a set number of epochs. The `ReduceLROn-Plateau` callback function is also part of the Keras library that can be used to reduce the learning rate if the value of the evaluation metric (accuracy) of the model has not improved for a set number of epochs. The `ModelCheckpoint` function is perhaps one of the most commonly used callback functions. It saves the best copy of your model through each epoch of the training process.

The code to train the model is provided in a separate Python file called `InceptionV4_model_training.py`. The training code is not included in the Jupyter Notebook file, because accidentally executing it on a computer without a GPU can freeze the notebook instance and cause you to lose unsaved changes. The Inception-v4 model was trained on a Windows 10 computer workstation with 64GB of RAM and an NVIDIA RTX 2080Ti 11Gb graphics card. It took about three hours to train 30 epochs, with the best model having an accuracy of 87.9 percent. The output of the training process is presented here:

```
Epoch 1/30
782/782 [==============================] - 455s 582ms/step - loss: 1.9923 - acc:
0.5955 - val_loss: 1.7204 - val_acc: 0.5541

Epoch 00001: val_loss improved from inf to 1.72038, saving model to inceptionv4_
checkpoint_weights.h5
Epoch 2/30
782/782 [==============================] - 364s 466ms/step - loss: 1.4701 - acc:
0.6391 - val_loss: 1.3388 - val_acc: 0.6702

Epoch 00002: val_loss improved from 1.72038 to 1.33879, saving model to
inceptionv4_checkpoint_weights.h5
Epoch 3/30
```

```
782/782 [==============================] - 364s 465ms/step - loss: 1.2062 - acc:
0.6821 - val_loss: 1.2906 - val_acc: 0.6776

Epoch 00003: val_loss improved from 1.33879 to 1.29060, saving model to
inceptionv4_checkpoint_weights.h5
Epoch 4/30
782/782 [==============================] - 368s 471ms/step - loss: 1.0563 - acc:
0.6919 - val_loss: 1.0982 - val_acc: 0.5832

Epoch 00004: val_loss improved from 1.29060 to 1.09822, saving model to
inceptionv4_checkpoint_weights.h5
Epoch 5/30
782/782 [==============================] - 369s 472ms/step - loss: 0.9522 - acc:
0.7056 - val_loss: 3.3594 - val_acc: 0.5000

Epoch 00005: val_loss did not improve from 1.09822
Epoch 6/30
782/782 [==============================] - 367s 470ms/step - loss: 0.9249 - acc:
0.6946 - val_loss: 0.7992 - val_acc: 0.7469

Epoch 00006: val_loss improved from 1.09822 to 0.79921, saving model to
inceptionv4_checkpoint_weights.h5
Epoch 7/30
782/782 [==============================] - 368s 470ms/step - loss: 0.7862 - acc:
0.7329 - val_loss: 1.2728 - val_acc: 0.5000

Epoch 00007: val_loss did not improve from 0.79921
Epoch 8/30
782/782 [==============================] - 366s 468ms/step - loss: 0.7180 - acc:
0.7590 - val_loss: 0.6778 - val_acc: 0.7598

Epoch 00008: val_loss improved from 0.79921 to 0.67780, saving model to
inceptionv4_checkpoint_weights.h5
Epoch 9/30
782/782 [==============================] - 361s 462ms/step - loss: 0.6508 - acc:
0.7682 - val_loss: 0.6151 - val_acc: 0.7851

Epoch 00009: val_loss improved from 0.67780 to 0.61506, saving model to
inceptionv4_checkpoint_weights.h5
Epoch 10/30
782/782 [==============================] - 360s 461ms/step - loss: 0.5999 - acc:
0.7832 - val_loss: 0.5462 - val_acc: 0.8118

Epoch 00010: val_loss improved from 0.61506 to 0.54624, saving model to
inceptionv4_checkpoint_weights.h5
Epoch 11/30
782/782 [==============================] - 359s 460ms/step - loss: 0.5608 - acc:
0.8045 - val_loss: 0.6611 - val_acc: 0.0992
```

```
Epoch 00011: val_loss did not improve from 0.54624
Epoch 12/30
782/782 [==============================] - 360s 460ms/step - loss: 0.5281 - acc:
0.8107 - val_loss: 0.8895 - val_acc: 0.5246

Epoch 00012: val_loss did not improve from 0.54624
Epoch 13/30
782/782 [==============================] - 360s 460ms/step - loss: 0.5044 - acc:
0.8209 - val_loss: 6.8722 - val_acc: 0.5019

Epoch 00013: val_loss did not improve from 0.54624
Epoch 14/30
782/782 [==============================] - 370s 473ms/step - loss: 0.4812 - acc:
0.8283 - val_loss: 0.5009 - val_acc: 0.8216

Epoch 00014: val_loss improved from 0.54624 to 0.50094, saving model to
inceptionv4_checkpoint_weights.h5
Epoch 15/30
782/782 [==============================] - 359s 459ms/step - loss: 0.4595 - acc:
0.8388 - val_loss: 0.6911 - val_acc: 0.7666

Epoch 00015: val_loss did not improve from 0.50094
Epoch 16/30
782/782 [==============================] - 359s 460ms/step - loss: 0.4486 - acc:
0.8398 - val_loss: 0.6691 - val_acc: 0.8318

Epoch 00016: val_loss did not improve from 0.50094
Epoch 17/30
782/782 [==============================] - 359s 459ms/step - loss: 0.4379 - acc:
0.8469 - val_loss: 0.5600 - val_acc: 0.7950

Epoch 00017: val_loss did not improve from 0.50094
Epoch 18/30
782/782 [==============================] - 359s 459ms/step - loss: 0.4295 - acc:
0.8511 - val_loss: 0.4946 - val_acc: 0.8283

Epoch 00018: val_loss improved from 0.50094 to 0.49464, saving model to
inceptionv4_checkpoint_weights.h5
Epoch 19/30
782/782 [==============================] - 360s 460ms/step - loss: 0.4087 - acc:
0.8630 - val_loss: 3.8307 - val_acc: 0.5000

Epoch 00019: val_loss did not improve from 0.49464
Epoch 20/30
782/782 [==============================] - 359s 459ms/step - loss: 0.4119 - acc:
0.8615 - val_loss: 1.3125 - val_acc: 0.3493
```

```
Epoch 00020: val_loss did not improve from 0.49464
Epoch 21/30
782/782 [==============================] - 359s 460ms/step - loss: 0.3881 - acc:
0.8698 - val_loss: 1.1232 - val_acc: 0.5539


Epoch 00021: val_loss did not improve from 0.49464
Epoch 22/30
782/782 [==============================] - 359s 459ms/step - loss: 0.4009 - acc:
0.8704 - val_loss: 0.8475 - val_acc: 0.6339


Epoch 00022: val_loss did not improve from 0.49464
Epoch 23/30
782/782 [==============================] - 360s 460ms/step - loss: 0.3766 - acc:
0.8763 - val_loss: 0.3672 - val_acc: 0.8741


Epoch 00023: val_loss improved from 0.49464 to 0.36720, saving model to
inceptionv4_checkpoint_weights.h5
Epoch 24/30
782/782 [==============================] - 360s 461ms/step - loss: 0.3674 - acc:
0.8764 - val_loss: 1.0319 - val_acc: 0.7494


Epoch 00024: val_loss did not improve from 0.36720
Epoch 25/30
782/782 [==============================] - 360s 460ms/step - loss: 0.3702 - acc:
0.8804 - val_loss: 0.3672 - val_acc: 0.8834


Epoch 00025: val_loss did not improve from 0.36720
Epoch 26/30
782/782 [==============================] - 359s 459ms/step - loss: 0.3523 - acc:
0.8849 - val_loss: 0.8007 - val_acc: 0.7058


Epoch 00026: val_loss did not improve from 0.36720
Epoch 27/30
782/782 [==============================] - 359s 459ms/step - loss: 0.3492 - acc:
0.8860 - val_loss: 6.7610 - val_acc: 0.5539


Epoch 00027: val_loss did not improve from 0.36720
Epoch 28/30
782/782 [==============================] - 359s 459ms/step - loss: 0.3485 - acc:
0.8882 - val_loss: 0.4005 - val_acc: 0.8629


Epoch 00028: ReduceLROnPlateau reducing learning rate to 0.00010000000474974513.

Epoch 00028: val_loss did not improve from 0.36720
Epoch 29/30
782/782 [==============================] - 361s 461ms/step - loss: 0.2923 - acc:
0.9104 - val_loss: 0.2640 - val_acc: 0.9285
```

```
Epoch 00029: val_loss improved from 0.36720 to 0.26402, saving model to
inceptionv4_checkpoint_weights.h5
Epoch 30/30
782/782 [==============================] - 359s 459ms/step - loss: 0.2673 - acc:
0.9183 - val_loss: 0.3109 - val_acc: 0.9037

Epoch 00030: val_loss did not improve from 0.26402
training completed in:
3:04:34.654725
```

As you can see, the model on the 29th epoch has a validation accuracy of 92.85 percent, whereas the model on the 30th (final) epoch has a lower accuracy of 90.37.

```
Epoch 29/30
782/782 [==============================] - 361s 461ms/step - loss: 0.2923 - acc:
0.9104 - val_loss: 0.2640 - val_acc: 0.9285

Epoch 30/30
782/782 [==============================] - 359s 459ms/step - loss: 0.2673 - acc:
0.9183 - val_loss: 0.3109 - val_acc: 0.9037
```

Since you used the ModelCheckpoint callback function at the start of the training process, the weights for the best model (epoch 29) will be available in the inception_v4_checkpoint_weights.h5 file.

```
ModelCheckpoint('inceptionv4_checkpoint_weights.h5', verbose=1, save_best_
only=True, save_weights_only=True)
```

The model and weights at the end of the final (30th) epoch are available in the inceptionv4_dogscats_fullmodel.mod and inceptionv4_dogscats_weights.h5 files.

```
model.save('./inceptionv4_dogscats_fullmodel.mod')
model.save_weights('inceptionv4_dogscats_weights.h5')
```

It is sometimes useful to visualize the value of the loss function and performance metric on the training and test datasets at each epoch. The result of the fit_generator() function is a History object that contains this data. The following code can be used to plot the data in the History object. Figure 10.15 depicts the resulting plot.

```
# display a graph of the training process
import numpy as np
import matplotlib.pyplot as plt

def plot_training_stats(stats):
    plt.figure(figsize=(8, 8))
    plt.title("Learning curve")
```

```
plt.plot(stats.history["loss"], label="loss")
plt.plot(stats.history["val_loss"], label="val_loss")
plt.plot(stats.history["acc"], label="acc")
plt.plot(stats.history["val_acc"], label="val_acc")

plt.plot( np.argmin(stats.history["val_loss"]), np.min(stats.history["val_
loss"]), marker="x", color="r", label="best model")
plt.xlabel("Epochs")
plt.ylabel("accuracy and loss")
plt.legend();

plot_training_stats(history)
```

FIGURE 10.15

A plot of the train-
ing history

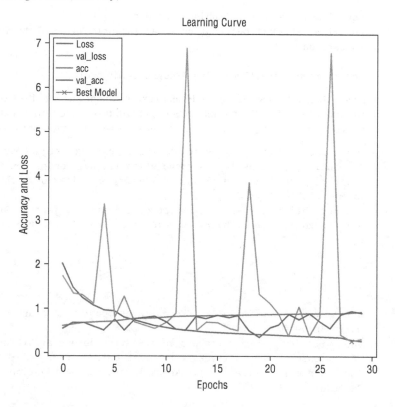

Now that you have a Keras Inception-v4 model, you need to use Core ML tools to export the
model into the Core ML format. This is covered in the next section.

Exporting the Keras Inception-v4 Model to the Core ML Format

Regardless of whether you have trained the model from scratch or loaded pre-trained weights
into the compiled model, you will need to convert the Keras InceptionV4 model into the Core ML
format before you can use the model in an iOS app.

Execute the following code in an empty notebook cell to save the Keras model to the Core ML format:

```
# export the model to Core ML format
import coremltools

coreml_model = coremltools.converters.keras.convert(model,
                                        input_names=['image'],
                                        output_names=['output'],
                                        class_labels=['0', '1'],
                                        image_input_names='image')


coreml_model.author = 'Abhishek Mishra'
coreml_model.short_description = 'An InceptionV4 model trained on the Kaggle Dogs
vs Cats dataset.'

coreml_model.save('Inceptionv4-dogscats.mlmodel')
```

This code snippet uses Core ML tools to export the model into the Core ML format. Owing to the number of layers in the model, the snippet will take some time to execute. The output of the conversion process will list each layer as it is exported. A section of the output is presented here:

```
0 : input_1, <keras.engine.input_layer.InputLayer object at 0x7fc54be9aba8>
1 : conv2d_1, <keras.layers.convolutional.Conv2D object at 0x7fc54be9a9b0>
2 : batch_normalization_1, <keras.layers.normalization.BatchNormalization object
at 0x7fc5682ec160>
3 : activation_1, <keras.layers.core.Activation object at 0x7fc5682ecf98>
4 : conv2d_2, <keras.layers.convolutional.Conv2D object at 0x7fc54bec60b8>

...
...
...

485 : average_pooling2d_15, <keras.layers.pooling.AveragePooling2D object at
0x7fc54be9a240>
486 : flatten_1, <keras.layers.core.Flatten object at 0x7fc5684fe2e8>
487 : dense_1, <keras.layers.core.Dense object at 0x7fc5684ad518>
488 : dense_1__activation__, <keras.layers.core.Activation object at
0x7fc4d9f50cc0>
```

As you can see, Core ML tools has exported a Keras model with 488 layers into the Core ML format. You will use this model in the app you will create in the next section.

Creating the iOS Project

After exporting the Keras model to the Core ML format, launch Xcode on your Mac and create a new project using the Single View App template (see Figure 10.16).

FIGURE 10.16
Creating a new iOS
project using the Single
View App template

When prompted, use the following project options:

◆ **Product Name:** PetDetector

◆ **Organization Name:** *Provide a suitable value*

◆ **Organization Identifier:** *Provide a suitable value*

◆ **Language:** Swift

◆ **User Interface:** Storyboard

◆ **Use Core Data:** Unchecked

◆ **Include Unit Tests:** Unchecked

◆ **Include UI Tests:** Unchecked

Creating the User Interface

With the project created, set up the user interface of the project using these steps:

1. Open the Main.storyboard file and use the View ➤ Show Library menu item to access the object library window. Drag and drop an image view, two button instances, and a label from the object library onto the default view controller scene.

2. Using the Attributes Inspector, change the caption of one of the buttons to Select an Image, and change the caption of the other button to Capture an Image. Change the background color of both buttons to a shade of gray to make them easier to see on the storyboard scene. You can access the Attributes Inspector using the View ➤ Inspectors ➤ Show Attributes Inspector menu item.

3. Organize the elements on the default view controller scene to resemble Figure 10.17 and set up the appropriate storyboard constraints.

FIGURE 10.17
Application storyboard with default view controller scene

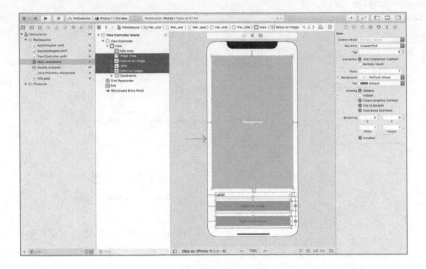

4. Use the Editor ➤ Assistant menu item to access the Assistant Editor and ensure the `ViewController.swift` file is open in the Assistant Editor. Create two outlets in the view controller class called `imageView` and `resultLabel`. Associate these outlets with the image view and label object of the storyboard scene (see Figure 10.18).

FIGURE 10.18
Using the Assistant Editor to create outlets

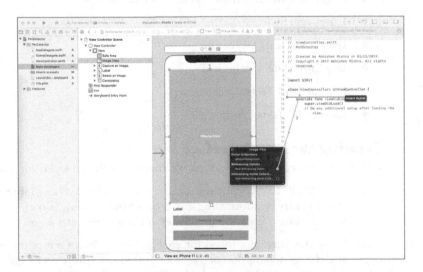

5. Create two action methods in the `ViewController.swift` file called `onSelectImage-FromPhotoLibrary(_ sender: Any)` and `onSelectImageFromCamera(_ sender: Any`. Associate these methods with the `Touch Up Inside` event of the buttons labeled Select an

Image and Capture an Image, respectively. The code in your `ViewController.swift` file should now resemble Listing 10.1.

LISTING 10.1:   ViewController.swift File with Outlets and Actions

```swift
import UIKit

class ViewController: UIViewController {

    @IBOutlet weak var imageView: UIImageView!
    @IBOutlet weak var resultLabel: UILabel!

    override func viewDidLoad() {
        super.viewDidLoad()
        // Do any additional setup after loading the view.
    }

    @IBAction func onSelectImageFromPhotoLibrary(_ sender: Any) {
    }

    @IBAction func onSelectImageFromCamera(_ sender: Any) {
    }

}
```

6. Add a method called `detectPet(in image: UIImage)` in your `ViewController.swift` file and implement it as follows:

```swift
func detectPet(in image: UIImage) {
    // to do: write code to perform object detection with Core ML
}
```

The implementation of the method will be presented later in this chapter and will use a Core ML model to detect the dominant object in the image selected by the user.

7. Update the implementation of the `OnSelectImageFromPhotoLibrary(_ sender: Any)` method to the following:

```swift
@IBAction func onSelectImageFromPhotoLibrary(_ sender: Any) {
    let picker = UIImagePickerController()
    picker.delegate = self
    picker.sourceType = .photoLibrary
    present(picker, animated: true)
}
```

This code uses a `UIKit UIImagePickerController` object to allow the user to select a photo from the photo library of the iOS device.

8. Update the implementation of the `OnSelectImageFromCamera(_ sender: Any)` method to the following:

```
@IBAction func onSelectImageFromCamera(_ sender: Any) {
    // ensure camera is available.
    guard UIImagePickerController.isSourceTypeAvailable(.camera) else {

        let alertController = UIAlertController(title: "Error",
                                message: "Could not access the camera.",
                                preferredStyle: .alert)
alertController.addAction(UIAlertAction(title: "Ok",
                                    style: .cancel, handler: nil))
        self.present(alertController, animated: true, completion: nil)
        return
    }

    let picker = UIImagePickerController()
    picker.delegate = self
    picker.sourceType = .camera
    present(picker, animated: true)
}
```

This code checks to see whether the device has a camera and that the user has granted the app access to the camera. If there is no problem accessing the camera, the code creates a `UIKit UIImagePickerController` object to allow the user to use the camera to take a picture.

9. Add the following snippet to the bottom of `ViewController.swift` to implement the `UIImagePickerControllerDelegate` method func `imagePickerController (_ picker:, didFinishPickingMediaWithInfo:)` in a class extension:

```
extension ViewController: UIImagePickerControllerDelegate,
                    UINavigationControllerDelegate {

    func imagePickerController(_ picker: UIImagePickerController,
        didFinishPickingMediaWithInfo info:
        [UIImagePickerController.InfoKey : Any]) {
        picker.dismiss(animated: true)
        let image = info[UIImagePickerController.InfoKey.originalImage]
                    as! UIImage
        imageView.image = image
        detectPet(in: image)
    }
}
```

This code displays the picture selected by the user (or taken with the camera) in the image view object of the application's user interface and calls the `detectPet(in:)` method to perform object detection. The code in `ViewController.swift` should resemble Listing 10.2.

LISTING 10.2:   ViewController.swift File with UIImagePicker Integration

```swift
import UIKit

class ViewController: UIViewController {

    @IBOutlet weak var imageView: UIImageView!
    @IBOutlet weak var resultLabel: UILabel!

    override func viewDidLoad() {
        super.viewDidLoad()
        // Do any additional setup after loading the view.
    }

    @IBAction func onSelectImageFromPhotoLibrary(_ sender: Any) {
        let picker = UIImagePickerController()
        picker.delegate = self
        picker.sourceType = .photoLibrary
        present(picker, animated: true)
    }

    @IBAction func onSelectImageFromCamera(_ sender: Any) {
        // ensure camera is available.
        guard UIImagePickerController.isSourceTypeAvailable(.camera) else {

            let alertController = UIAlertController(title: "Error",
                                    message: "Could not access the camera.",
                                    preferredStyle: .alert)

            alertController.addAction(UIAlertAction(title: "Ok",
                                        style: .cancel, handler: nil

            self.present(alertController,
                            animated: true, completion: nil)
            return
        }

        let picker = UIImagePickerController()
        picker.delegate = self
        picker.sourceType = .camera
        present(picker, animated: true)
    }
```

```
    func detectPet(in image: UIImage) {
        // to do: write code to perform object detection with Core ML
    }
}

extension ViewController: UIImagePickerControllerDelegate,
                          UINavigationControllerDelegate {

    func imagePickerController(_ picker: UIImagePickerController,
        didFinishPickingMediaWithInfo info:
        [UIImagePickerController.InfoKey : Any]) {
        picker.dismiss(animated: true)
        let image = info[UIImagePickerController.InfoKey.originalImage]
                as! UIImage
        imageView.image = image
        detectPet (in: image)
    }
}
```

Updating Privacy Settings

Before your app can access the camera on the device, you need to ask the user's permission and provide a short description of what your app intends to do with the camera. The `UIImagePickerController` class automatically asks the user for permission. All you need to do is add a key to the application's `Info.plist` file and set the value of this key to a user-friendly message that will inform the user what your app intends to do with the camera.

Click the `Info.plist` file in the Project Navigator to open it in the plist editor. Click the Editor ➢ Add Item menu to insert a new key into the `Info.plist` file. Select the Privacy – Camera Usage Description key from the list of available keys and provide a short string of text that describes how your app will use the camera (see Figure 10.19).

FIGURE 10.19
Editing the application's
`Info.plist` file

Using the Inception-v4 Model in the iOS Project

Now that you have built the app's user interface, it is time to use the Inception-v4 model that was built in an earlier section to detect objects on the image selected by the user. Perform the following steps:

1. Control-click the `PetDetector` folder group in the Project Navigator window and select the Add Files to PetDetector menu item. Navigate to the `Inceptionv4-dogscats.mlmodel` file in your notebook folder and ensure that the Copy Items if Needed option is checked and the `PetDetector` target is selected in the dialog box (see Figure 10.20).

FIGURE 10.20
Import settings for the Inceptionv4-dogscats.mlmodel file

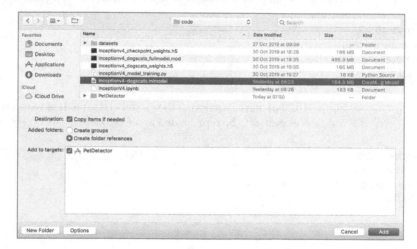

2. Select the `Inceptionv4-dogscats.mlmodel` file in the Project Navigator to get an overview of the model (see Figure 10.21).

FIGURE 10.21
Overview of the Inceptionv4-dogscats.mlmodel file

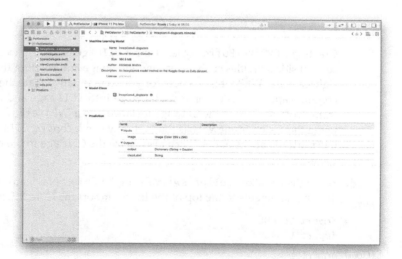

As you can see from the model overview screen, the size of the model is just over 164 MB, and the inputs to the model are RGB (color) images of dimension 229×229 pixel. The image that you select from the photo library (or camera) is much larger than this and will need to be downsampled to this size.

It is also evident from the model overview page that there are two outputs from the model. The first is a dictionary of class-wise probabilities called `output`, and the second output is the name of the most likely class of the image, called `classLabel`. The most likely class is simply the class with the highest probability. You can access this Swift class from the Model Class section of the model overview page (see Figure 10.22).

FIGURE 10.22

Accessing the Swift interface to the Core ML model file

Figure 10.23 depicts a section of the model class file. It is worth noting that the input image is expected to be represented as a `CVPixelBuffer` object and not a `UIImage`.

FIGURE 10.23

A section of the Inceptionv4-dogscats. Swift file

Creating a `CVPixelBuffer` object from a `UIImage` is a complex task, and it involves several side activities such as resizing the image and rotating the image to ensure it is right-side up. While it is possible for you to manually create the `CVPixelBuffer`, the most common approach is to convert a `UIImage` into a `CIImage` and then use the Vision framework to convert the `CIImage` instance into a `CVPixelBuffer`. The advantage of using the Vision framework is that not only can it convert `CIImage` instances into `CVPixelBuffer` instances, it can also resize the `CIImage` to the dimensions expected by the model.

3. Select the `ViewController.swift` file in the Project Navigator and add the following `import` statements to the top of the file to import the Core ML and Vision frameworks.

```
import CoreML
import Vision
```

4. To use the Vision framework to perform object detection with a custom Core ML model, you need to encapsulate your request into a VNCoreMLRequest object and then use a VNImageRequestHandler object to execute the request. Add the following lazy variable to the ViewController.swift file:

```
lazy var classificationRequest: VNCoreMLRequest = {
    do {
        let model = try VNCoreMLModel(for: Inceptionv4_dogscats().model)

        let request = VNCoreMLRequest(model: model,
            completionHandler: { [weak self] request, error in
                self?.processResults(for: request, error: error)
        })

        request.imageCropAndScaleOption = .scaleFit
        return request
    } catch {
        fatalError("Failed to load Core ML model")
    }
}()
```

By using a lazy variable, you are ensuring that this code will not be executed when the class is loaded but instead when you eventually access the classificationRequest variable from your code.

This code creates a VNCoreMLModel instance from the autogenerated Core ML model class Inceptionv4_dogscats and then creates a VNCoreMLRequest instance by passing the VNCoreMLModel and a completion handler as parameters.

The VNCoreMLRequest object has a method called perform() that takes care of the heavy lifting of converting the image to a CVPixelBuffer and using the model to perform object detection. You will call the perform() method later in this chapter. The completion handler that you supplied while creating the VNCoreMLRequest object is called when the operation completes, and in this snippet, the completion handler calls a method called processResults(for:, error:), which you will create next.

Before returning the VNCoreMLRequest instance, the imageCropAndScaleOption property is set to scaleFit. This property is used by Vision to determine how it should scale the image down to the dimensions required by the model. Since the image taken by the camera is rectangular and the image required by the model is a square, some cropping will also occur. There are three potential options you can specify.

◆ centerCrop: This option resizes the image proportionally until the smallest dimension of the image matches the dimensions expected by the model. The resized image (which is still a rectangle) is cropped into a square by using the central portion. This option can end up cropping off parts of the object in the center of the image.

◆ scaleFill: This option resizes the image disproportionally until both dimensions of the image match the dimensions expected by the model. The resized image will appear to be squashed.

◆ scaleFit: This option resizes the image proportionally until the longest dimension of the image matches the dimensions expected by the model, and the resized image is converted into a square by padding the shorter dimension with black pixels.

5. Implement the processResults(for:, error:) method in the ViewController.swift file as follows:

```swift
func processResults(for request: VNRequest, error: Error?) {
    DispatchQueue.main.async {
        guard let results = request.results else {
            print("Unable to classify image.\n\(error!.localizedDescription)")
            self.resultLabel.text = "Unable to classify image."
            return
        }

        let classifications = results as! [VNClassificationObservation]

        if classifications.isEmpty {
            self.resultLabel.text = "Did not recognize anything."
        } else {

            // convert from objectType = 0, 1 to cat, dog
            var objectType:String = "Cat"
            if (classifications[0].identifier.compare("1") == .orderedSame) {
                objectType = "Dog"
            }

            self.resultLabel.text = String(format: "%@ %.1f%%",
                            objectType,
                        classifications[0].confidence * 100)
        }
    }
}
```

This method is called from the completion handler of the VNCoreMLRequest object. The method accepts two parameters. The first is a VNRequest instance called request, and the other is an optional error object. You can access the results of the classification in using the results member of the VNRequest object. The results of the classification are returned as an array of VNClassificationObservation objects. Each object has two member variables: identifier, which represents the class of the detected object, and confidence, which represents the probability of that class. The results are sorted in descending order of probability, with the first item in the array being the most probable object class.

It is important to note that this method is not called on the main UI thread and, therefore, any updates to the user interface must be wrapped in a DispatchQueue.main .async{} block.

6. Now that you have written the code to create a VNCoreMLRequest and processed the results of the image classification, all you need to do is write code to create and execute the VNCoreMLRequest when the user selects an image. Earlier in this chapter you created an empty method called func detectPet(in image: UIImage). Replace the empty method with the following:

```
func detectPet(in image: UIImage) {
    resultLabel.text = "Processing..."

    guard let ciImage = CIImage(image: image),
        let orientation = CGImagePropertyOrientation(rawValue:
                        UInt32(image.imageOrientation.rawValue))
    else {
        print("Unable to create CIImage instance")
        resultLabel.text = "Failed."
        return
    }

    DispatchQueue.global(qos: .userInitiated).async {
        let handler = VNImageRequestHandler(ciImage: ciImage,
                                orientation: orientation)
        do {
            try handler.perform([self.classificationRequest])
        } catch {
            print("Failed to perform
                    classification.\n\(error.localizedDescription)")
        }
    }
}
```

This function is already wired to be called from the UIImagePickerController delegate method. It receives a UIImage instance that represents the image selected by the user from the photo library or captured with the camera. The code in this function converts the UIImage instance into a CIImage instance and then creates a VNImageRequestHandler object with the CIImage instance:

```
guard let ciImage = CIImage(image: image),
    let orientation = CGImagePropertyOrientation(rawValue:
                    UInt32(image.imageOrientation.rawValue))
else {
    print("Unable to create CIImage instance")
    resultLabel.text = "Failed."
    return
}
```

Recall that the `VNImageRequestHandler` object can be used to execute a `VNCoreMLRequest`, which is performed by calling `perform` on the handler object.

```
let handler = VNImageRequestHandler(ciImage: ciImage,
                                    orientation: orientation)
do {
    try handler.perform([self.classificationRequest])
} catch {
    print("Failed to perform
            classification.\n\(error.localizedDescription)")
}
```

Since object detection is a time-consuming operation and you do not want to block your application user interface while Core ML is executing the model, the call to create the `VNImageRequestHandler` and execute the `VNCoreMLRequest` is wrapped in a `DispatchQueue.global(qos: .userInitiated).async` block. The code in the `ViewController.swift` file should now resemble Listing 10.3.

LISTING 10.3:   Completed ViewController.swift File

```
import UIKit
import CoreML
import Vision

class ViewController: UIViewController {

    @IBOutlet weak var imageView: UIImageView!
    @IBOutlet weak var resultLabel: UILabel!

    lazy var classificationRequest: VNCoreMLRequest = {
        do {
            let model = try VNCoreMLModel(for: Inceptionv4_dogscats().model)

            let request = VNCoreMLRequest(model: model,
                completionHandler: { [weak self] request, error in
                    self?.processResults(for: request, error: error)
            })

            request.imageCropAndScaleOption = .scaleFit
            return request
        } catch {
            fatalError("Failed to load Core ML model")
        }
    }()


    override func viewDidLoad() {
        super.viewDidLoad()
```

```
        // Do any additional setup after loading the view.
    }

    @IBAction func onSelectImageFromPhotoLibrary(_ sender: Any) {
        let picker = UIImagePickerController()
        picker.delegate = self
        picker.sourceType = .photoLibrary
        present(picker, animated: true)
    }

    @IBAction func onSelectImageFromCamera(_ sender: Any) {
        // ensure camera is available.
        guard UIImagePickerController.isSourceTypeAvailable(.camera) else {

            let alertController = UIAlertController(title: "Error",
                                message: "Could not access the camera.",
                                preferredStyle: .alert)

            self.present(alertController, animated: true, completion: nil)
            return
        }

        let picker = UIImagePickerController()
        picker.delegate = self
        picker.sourceType = .camera
        present(picker, animated: true)

    }

    func detectPet(in image: UIImage) {
        resultLabel.text = "Processing..."

        guard let ciImage = CIImage(image: image),
            let orientation = CGImagePropertyOrientation(rawValue:
                            UInt32(image.imageOrientation.rawValue))
        else {
            print("Unable to create CIImage instance")
            resultLabel.text = "Failed."
            return
        }

        DispatchQueue.global(qos: .userInitiated).async {
            let handler = VNImageRequestHandler(ciImage: ciImage,
                                    orientation: orientation)
            do {
                try handler.perform([self.classificationRequest])
            } catch {
                print("Failed to perform
```

```swift
                                    classification.\n\(error.localizedDescription)")
                }
            }
        }

    func processResults(for request: VNRequest, error: Error?) {
        DispatchQueue.main.async {
            guard let results = request.results else {
                print("Unable to classify image.\n\(error!.localizedDes
    cription)")
                self.resultLabel.text = "Unable to classify image."
                return
            }

            let classifications = results as! [VNClassificationObservation]

            if classifications.isEmpty {
                self.resultLabel.text = "Did not recognize anything."
            } else {

                let catProbability = classifications[0].confidence * 100.0
                let dogProbability = classifications[1].confidence * 100.0

                self.resultLabel.text = String(format: "Cat probability=%.1f%,
                                                Dog probability=%.1f%",
                                    catProbability, dogProbability)
            }
        }
    }

}


extension ViewController: UIImagePickerControllerDelegate,
                        UINavigationControllerDelegate {

    func imagePickerController(_ picker: UIImagePickerController,
        didFinishPickingMediaWithInfo info:
        [UIImagePickerController.InfoKey : Any]) {
        picker.dismiss(animated: true)
        let image = info[UIImagePickerController.InfoKey.originalImage]
                    as! UIImage
        imageView.image = image
        detectPet(in: image)
    }
}
```

Save your project and run the app on an iOS device. Use the camera to take a picture of a dog or a cat. You should see the results of the object detection process on the screen. Figure 10.24 depicts the results of running the app on a device and selecting the picture of a dog from the photo library.

NOTE   If you do not want to test this app on a real phone, launch Safari on the iOS Simulator and drag a few images of dogs and cats from your macOS finder into Safari on the iOS Simulator.

You can now run the app on the iOS Simulator and select these images from the photo library on the simulator.

FIGURE 10.24

Results of running the app with the picture of a dog

As you can see, the result indicates that the model has successfully detected the image as that of a dog, with 100 percent confidence. Keep in mind that you have set the value of the image-CropAndScale option of the VNCoreMLRequest object to .scaleFilt. You can try different imageCropAndScale values to gauge the performance of the model with these values.

NOTE   You can download the code files for this chapter from wrox.com or from GitHub using the following URL:

https://github.com/asmtechnology/iosmlbook-chapter10.git

Summary

- The first version of the Inception deep learning network was proposed in 2014 by Christian Szegedy et al.

- There are several revisions to the original Inception architecture, with the latest being the Inception-v4 and Inception-ResNet architectures.

- The core idea in an inception-style network is that of an Inception block. There are different types of Inception blocks, and the network architecture consists of stacking these blocks.

- Keras is a popular Python-based deep learning framework created by François Chollet.

- Keras provides a layer of abstraction on top of other deep-learning libraries such as Google TensorFlow.

- Keras provides two model-building APIs, the sequential API and the functional API.

- The Keras functional API allows you to represent each layer of the network as a function and apply this function to the output of the previous layer.

- Training a deep neural network such as Inception-v4 from scratch requires a computer with a high-end NVIDIA GPU.

- Keras uses Python generators. A generator is a function that generates some data and in the context of the training process will generate a batch of samples.

- Generators provide a layer of abstraction between the actual training data and the model. You can modify the data as it flows through the generator and even generate data algorithmically.

- Keras provides a limited degree of image preprocessing support that can be used to modify the training data before it is presented to the network. These modifications (also known as *augmentations*) are used to make the network more robust to subtle changes in the size, shape, and orientation of objects in images.

- Core ML Tools can be used to export a Keras model to the Core ML format.

Appendix A

Anaconda and Jupyter Notebook Setup

WHAT'S IN THIS APPENDIX

◆ Installing the Anaconda distribution

◆ Setting up a Python environment

◆ Setting up Jupyter Notebook

In this appendix, you learn to install Anaconda Navigator on your computer, set up a Python environment that includes several common machine learning libraries, and configure Jupyter Notebook.

Installing the Anaconda Distribution

Anaconda is a Python *distribution* (prebuilt and preconfigured collection of packages) that is commonly used for data science. The Anaconda distribution includes the Conda package manager in addition to the preconfigured Python packages and other tools. The Conda package manager can be used from the command line to set up Python environments and install additional packages that come with the default Anaconda distribution.

Anaconda Navigator is a GUI tool that is included in the Anaconda distribution and makes it easy to configure, install, and launch tools such as Jupyter Notebook. Although we use the Anaconda Navigator in this book, keep in mind that you can do everything through the command line using the conda command.

To begin the Anaconda Navigator installation process, visit https://www.anaconda.com and click the Downloads link at the top-right corner of the page (see Figure A.1).

On the Downloads page, locate the download link for a version that includes Python 3.7 or higher (see Figure A.2). Click the Download link to download the installer for your operating system.

Locate the installer on your computer's download folder and launch it to begin the installation process (see Figure A.3).

At some point in the installation process, you may be asked if you want to install an IDE such as Microsoft Visual Studio Code or JetBrain PyCharm (see Figure A.4). Installing an IDE is optional, and in this book we do not use any third-party IDE. If you want to install a third-party IDE, you can do so either during the Anaconda distribution installation process or later from the Anaconda Navigator user interface.

FIGURE A.1
Anaconda
.com home page

FIGURE A.2
Downloading the
appropriate version of
Anaconda distribution

The Anaconda distribution will be installed on your computer when the installer completes successfully (see Figure A.5).

Creating a Conda Python Environment

A fresh Anaconda installation comes with a single Conda Python environment called *base (root)*, and it includes a set of pre-installed packages. In this section, you will create a new Conda Python environment and install a set of packages that have been used for the examples in this book. A Conda Python environment is an isolated environment and allows you to install packages without modifying your system's Python installation.

FIGURE A.3
Anaconda distribution
installer on macOS X

FIGURE A.4
Anaconda installer
provides the option to
install third-party IDEs

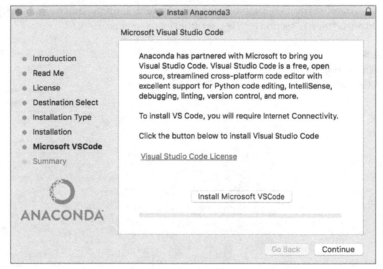

Python's officially sanctioned package manager is called PiP (Pip Installs Packages). It gets its packages from an online repository called the Python Package Index (PyPI). Conda is a language-agnostic package manager and is used to install packages within Conda environments. This is an important distinction—Conda cannot help you install packages on your system Python installation.

A number of tools that are included with Anaconda Navigator, such as Jupyter Notebook and Spyder IDE, will pick up the Conda environments available on your computer and allow you to switch between different environments with little overhead.

FIGURE A.5
Anaconda has been
successfully installed.

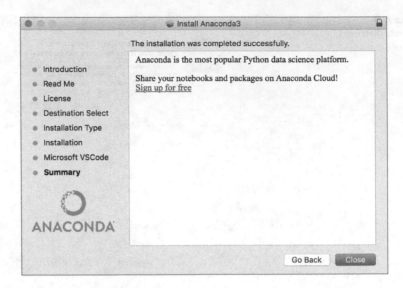

To get started creating a new environment, launch Anaconda Navigator and switch to the Environments section of the user interface (see Figure A.6).

FIGURE A.6
Environment settings in
Anaconda Navigator

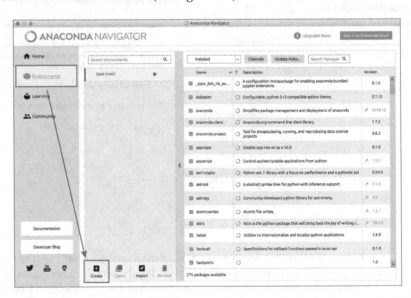

You will see the *base (root)* environment created by the Anaconda installer along with all the packages contained in the environment. Click the Create button to create a new Conda environment.

Provide a name for the new Conda environment (see Figure A.7). Ensure that the Python language is checked, and the Python version is set to 3.7 or higher. Ensure that the R language checkbox is unchecked. The Python examples in this book assume the Conda environment is called *IOS_ML_Book*. However, you are free to use your own name. Remember to select the appropriate environment while trying out the examples in this book. Click the Create button in the Create New Environment dialog box to finish creating the environment.

FIGURE A.7
Creating a new Conda
Python environment

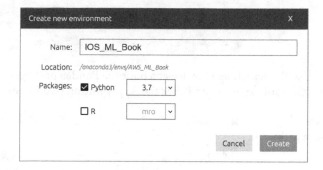

After a few minutes, a new Conda environment will be created on your computer, and you will see it listed in Anaconda Navigator (see Figure A.8).

FIGURE A.8
Switching to the IOS_
ML_Book Conda
environment

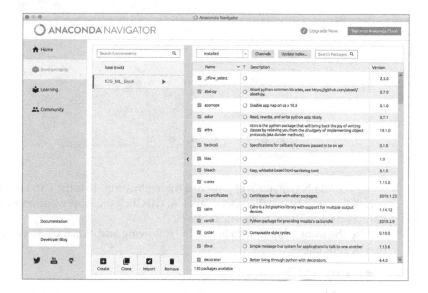

Clicking the new environment will display a list of packages in this environment. By default, all new Conda environments are created with a minimal set of packages.

Installing Python Packages

In this section, you will install a number of Python packages in your new Conda environment. To start with, ensure your Conda environment is selected in the Anaconda Navigator application. Select the All option in the package type combo box (see Figure A.9).

FIGURE A.9
Displaying all available
Python packages

Use the search text box to search for the Pandas package. Locate the Pandas package in the search result, select it, and click the Apply button (see Figure A.10).

FIGURE A.10
Searching for a package

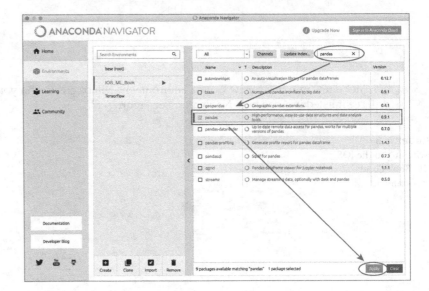

Anaconda Navigator will present a dialog box that lists the Pandas package and all dependencies that will be installed (see Figure A.11). Click the Apply button to finish installing the Pandas package and its dependencies.

Use the same technique to install the following additional packages along with their respective dependencies:

◆ `matplotlib`

◆ `pillow`

◆ `scikit-learn`

◆ `tensorflow`

◆ `keras`

NOTE   If your computer has an Nvidia GPU, you will have the option to install a GPU-accelerated version of TensorFlow called TensorFlow-GPU.

FIGURE A.11
Package dependencies
dialog box

Installing Jupyter Notebook

In this section, you will install Jupyter Notebook in the Conda environment that you created earlier in this appendix. Launch Anaconda Navigator and switch to the Home tab. Locate the Jupyter Notebook icon and click the Install button (see Figure A.12). This action will install Jupyter Notebook in the default base (root) environment.

FIGURE A.12
Installing
Jupyter Notebook

After Jupyter Notebook has been installed, launch a Terminal window on your Mac (or Command Prompt in Windows) and type the following command to list all Conda environments on your computer. Press the Enter key after typing the command. This command assumes the location of the conda command-line tool referenced by your system $PATH variable.

```
$ conda info -envs
```

The output on your computer should resemble the following:

```
AMBP:~ abhishekmishra$ conda info -envs
# conda environments:
#
base                     *  /anaconda3
IOS_ML_Book                 /anaconda3/envs/IOS_ML_Book
```

You should see the Conda environment you created earlier in this appendix along with any other Conda environments that exist on your computer.

Type the following command to switch to the Conda environment you created earlier in this appendix. Replace IOS_ML_Book with the name of the environment you created. Press the Enter key after typing the command.

```
$ conda activate IOS_ML_Book
```

Type the following command to install Jupyter Notebooks in the Conda environment you have just activated with the previous command.

```
$ conda install jupyter
```

The output on your computer should resemble the following:

```
$ conda install jupyter
Solving environment: done

## Package Plan ##

  environment location: /anaconda3/envs/IOS_ML_Book

  added / updated specs:
    - jupyter


The following packages will be downloaded:

    package                    |              build
    ---------------------------|-----------------
    widgetsnbextension-3.4.2   |          py36_0        1.7 MB
    ipywidgets-7.4.2           |          py36_0        151 KB
    qtconsole-4.4.2            |          py36_0        157 KB
    pyqt-5.9.2                 |    py36h655552a_2       4.4 MB
    jupyter-1.0.0              |          py36_7          6 KB
    sip-4.19.8                 |    py36h0a44026_0       252 KB
    jupyter_console-6.0.0      |          py36_0         35 KB
    ---------------------------------------------------------
                                          Total:         6.7 MB
```

```
The following NEW packages will be INSTALLED:

    dbus:               1.13.2-h760590f_1
    expat:              2.2.6-h0a44026_0
    gettext:            0.19.8.1-h15daf44_3
    glib:               2.56.2-hd9629dc_0
    icu:                58.2-h4b95b61_1
    ipywidgets:         7.4.2-py36_0
    jupyter:            1.0.0-py36_7
    jupyter_console:    6.0.0-py36_0
    libiconv:           1.15-hdd342a3_7
    pcre:               8.42-h378b8a2_0
    pyqt:               5.9.2-py36h655552a_2
    qt:                 5.9.6-h45cd832_2
    qtconsole:          4.4.2-py36_0
    sip:                4.19.8-py36h0a44026_0
    widgetsnbextension: 3.4.2-py36_0
```

```
Proceed ([y]/n)?
```

You will be presented with a summary of the packages that will be installed in the environment and asked if you want to proceed. Press the Y key on your keyboard and then Enter to continue.

After Jupyter Notebook has finished installing in the new Conda environment, type the following command to create a new kernel specification in Jupyter Notebook. A kernel specification will allow you to switch to your new Conda environment from within Jupyter Notebook. Replace *IOS_ML_BOOK* with the name of your environment. Press the Enter key after typing the command.

```
$ python -m ipykernel install --user --name IOS_ML_BOOK --display-name "Python
(IOS_ML_BOOK)"
```

You should see a message on your computer confirming that the kernel specification has been installed:

```
Installed kernelspec IOS_ML_BOOK in /Users/abhishekmishra/Library/Jupyter/
kernels/ios_ml_book
```

Type the following command to install the `nb-conda-kernels` package from the `conda-forge` repository (also known as a *channel*). Press the Enter key after typing the command.

```
$ conda install --channel=conda-forge nb_conda_kernels
```

You will once again be asked to confirm whether you want to download and install the `nb_conda_kernels` package along with dependencies. Press the Y key on your keyboard when asked to finish installing the packages.

You can now use Anaconda Navigator to launch Jupyter Notebook. The notebook is launched in your default web browser and configured to display the contents of your user directory (see Figure A.13).

FIGURE A.13
Jupyter Notebook
running in a
web browser

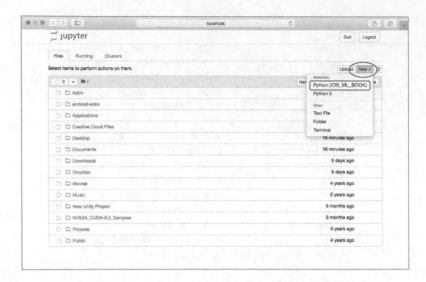

Clicking the New button from the Jupyter Notebook page within your web browser will display a drop-down menu allowing you to create a new notebook using one of the kernels installed on your computer. A kernel corresponding to the new Conda environment you created earlier in this appendix should be listed in the drop-down menu.

You can also launch Jupyter Notebook using the command line by typing the following command in a Terminal (or Command Prompt) window and pressing Enter:

```
$ jupyter notebook
```

Summary

◆ Anaconda is a Python distribution (prebuilt and preconfigured collection of packages) that is commonly used for data science. The Anaconda distribution includes the Conda package manager in addition to the preconfigured Python packages and other tools.

◆ Anaconda Navigator is a GUI tool that is included in the Anaconda distribution and makes it easy to configure, install, and launch tools such as Jupyter Notebook.

◆ A Conda Python environment is an isolated environment. It allows you to install packages without modifying your system's Python installation.

Appendix B

Introduction to NumPy and Pandas

WHAT'S IN THIS APPENDIX

- ◆ Learning the basics of the NumPy Python library
- ◆ Learning the basics of the Pandas Python library

In this appendix you will learn to use two popular Python libraries used by data scientists— NumPy and Pandas. These libraries are commonly used during the data exploration and feature engineering phase of a project. The examples in this appendix require the use of Jupyter Notebooks.

NOTE To follow along with this appendix, ensure you have installed Anaconda Navigator and Jupyter Notebooks, as described in Appendix A.

You can download the code files for this appendix from `Wrox.com` or from GitHub using the following URL:

```
https://github.com/asmtechnology/awsmlbook-appendixb.git
```

NumPy

NumPy is a math library for Python that allows for fast and efficient manipulation of arrays. The main object provided by NumPy is a homogenous multidimensional array called an *ndarray*. All the elements of an ndarray must be of the same data type, and dimensions are referred to as *axes* in NumPy terminology.

To use NumPy in a Python project, you typically add the following import statement to your Python file:

```
import numpy as np
```

The lowercase alias np is a standard convention for referring to NumPy in Python projects.

Creating NumPy Arrays

There are a number of ways in which you can create an ndarray. To create an ndarray object out of a three-element Python list, use the np.array() statement. The following code snippet, when typed in a Jupyter notebook, will result in an NumPy array created with three elements:

```
# creating an ndarray
x = np.array([10, 27, 34])
```

```
print (x)
```

```
[10 27 34]
```

Note the use of the square brackets within the parentheses. Omitting the square brackets will result in an error. The ndarray x has one axis and three elements. Unlike arrays created using the Python library class called array, NumPy arrays can be multidimensional. The following statements create a NumPy array with two axes and print the contents of the ndarray object:

```
# creating a two-dimensional ndarray
points = np.array([[11, 28, 9], [56, 38, 91], [33,87,36], [87,8,4]])
print (points)
```

```
[[11 28  9]
 [56 38 91]
 [33 87 36]
 [87  8  4]]
```

The ndarray created by this statement will have two axes and can be represented for visualization purposes as a two-dimensional matrix with four rows and three columns.

11	28	9
56	38	91
33	87	36
87	8	4

The first axis contains four elements (the number of rows), and the second axis contains three elements (the number of columns). Table B.1 contains some of the commonly used attributes of ndarrays.

TABLE B.1:   Commonly Used ndarray Attributes

ATTRIBUTE	DESCRIPTION
ndim	Returns the number of axes
shape	Returns the number of elements along each axis
size	Returns the total number of elements in the ndarray
dtype	Returns the data type of the elements in the ndarray

All elements in an ndarray must have the same data type. NumPy provides its own data types, the most commonly used of which are np.int16, np.int32, and np.float64. Unlike Python, NumPy provides multiple data types for a particular data class. This is similar to the C language concept of short, int, long, signed, and unsigned variants of a data class. For example, NumPy provides the following data types for signed integers:

◆ byte: This is compatible with a C char.

◆ short: This is compatible with a C short.

◆ intc: This is compatible with a C int.

◆ int_: This is compatible with a Python int and a C long.

◆ longlong: This is compatible with a C long long.

◆ intp: This data type can be used to represent a pointer, the number of bytes depend on the processor architecture and operating system your code is running on.

◆ int8: A 8 bit signed integer. This is the same as int8_t in C.

◆ int16: A 16 bit signed integer. This is the same as int16_t in C.

◆ int32: A 32 bit signed integer. This is the same as int32_t in C.

◆ int64: A 64 bit signed integer. This is the same as int64_t in C.

Some NumPy data types are compatible with Python. These usually end in an underscore character (such as int_, float_). A complete list of NumPy data types can be found at https://docs.scipy.org/doc/numpy-1.15.1/reference/arrays.scalars.html#arrays-scalars-built-in.

You can specify the data type when creating ndarrays, as illustrated in the following snippet:

```
#creating a one dimensional array, whilst specifying the data type
y = np.array([10, 27, 34], dtype=np.float64)
print (y)
```

```
[10. 27. 34.]
```

When you specify the elements in the array at the time of creation but do not specify the data type, NumPy attempts to guess the most appropriate data type. The default data type is float_, which is compatible with a Python float.

When creating a NumPy array, if you do not know the values of the elements but know the size and number of axes, you can use one of the following functions to create ndarrays with placeholder content:

◆ zeros: Creates an ndarray of specified dimensions, with each element being zero

◆ ones: Creates an ndarray of specified dimensions, with each element being one

◆ empty: Creates an unintialized ndarray of specified dimensions

◆ random.random: Creates an array of random values that lie in the half-open interval [0.0, 1.0)

As an example, if you wanted to create an ndarray with four rows and three columns, where each element is an int16 with value 1, you would use a statement similar to the following:

```
# create an array with ones
a = np.ones((4,3), dtype=np.int16)
```

```
print (a)
```

```
[[1 1 1]
 [1 1 1]
 [1 1 1]
 [1 1 1]]
```

The following statement would create an ndarray with two rows and three columns populated with random numbers. The data type of random numbers is `float_`.

```
# create an array with random numbers
r = np.random.random([2,3])
print (r)
```

```
[[0.48746158 0.93214926 0.1450121 ]
 [0.69303901 0.43758922 0.62645661]]
```

NumPy provides methods to create sequences of numbers, the most commonly used are the following:

◆ `arange`: Creates a single axis ndarray with evenly spaced elements

◆ `linspace`: Creates a single axis ndarray with evenly spaced elements

The `arange` function is similar to the Python `range` function in functionality. The `arange` function takes four arguments. The first value is the start of the range, the second is the end of the range, the third is the step increment between numbers within the range, and the fourth is an optional parameter that allows you to specify the data type.

For example, the following snippet creates an ndarray, the elements of which lie in the range `[0,9(`. Each element in the ndarray is greater than the previous element by three.

```
# use the arange function to create a sequence of numbers
sequence1 = np.arange(0, 9, 3)
print (sequence1)
```

```
[0 3 6]
```

The upper limit of the range is not included in the numbers that are generated by the `arange` function. Therefore, the ndarray generated by the previous statement will have the following elements, and not include the number 9:

```
0, 3, 6
```

If you want a sequence of integers from 0 up until a specific number, you can call the `arange` function with a single argument. The following statements achieve identical results:

```
# these arange statements achieve identical results.
sequence2 = np.arange(5)
sequence3 = np.arange(0,5,1)

print (sequence2)
[0 1 2 3 4]
```

```
print (sequence3)
0 1 2 3 4]
```

The linspace function is similar to arrange in that it generates a sequence of numbers that lie within a range. The difference is that the third element is the number of values that are required between the start and end values. The following statement created an ndarray with three elements, between 0 and 9:

```
# the linspace function can also be used to obtain a sequence
sequence4 = np.linspace(0, 9, 3)
print (sequence4)
```

```
[0.     4.5     9. ]
```

Unlike the arrange function, the linspace function ensures that the specified lower and upper bounds are part of the sequence.

Modifying Arrays

NumPy provides several functions that allow you to modify the contents of arrays. While it is not possible to cover each of them in this appendix, the most commonly used operations will be discussed.

ARITHMETIC OPERATIONS

NumPy allows you to perform element-wise arithmetic operations between two arrays. The result of the operation is stored in a new array. The +, -, /, and * operators retain their arithmetic meaning. The following code snippet demonstrates how to perform arithmetic operations on two ndarrays:

```
# Elementwise Arithmetic operations can be performed on ndarrays
array1 = np.array([[1,2,3], [2, 3, 4]])
array2 = np.array([[3,4,5], [4, 5, 6]])

Sum = array1 + array2
Difference = array1 - array2
Product = array1 * array2
Division = array1 / array2

print (Sum)
[[ 4  6  8]
 [ 6  8 10]]

print (Difference)
[[-2 -2 -2]
 [-2 -2 -2]]

print (Product)
[[ 3  8 15]
 [ 8 15 24]]
```

```
print (Division)
[[0.33333333 0.5        0.6        ]
 [0.5        0.6        0.66666667]]
```

You can use the +=, -=, *=, and /= operators to perform in-place element-wise arithmetic operations. The results of these operations are not stored in a new array. The use of these operators is demonstrated in the following snippet:

```
# in-place elementwise arithmetic operations
array1 = np.array([1,2,3], dtype=np.float64)
array2 = np.array([3,4,5], dtype=np.float64)
array3 = np.array([4,5,6], dtype=np.float64)
array4 = np.array([5,6,7], dtype=np.float64)

# in-place arithmetic and can be performed using arrays of the same size
array1 += np.array([10,10,10], dtype=np.float64)
array2 -= np.array([10,10,10], dtype=np.float64)
array3 *= np.array([10,10,10], dtype=np.float64)
array4 /= np.array([10,10,10], dtype=np.float64)

# in-place arithmetic can be performed using a scalar value
array1 +  = 100.0
array2 -= 100.0
array3 *= 100.0
array4 /= 100.0

print (array1)
[111. 112. 113.]

print (array2)
[-107. -106. -105.]

print (array3)
[4000. 5000. 6000.]

print (array4)
[0.005 0.006 0.007]
```

The exponent operator is represented by two asterisk symbols, **. The following statements demonstrate the use of the exponent operator:

```
# the exponent operator
array1 = np.arange(4, dtype=np.float64)
array1 **= 4
print (array1)

[ 0.  1. 16. 81.]
```

COMPARISON OPERATIONS

NumPy provides the standard comparison operators <, >, <= , >=, ! = , and ==. The comparison operators can be used with ndarrays of the same size or a scalar. The result of using a comparison operator is an ndarray of Booleans. The use of comparison operators is demonstrated in the following snippet:

```
array1 = np.array([1,4,5])
array2 = np.array([3,2,5])

# less than
print (array1 < array2)
[True False False]

# less than equal to
print (array1 <= array2)
[True False  True]

# greater than
print (array1 > array2)
[False  True False]

# greater than equal to
print (array1 >= array2)
[False  True  True]

# equal to
print (array1 == array2)
[False False  True]

# not equal to
print (array1 != array2)
[ True  True False]
```

MATRIX OPERATIONS

NumPy provides the ability to perform matrix operations on ndarrays. The following list contains some of the most commonly used matrix operations:

- ◆ inner: Performs a dot product between two arrays
- ◆ outer: Performs the outer product between two arrays
- ◆ cross: Performs the cross product between two arrays
- ◆ transpose: Swaps the rows and columns of an array

The use of matrix operations is demonstrated in the following snippet:

```
array1 = np.array([1,4,5], dtype=np.float_)
array2 = np.array([3,2,5], dtype=np.float_)
```

```
# inner (dot product)
print (np.inner(array1, array2))
36.0

# outer product
print (np.outer(array1, array2))
[[ 3.  2.  5.]
 [12.  8. 20.]
 [15. 10. 25.]]

# cross product
print (np.cross(array1, array2))
[ 10.  10. -10.]
```

Indexing and Slicing

NumPy provides the ability to index elements in an array as well as slice larger arrays into smaller ones. NumPy array indexes are zero-based. The following code snippet demonstrates how to index and slice one-dimensional arrays:

```
# create a one-dimensional array with 10 elements
array1 = np.linspace(0, 9, 10)

print (array1)
[0. 1. 2. 3. 4. 5. 6. 7. 8. 9.]

# get the third element. Indexes are zero-based.
print (array1[3])
3.0

# extracts elements 2 , 3, 4 into a sub array
print (array1[2:5])
[2. 3. 4.]

#extract first 6 elements of the array (elements 0 to 5)
print (array1[:6])
[0. 1. 2. 3. 4. 5.]

# extract elements 5 onwards
print(array1[5:])
[5. 6. 7. 8. 9.]

# extract every alternate element, step value is specified as 2
print (array1[::2])
[0. 2. 4. 6. 8.]

# reverse all the elements in array1
print (array1[::-1])
```

```
[9. 8. 7. 6. 5. 4. 3. 2. 1. 0.]
```

Indexing a multidimensional array requires you to provide a tuple with the value for each axis. The following code snippet demonstrates how to index and slice multidimensional arrays:

```
# create a two-dimensional array with 12 elements
array1 = np.array([[1,2,3,4], [5,6,7,8], [9, 10, 11, 12]])

print (array1)
[[ 1  2  3  4]
 [ 5  6  7  8]
 [ 9 10 11 12]]

# get the element in the second row, third column. Indexes are zero-based.
print (array1[1,2])
7

# get all the elements in the first column
print (array1[:,0])
[1 5 9]

#get all the elements in the first row
print (array1[0,:])
[1 2 3 4]

# get a sub 2-dimensional array
print (array1[:3, :2])
[[ 1  2]
 [ 5  6]
 [ 9 10]]
```

Pandas

Pandas is a free, open source data analysis library for Python and is one of the most commonly used tools for data munging. The key objects provided by Pandas are the series and dataframe. A Pandas series is similar to a one-dimensional list, and a dataframe is similar to a two-dimensional table. One of the key differences between Pandas dataframes and NumPy arrays is that the columns in a dataframe object can have different data types and can even handle missing values.

To use Pandas in a Python project, you typically add the following import statement to your Python file:

```
import pandas as pd
```

The lowercase alias pd is a standard convention for referring to Pandas in Python projects.

Creating Series and Dataframes

There are many ways to create a series and a dataframe object with Pandas. The simplest way is to create a Pandas series out of a Python list, as demonstrated in the following snippet:

```
# create a Pandas series from a Python list.
car_manufacturers = ['Volkswagen','Ford','Mercedes-Benz','BMW','Nissan']
pds_car_manufacturers = pd.Series(data=car_manufacturers)
print (pds_car_manufacturers)

0        Volkswagen
1              Ford
2     Mercedes-Benz
3               BMW
4            Nissan
dtype: object
```

A Pandas series contains an additional index column, which contains a unique integer value for each row of the series. In most cases, Pandas automatically creates this index column, and the index value can be used to select an item using square brackets, [ ]:

```
print (pds_car_manufacturers[2])
```

Mercedes-Benz

If your data is loaded into a Python dictionary, you can convert the dictionary into a Pandas dataframe. A dataframe built from a Python dictionary does not, by default, have an integer index for each row of the dataframe. The following example shows how to convert a Python dictionary into a Pandas dataframe:

```
# create a Pandas series from a Python dictionary
#
# Pandas does not generate a series index.
cars = {'RJ09VWQ':'Blue Volkswagen Polo',
        'WQ81R09':'Red Ford Focus',
        'PB810AQ':'White Mercedes-Benz E-Class',
        'TU914A8':'Silver BMW 1 Series'}

pds_cars = pd.Series(data=cars)

print (pds_cars)
RJ09VWQ           Blue Volkswagen Polo
WQ81R09                 Red Ford Focus
PB810AQ    White Mercedes-Benz E-Class
TU914A8            Silver BMW 1 Series
dtype: object
```

Even though the dataframe does not have a numeric index, you can still use numbers to select a value.

```
print (pds_cars[2])
```

White Mercedes-Benz E-Class

Since the dataframe was created from a Python dictionary, the keys of the dictionary can be used to select a value.

```
print (pds_cars['WQ81R09'])
```

Red Ford Focus

The reason you are able to use the keys from the dictionary object is that Pandas is clever enough to create an Index object for your dataframe. You can use the following statement to view the contents of the index of the data frame:

```
print (pds_cars.index)
```

```
Index(['RJ09VWQ', 'WQ81R09', 'PB810AQ', 'TU914A8'], dtype='object')
```

In most real-world use cases, you do not create Pandas dataframes from Python lists and dictionaries; instead, you will want to load the entire contents of a CSV file straight into a dataframe. The following snippet shows how to load the contents of a CSV file that is included with the resources that accompany this lesson into a Pandas dataframe:

```
# load the contents of a file into a pandas Dataframe
input_file = './titanic_dataset/original/train.csv'
df_iris = pd.read_csv(input_file)
```

The dataframe created in this case is a matrix of columns and rows. You can get a list of column names by using the columns attribute.

```
# print the names of the columns
print (df_iris.columns)
```

```
Index(['PassengerId', 'Survived', 'Pclass', 'Name', 'Sex', 'Age', 'SibSp',
       'Parch', 'Ticket', 'Fare', 'Cabin', 'Embarked'],
    dtype='object')
```

You can also create a dataframe by selecting a subset of named columns from an existing dataframe, as shown in the following example:

```
# create a Dataframe with a subset of the columns in df_iris
df_iris_subset = df_iris[['PassengerId', 'Survived', 'Pclass',
'Sex','Fare', 'Age']]
```

Getting Dataframe Information

Pandas provides several useful functions to inspect the contents of a dataframe, get information on the memory footprint of the dataframe, and get statistical information on the columns of a dataframe. Some of the commonly used functions to inspect the contents of a dataframe are listed here:

- ◆ shape(): Use this function to determine the number of columns and rows in a dataframe.

- ◆ head(n): Use this function to inspect the first *n* rows of the dataset. If you do not specify a value for n, the default used is 5.

◆ tail(n): Use this function to inspect the last *n* rows of the dataset. If you do not specify a value for n, the default used is 5.

◆ sample(n): Use this function to inspect a random sample of *n* rows from the dataset. If you do not specify a value for n, the default used is 1.

The following code snippet demonstrates the use of the shape(), head(), tail(), and sample() functions:

```
# how many rows and columns in the dataset
print (df_iris_subset.shape)
(891, 6)


# print first 5 rows
print (df_iris_subset.head())
```

	PassengerId	Survived	Pclass	Sex	Fare	Age
0	1	0	3	male	7.2500	22.0
1	2	1	1	female	71.2833	38.0
2	3	1	3	female	7.9250	26.0
3	4	1	1	female	53.1000	35.0
4	5	0	3	male	8.0500	35.0

```
# print last 3 rows
print (df_iris_subset.tail(3))
```

	PassengerId	Survived	Pclass	Sex	Fare	Age
888	889	0	3	female	23.45	NaN
889	890	1	1	male	30.00	26.0
890	891	0	3	male	7.75	32.0

```
# print a random sample of 10 rows
print (df_iris_subset.sample(10))
```

	PassengerId	Survived	Pclass	Sex	Fare	Age
710	711	1	1	female	49.5042	24.0
127	128	1	3	male	7.1417	24.0
222	223	0	3	male	8.0500	51.0
795	796	0	2	male	13.0000	39.0
673	674	1	2	male	13.0000	31.0
115	116	0	3	male	7.9250	21.0
451	452	0	3	male	19.9667	NaN
642	643	0	3	female	27.9000	2.0
853	854	1	1	female	39.4000	16.0
272	273	1	2	female	19.5000	41.0

Pandas provides several useful functions to get information on the statistical characteristics and memory footprint of the data. These are some of the most commonly used functions to obtain statistical information:

- ◆ describe(): Provides information on the number of non-null values, mean, standard deviation, minimum value, maximum value, and quartiles of all numeric columns in the dataframe.

- ◆ mean(): Provides the mean value of each column.

- ◆ median(): Provides the median value of each column.

- ◆ std(): Provides the standard deviation of the values of each column.

- ◆ count(): Returns the number of non-null values in each column.

- ◆ max(): Returns the largest value in each column.

- ◆ min(): Returns the smallest value in each column.

The following snippet demonstrates the use of some of these statistical functions:

```
# get statistical information on numeric columns
print (df_iris_subset.describe())
```

	PassengerId	Survived	Pclass	Fare	Age
count	891.000000	891.000000	891.000000	891.000000	714.000000
mean	446.000000	0.383838	2.308642	32.204208	29.699118
std	257.353842	0.486592	0.836071	49.693429	14.526497
min	1.000000	0.000000	1.000000	0.000000	0.420000
25%	223.500000	0.000000	2.000000	7.910400	20.125000
50%	446.000000	0.000000	3.000000	14.454200	28.000000
75%	668.500000	1.000000	3.000000	31.000000	38.000000
max	891.000000	1.000000	3.000000	512.329200	80.000000

```
# mean of all columns
print (df_iris_subset.mean())
```

```
PassengerId    446.000000
Survived         0.383838
Pclass           2.308642
Fare            32.204208
Age             29.699118
dtype: float64
```

```
# the following statement is identical to the previous one,
# as axis = 0 implies columns.
print (df_iris_subset.mean(axis=0))
```

```
PassengerId    446.000000
Survived         0.383838
Pclass           2.308642
Fare            32.204208
Age             29.699118
dtype: float64
```

```
#correlation between columns
print (df_iris_subset.corr())
```

```
             PassengerId   Survived     Pclass       Fare        Age
PassengerId     1.000000  -0.005007  -0.035144   0.012658   0.036847
Survived       -0.005007   1.000000  -0.338481   0.257307  -0.077221
Pclass         -0.035144  -0.338481   1.000000  -0.549500  -0.369226
Fare            0.012658   0.257307  -0.549500   1.000000   0.096067
Age             0.036847  -0.077221  -0.369226   0.096067   1.000000
```

```
# number of non-null values in each column
print (df_iris_subset.count())
```

```
PassengerId   891
Survived      891
Pclass        891
Sex           891
Fare          891
Age           714
dtype: int64
```

The info() function provides information on the data type of each column and the total memory required to store the dataframe. The following snippet demonstrates the use of the info() function:

```
# get information on data types and memory footprint
print (df_iris_subset.info())
```

```
<class 'pandas.core.frame.DataFrame'>
RangeIndex: 891 entries, 0 to 890
Data columns (total 6 columns):
PassengerId    891 non-null int64
Survived       891 non-null int64
Pclass         891 non-null int64
Sex            891 non-null object
Fare           891 non-null float64
Age            714 non-null float64
dtypes: float64(2), int64(3), object(1)
memory usage: 41.8+ KB
```

The isnull() function can be used to highlight the null values in a dataframe. The output of the isnull() function is a dataframe of the same dimensions as the original, with each location containing a Boolean value that is true if the corresponding location in the original dataframe is null. The isnull() function is demonstrated in the following snippet:

```
# highlight the null values in a random sample of data
print (df_iris_subset.sample(10).isnull())
```

	PassengerId	Survived	Pclass	Sex	Fare	Age
385	False	False	False	False	False	False
530	False	False	False	False	False	False
166	False	False	False	False	False	True
334	False	False	False	False	False	True
603	False	False	False	False	False	False
807	False	False	False	False	False	False
819	False	False	False	False	False	False
99	False	False	False	False	False	False
767	False	False	False	False	False	False
480	False	False	False	False	False	False

If you want to quickly determine the number of null values in each column of the dataframe, use the sum() function with the isnull() function, as demonstrated in the following snippet:

```
# find out if there are any missing values in the data
print (df_iris_subset.isnull().sum())
```

```
PassengerId       0
Survived          0
Pclass            0
Sex               0
Fare              0
Age             177
dtype: int64
```

Selecting Data

Pandas provides powerful functions to select data from a dataframe. You can create a dataframe (or series) that contains a subset of the columns in an existing dataframe by specifying the names of the columns you want to select:

```
# extract a single column as a series object
pds_class = df_iris_subset[['Pclass']]
print (pds_class.head())
```

```
   Pclass
0       3
1       1
2       3
3       1
4       3
```

```
# extract a specific subset of named columns into a new dataframe
df_test1 = df_iris_subset[['PassengerId', 'Age']]
print (df_test1.head())
```

```
   PassengerId   Age
0            1  22.0
1            2  38.0
```

```
2              3  26.0
3              4  35.0
4              5  35.0
```

You can create a dataframe that contains a subset of the rows in an existing dataframe by specifying a range of row index numbers.

```
# extract first 3 rows into a new data frame
df_test2 = df_iris_subset[0:3]
print (df_test2.head())
```

```
   PassengerId  Survived  Pclass     Sex     Fare   Age
0            1         0       3    male   7.2500  22.0
1            2         1       1  female  71.2833  38.0
2            3         1       3  female   7.9250  26.0
```

You can use the iloc() function to extract a submatrix from an existing dataframe.

```
# extract first 3 rows and 3 columns into a new dataframe
df_test3 = df_iris_subset.iloc[0:3,0:3]
print (df_test3.head())
```

```
   PassengerId  Survived  Pclass
0            1         0       3
1            2         1       1
2            3         1       3
```

You can also use comparison operators to extract all rows from a dataframe that fulfill a specific criteria; for example, the following snippet will extract all rows from the df_iris_subset dataframe that have a value greater than 26 in the Age column:

```
# extracting all rows where Age > 26 into a new dataframe
df_test4 = df_iris_subset[df_iris_subset['Age'] > 26]
print (df_test4.count())
```

```
>>> PassengerId    395
Survived           395
Pclass             395
Sex                395
Fare               395
Age                395
dtype: int64
```

Besides the functions covered in this appendix, Pandas provides several others, including functions that can be used to sort data and techniques to use a standard Python function as a filter function over all the values of a dataframe. To find out more about the capabilities of Pandas, visit http://pandas.pydata.org.

Summary

◆ NumPy is a math library for Python that allows for fast and efficient manipulation of multidimensional arrays.

◆ The lowercase alias np is a standard convention for referring to NumPy in Python projects.

◆ All elements in an ndarray must have the same data type. NumPy provides its own data types, some of which are compatible with Python data types.

◆ Pandas is a free, open source data analysis library for Python and is commonly used for data munging.

◆ The key objects provided by Pandas are the series and dataframe.

◆ A Pandas series is similar to a one-dimensional list, and a dataframe is similar to a two-dimensional table.

◆ The columns in a Pandas dataframe object can have different data types, and can even handle missing values.

◆ The lowercase alias pd is a standard convention for referring to Pandas in Python projects.

Index

Google ML Kit, 78
Google TensorFlow, 5, 245
Google TensorFlow-Lite, 78
Handwritten digits dataset, 26
ImageDataGenerator class, 262
"Inception-v4, Inception-ResNet, and
   the Impact of Residual Connections
   on Learning," 239
Iris plants dataset, 26
Jupyter Notebook, 4
Kaggle competitions, 27
Keras, 5
Keras activation layers, 249
Keras callbacks, 264
Linnerud dataset, 26
Matplotlib, 5, 54
Microsoft Cognitive Toolkit, 245
Natural Language framework, 76
"Network in Network" (Lin), 237
NumPy, 5
NumPy data types, 298
Onset of diabetes dataset, 26

Pandas, 5, 312
Pillow, 5
Pima Indians diabetes dataset, 203
"Rethinking the Inception Architecture
   for Computer Vision," 238
Scikit-learn, 5, 79
Speech framework, 76
tf-coreml, 76
Theano, 245
Titanic dataset, 48
UCI Machine Leaning Repository,
   27
Vision framework, 75
Wine recognition dataset, 26
white-box models, 21
Wine recognition dataset, 26
WineClassifierOutput class, 165
wines dataset, 135–143

Z

zeros function, 298
Zisserman, Andrew, 92